Dark Bargain

We the People

of the United States,

Article. I

Section. 1. All legislative Powers herein granted shall be vested in a Congress of the United States...

Section. 2. The House of Representatives shall be composed of Members chosen every...

Dark Bargain

SLAVERY, PROFITS,

AND THE STRUGGLE

FOR THE CONSTITUTION

LAWRENCE GOLDSTONE

WALKER & COMPANY
NEW YORK

First published in the United States of America in 2005 by
Walker Publishing Company, Inc.
Distributed to the trade by Holtzbrinck Publishers

For information about permission to reproduce selections from this book,
write to Permissions, Walker & Company, 104 Fifth Avenue, New York,
New York 10011.

Art Credits
Frontispiece: National Archives. Pages 5, 15, 23, 25, 33, 62, 71, 76, 83, 88, 106,
109, 114, 124, 128, 131, 134, 150, 151, 167, and 172: Library of Congress.
Pages 94, 153, 183, and 185: Independence National Historic Park.
Pages 44 and 58: New York Public Library.

Library of Congress Cataloging-in-Publication Data
Goldstone, Lawrence, 1947-
Dark bargain : slavery, profits, and the struggle for the Constitution /
Lawrence Goldstone.
p. cm.
Includes bibliographical references and index.
ISBN 0-8027-1460-9 (alk. paper : hardcover)
ISBN-13 978-0-8027-1460-2 (alk. paper : hardcover)
1. United States. Constitutional Convention (1787)—History.
2. Constitutional history—United States.   3. Slavery—Law and
legislation—United States—History.   4. United States—Politics and
government—1783-1789.   I. Title.

KF4510.G65 2005
342.7302'9—dc22
2005042315

Book design by Maura Fadden Rosenthal/Mspace

Visit Walker & Company's Web site at www.walkerbooks.com

Typeset by Westchester Book Group

Printed in the United States of America
by Quebecor World Fairfield

2 4 6 8 10 9 7 5 3 1

For Nancy and Emily

CONTENTS

Dark Bargain

PROLOGUE

Fulcrum

*O*n the morning of Thursday, January 17, 1788, General Charles Cotesworth Pinckney rose to address his colleagues in the South Carolina General Assembly. One of the state's most distinguished and respected citizens, famed for his exploits in both peace and war, the general was a fourth-generation Carolinian who could trace his lineage to a vassal of William the Conqueror.

Born in 1746, son of a future chief justice of the South Carolina courts, Pinckney had been sent to Oxford to study law, where he read with the great legal theorist William Blackstone. He had returned to set up his own practice, but soon joined the struggle for independence as an aide-de-camp to General Washington. Pinckney won quick promotion and in 1780 was one of the officers charged with resisting the British siege at Charleston. Even in the face of overwhelming force, he had advocated fighting on, only agreeing to surrender after intense persuasion by his fellow officers. As a result, he spent the next year as a British prisoner of war. When his captors tried to persuade him to change sides, Pinckney said, "If I had a vein that did not beat with the love of my Country, I myself would open it. If I had a drop of blood that could flow dishonourable, I myself would let it out."[1]

For all his lineage and fame, however, on that January morning in 1788, General Pinckney, described as "an indifferent Orator,"[2] faced possibly the greatest challenge of his life. The debate he was about to join, which had begun the previous day and would continue for two more, was crucial not only to the future of his state, but quite possibly would determine the very survival of the fledgling nation he had battled for and been imprisoned to secure. The subject was whether to call a convention to ratify the proposed new Constitution.

The Constitution had been drafted the previous summer in Philadelphia, fifty-five men from twelve states participating in often rancorous debate on how best to rescue the United States from the obviously inadequate Articles of Confederation.* General Pinckney, along with his younger cousin Charles,[3] had been one of the four delegates chosen to represent South Carolina.

According to the plan that had emerged from the convention, nine states would have to ratify the new Constitution if the Articles were to be replaced.

---

*Rhode Island—"Rogue's Island" to some—by this time dominated by what was popularly seen as a radical agrarian government, had refused to send a delegation.

1

By the time the South Carolina legislature took up the question of whether to authorize a ratifying convention, five states had already approved the document and conventions to take up the question were scheduled in a number of others. Still, adoption was very much in doubt. Intense opposition existed in New York, and ratification was far from certain in Massachusetts. Virginia, perhaps the most important state in the Union in terms of wealth and strategic location, would not even meet to consider the new Constitution for months, and sentiment in the Old Dominion was not encouraging. Virginia's governor, Patrick Henry, a rabid opponent of ratification, was already famous for his refusal to even attend the convention. "I smelt a rat," he had noted with typical understatement. If the South Carolina legislature declined to call a ratifying convention, it could well start a cascade of rejection.

Many South Carolinians were leery of ceding local prerogative to a central government, particularly one that might be dominated by the North. Under the Articles, each state voted as a unit, and at least nine votes were required to pass even the most basic legislation. As a result, the five southern states effectively maintained veto power over any measure that might be rammed through by the eight states to the north. Under the voting rules of the new Constitution, that blanket veto would be lost. Fear that tyranny and despotism were therefore just around the corner had to be overcome if South Carolina were to approve the new Constitution.

Heading the opposition was a figure of equal stature, Rawlins Lowndes, who had been South Carolina's second president.[4] At the close of the Wednesday session, Lowndes had insisted that while "he believed the gentlemen that went from this state to represent us in Convention possessed as much integrity, and stood as high in point of character, as any gentlemen that could have been selected," the plan would be a disaster.[5]

"It has been said that this new government was to be considered as an experiment," Lowndes had said.* "He really was afraid it would prove a fatal one to our peace and happiness. An experiment! What, risk the loss of political existence on experiment! So far from having any expectation of success from such experiments, he sincerely believed that, when this new Constitution should

---

*Both in the records of legislative meetings and the notes to the Constitutional Convention, speakers were often referred to in the third person by whoever was taking the notes. Although encountering a speaker referred to as "he" takes some getting used to, for accuracy and to give a flavor of the proceedings, these records will always be cited as written. In this case, for example, the "he" in the following sentence is Lowndes himself and the statement is a quote, not a paraphrase. This treatment will be adhered to with respect to convention delegates as well. Therefore, unless specifically noted to the contrary, quoted passages will always be those of the speaker indicated.

be adopted, the sun of the Southern States would set, never to rise again."[6]

Lowndes's proclamation had ended a day of long and grueling debate. It had begun with Charles Pinckney, the general's cousin, giving a lengthy description of the plan that had emerged the previous September. The younger Pinckney, headstrong and brilliant—he had lied about his age so as to appear to be the youngest delegate in Philadelphia—had spoken for most of the morning. When he finally concluded his remarks, the delegates had eschewed a paragraph-by-paragraph reading of the new Constitution, but had instead launched immediately into a debate on the aspect of the plan that they found most frightening. Since, as one of the representatives put it, the president of the United States "was not likely ever to be chosen from South Carolina or Georgia" (a prediction that remained accurate for almost two centuries),[7] executive power seemed to be of the most concern. Curiously, of all the powers of the presidency, it was the authority to negotiate treaties on which the delegates focused.

Almost the entire afternoon was spent discussing the treaty power, both in terms of its being binding on individual states and the need for a two-thirds vote in the Senate to ratify. Still, there was a surprising lack of specifics as to just what sort of treaties the South Carolinians found most objectionable. Instead, the debate was conducted on a philosophical plane, filled with comparisons to other governments—England and France, especially—and the theoretical dangers of treaty making and the potential for despotism. Then, just before the delegates were to adjourn for the day, Lowndes rose to speak, and the meaning of the previous debates became clear.

"The interest of the Northern States would so predominate, as to divest us of any pretensions to the title of a republic," he protested. "In the first place, what cause was there for jealousy of our importing negroes? Why confine us to twenty years* or rather why limit us at all? For his part, he thought this trade could be justified on the principles of religion, humanity, and justice; for certainly to translate a set of human beings from a bad country to a better, was fulfilling every part of these principles.[8] But they don't like our slaves, because they have none themselves, and therefore want to exclude us from this great advantage. Why should the Southern States allow of this . . . ?"

Slavery, as Lowndes made clear, was at the very heart of the matter. "Without negroes, this state is one of the most contemptible in the Union . . . Negroes were our wealth, our only natural resource; yet behold how our kind

---

*Alluding to a prohibition on the slave trade that was to take effect in 1808.

friends in the north were determined soon to tie up our hands, and drain us of
what we had!"

The session ended and the delegates were left to spend the night pondering
a South Carolina in which, because of treaties with foreign powers or Congressional fiat, slavery had withered away or had been prohibited altogether. Thus,
when General Pinckey rose to speak on Thursday morning, he likely felt that
in order to save the United States, he had to persuade his fellow Carolinians of
what he himself was already convinced and had struggled for four long months
to achieve—that the new Constitution did, in fact, protect and even encourage
the institution of slavery.

He immediately went on the attack, refuting Lowndes point by point. Due
to the rule of secrecy under which the debates in Philadelphia had been conducted, only the general and the other three members of the South Carolina
delegation had any idea of what had actually been said, and all of them favored
the plan. He was therefore able to both slant his description of the proceedings
and assure his suspicious fellow planters that the Yankees were not the conniv-
ing ogres that Lowndes had made them out to be. The northerners, in fact,
General Pinckney observed, had turned out to be a group of quite reasonable
fellows, eager to find middle ground.

When, for example, he described the compromise over apportionment, the
general noted, "As we have found it necessary to give very extensive powers to
the federal government both over the persons and estates of the citizens, we
thought it right to draw one branch of the legislature immediately from the
people, and that both wealth and numbers should be considered in the representation. We were at a loss, for some time, for a rule to ascertain the propor-
tionate wealth of the states. At last we thought that the productive labor of the
inhabitants was the best rule for ascertaining their wealth."

Not having been present in Philadelphia, Lowndes and the other opponents of the plan could not have known that this statement was patently false,
that wealth had been repeatedly rejected as a means of apportionment, and
productive labor had never been seriously considered as a standard.

"In conformity to this rule, joined to a spirit of concession," General
Pinckney went on, "we determined that representatives should be apportioned
among the several states, by adding to the whole number of free persons three
fifths of the slaves. We thus obtained a representation for our property; and I
confess I did not expect that we had conceded too much to the Eastern States,
when they allowed us a representation for a species of property which they
have not among them."

Charles Cotesworth Pinckney

This was, once again, less than a fully accurate account. Northern acquiescence in allowing slaves to be counted in apportionment of legislators was a victory for southerners, to be sure, but Pinckney and the rest of the South Carolina delegation had continually urged that slaves be counted in full and been rebuffed not just by northerners, but even by their slaveholding brethren in Virginia and Maryland.

"The first House of Representatives will consist of sixty-five members," the general continued. "South Carolina will send five of them. Each state has the same representation in the Senate that she has at present; so that South Carolina will have, under the new Constitution, a thirteenth share in the government, which is the proportion she has under the old Confederation: and when it is considered that the Eastern States are full of men, and that we must necessarily increase rapidly to the southward and south-westward,

I do not think that the Southern States will have an inadequate share in the representation. The honorable gentleman alleges that the Southern States are weak. I sincerely agree with him. We are so weak that by ourselves we could not form a union strong enough for the purpose of effectually protecting each other. Without union with the other states, South Carolina must soon fall."

When Pinckney moved on to the most volatile issue of all, that of the slave trade, he was on firmer ground. "By this settlement we have secured an unlimited importation of negroes for twenty years. Nor is it declared that the importation shall be then stopped; it may be continued."*

"I am of the same opinion now as I was two years ago . . . that, while there remained one acre of swampland uncleared of South Carolina, I would raise my voice against restricting the importation of negroes. I am as thoroughly convinced as that gentleman is, that the nature of our climate, and the flat, swampy situation of our country, obliges us to cultivate our lands with negroes, and that without them South Carolina would soon be a desert waste."

General Pinckney then persuasively summed up the many advantages that the new Constitution offered to slaveholders. "We have a security that the general government can never emancipate them, for no such authority is granted; and it is admitted, on all hands, that the general government has no powers but what are expressly granted by the Constitution, and that all rights not expressed were reserved by the several states. We have obtained a right to recover our slaves in whatever part of America they may take refuge, which is a right we had not before. In short, considering all circumstances, we have made the best terms for the security of this species of property it was in our power to make. We would have made better if we could; but, on the whole, I do not think them bad."

Immediately after the general ended his remarks and took his seat, another legislator, Dr. David Ramsay, observed that he "thought our delegates had made a most excellent bargain for us, by transferring an immense sum of Continental debt, which we were pledged to pay, upon the Eastern States, some of whom (Connecticut, for instance) could not expect to receive any material advantage from us. He considered the old Confederation as dissolved."

Lowndes continued to oppose the Constitution personally, but Pinckney's performance had been powerful and persuasive. When the vote to call a

---

*This interpretation of the twenty-year extension of the slave trade was exactly the opposite of the argument that James Madison was making to the citizens of New York as "Publius" in the *Federalist*.

ratifying convention was held a day later, it passed unanimously. Even Lowndes himself was forced to grudgingly acknowledge that perhaps South Carolina should allow a ratifying convention to consider the plan. Charles Cotesworth Pinckney had convinced the planters of South Carolina. Acting in the interest of their social system, slaveholders had helped preserve the chance of union.

PART I

Reluctant Nation

1. DEVIL IN THE MIST

*F*ew milestones in the history of humanity's struggle for self-rule have been as significant as the United States Constitution. The four months in which the Constitution came into being—from May to September 1787—were as dramatic and compelling as the document itself, and the delegates as intriguing a group of characters as has ever sat down to create a country. Lawyers, farmers, shippers, plantation owners, scientists, a philosopher or two, and a lot of speculators—these men were a study in extremes, geographically, politically, and socially.

The youngest was not the thirty-year-old Charles Pinckney but rather a callow twenty-seven-year-old from New Jersey named Jonathan Dayton, who barely opened his mouth, but nonetheless later had a city in Ohio named for him. The oldest was the eighty-one-year-old, gout-ridden Benjamin Franklin, "a short, fat, trunched old man"[1] who was carried to the meetings on a chair borne by four convicts. From Massachusetts came the quixotic capitalist Elbridge Gerry; from North Carolina, the scientist and physician Hugh Williamson; and from Maryland, the besotted Luther Martin, about whom it was later said, "the times must be momentous indeed . . . for the whole week Luther Martin has resided in Washington, he has not once been seen intoxicated in the public streets!"[2] Sometimes extremes existed within delegations: John Langdon, the richest man in New Hampshire, was forced to pay the expenses of his fellow delegate Nicholas Gilman, who was virtually penniless. To add gravitas to the proceedings, a reluctant George Washington had been induced to once again leave his beloved Mount Vernon and join the Virginia delegation.

No Adams would be present, nor would a Lee. Patrick Henry stayed home and Thomas Jefferson was in Paris. But each delegate who did attend was a man of power and prestige in his home state—Jefferson called them "demi-Gods"— used to deference and respect, now thrown into a room with other men accustomed to the same treatment. Many were meeting for the first time after years of commitment to a similar cause. Others were meeting after years of contention. Vain, imperious George Mason of Virginia, one of the richest of the delegates, set eyes on Benjamin Franklin for the first time in May 1787, after more than two decades of furious competition with the crafty Pennsylvanian in the race to buy up and settle land in the West. Inevitably, the clash of personalities in Philadelphia would be as intense as the advocacy of ideas or ideals.

Although there was ample contrast in Philadelphia among individual delegates, the greatest disparity lay between the states themselves, and the deepest gulf was between South and North, slave states and free.

While only five of the thirteen states were primarily slaveholding,[3] each of the five—particularly Virginia and South Carolina—was ruled by a genteel, landed aristocracy whose members had more in common with the British upper classes they had just kicked out than with their new countrymen in the North. They were Church of England, owned sprawling estates, ruled tenant farmers in addition to slaves, wore powdered wigs, imported fine silks in the latest fashions, held fancy balls, and provided their children with a classical education, often in Europe. Although they loved wealth, they thought there was something unseemly about handling money, and as a result, many were in debt.

Northerners, on the other hand, were often flinty, parsimonious, hardheaded merchants or capitalists who dressed in dark wool, had few servants, no tenants, and only borrowed money to expand their businesses. Some were presbyters who didn't dance, carouse, or stay up late. They also loved wealth, but found nothing demeaning about counting their money, often repeatedly.

To add to the challenge, these delegates had no model on which to base their efforts—no document of this kind had ever been drafted before. In the drive to find a workable formula, they drew from the Greeks, French *philosophes,* and English reformers, but mostly they relied on their own sense of practicality. They might not have known exactly what they wanted the new government to look like, but they certainly knew what they did *not* want it to look like, although even here different delegates held different opinions as to what they most wished to avoid.

Sometimes they sought resolution through debate on the floor of the convention; other times by assigning committees to draft compromise agreements in secret; and still others by meeting at night in small groups in the back rooms of Philadelphia's inns and taverns. The debates themselves played out with high tension—grand declarations interspersed with sarcasm, spite, and invective, the future of the embryonic democracy teetering on every petty squabble. Delegates regularly threatened to walk out if a favored proposal were voted down or a repugnant one agreed to. Some did leave, becoming fierce opponents of ratification in their home states.

Aware of what was at stake, the delegates knew they had to speak candidly, expressing sentiments they dared not voice in public. In order that none would be held accountable for anything said in the chamber, the proceedings remained strictly secret, conducted behind locked doors that were guarded at all times by armed sentries. To bar eavesdropping, the windows of the State House were kept bolted, intensifying the already oppressive heat and humidity of a Philadelphia summer where, at one point, the temperature reached ninety-six degrees.

The public was meant to be unaware of the proceedings not just as they occurred, but in perpetuity. The official minutes were kept intentionally sketchy, little more than a journal of motions and the ensuing votes, and even that cursory record was not released to the public for decades afterward.* The most copious notes were kept by James Madison and these would not be published until 1840. To Madison (and, in the early weeks, Robert Yates of New York) we owe almost all of our knowledge as to what went on behind those locked doors.

That a Constitution was actually wrought from such secrecy and disarray has been called "a miracle," and, given the tone of the proceedings, that description may not be far off.[4] The delegates disagreed on almost everything. Should the legislature be one house or two? Should the president be elected by the people, by the congress, or by the state legislatures? Should new states be admitted as equals or subordinates? Should there be a standing army? What were to be the powers of the court system? Were the states to be subordinate to the federal government or the other way around? Should the new government assume the massive debt from the Revolution? How should commerce be regulated? What constituted treason? Each of these questions had different advocates proposing different resolutions, all with equal ardor.

But of all the issues that would arise in Philadelphia, the one that evoked the most passion, the one that left the least possibility of compromise, the one that would most pit morality against pragmatism, was the question of slavery. To a significant and disquieting degree, America's most sacred document was molded and shaped by the most notorious institution in its history.

For the longest time, however, almost nobody thought so. Throughout the nineteenth and most of the twentieth centuries, one prominent historian after

---

*This is why General Pinckney had felt free to misrepresent the proceedings. The general was not alone in employing this tactic. It was widely used by former delegates during the ratification process.

another examined the record and insisted that the economics of slavery was a minor factor in Philadelphia. The battle was fought between big states and small states, insisted some, while others saw the principal conflict as between those who owned real property and those whose wealth was largely on paper. For many, the debates were simply one of history's great intellectual exercises, a four-month colloquium on government and political philosophy conducted by a group of latter-day Athenians.

The United States Constitution is arguably the most analyzed document in the history of government, but it is not difficult to understand why slavery has so regularly been consigned to the shadows. "The peculiar institution"—an equally peculiar phrase—was an unpleasant and repugnant topic, a stain on America's honor, and, therefore, the less of a role it played in defining the nation's identity the better. Even in the debates, so repellent was slavery to northerners—and so embarrassing to southerners—that when the subject came up, the delegates often danced around it, employing euphemisms, such as "this unique species of property" or "this unhappy class," as stand-ins for the more disagreeable "slaves." Thus, the words "slave" and "slavery" never appeared in the original Constitution, nor would they until ninety-one years later when the thirteenth amendment abolished the practice forever.[5]

With all that, any fair reading of the record makes it difficult to deny that the sectional division, with slavery as its pivot, was the most crucial. Many of the delegates certainly saw things precisely that way. James Madison, for example, at one point observed that he "always conceived that the difference of interest in the U. States lay not between the large & small, but the N. & Southn States," and added that "it was pretty well understood that the institution of slavery & its consequences formed the line of discrimination."[6]

Almost from the day the convention adjourned on September 17, 1787, theorizing began as to what the delegates intended to say and the underlying meanings of the document they had produced. Theorizing was necessary since there were only fifty-five men in the entire nation who knew what had transpired inside the State House. Even among these fifty-five, only a handful could offer firsthand commentary on the full course of the proceedings.

In the months following the convention, the debate as to intent was particularly furious, since the outcome—as in South Carolina—would determine whether or not the necessary nine states would ratify. During the winter of

James Madison

1787 and through 1788, analysis sprang from everywhere. Meetings and rallies abounded. Printers lined their pocketbooks as newspapers took sides, and pamphlets and broadsides were issued in every state and major city. That no one could know for sure in those early days what the delegates really had in mind—or even had said—did nothing to stop those in favor and those opposed from issuing definitive judgments as to the intent of the framers and its effect on the nation.

Some of the tracts supporting the new Constitution, like the *Federalist*, penned by two men who were present at the convention (Madison and Alexander Hamilton, although the latter was absent for almost two months) and one who was not (John Jay), have become an integral part of our national heritage. Others, equally profound, pointing up the flaws and dangers of the plan, such as Luther Martin's *Genuine Information* and a series of sixteen incisive, elegantly rendered essays published in the *New York Journal* by "Brutus" (identity still unknown, although it is suspected to have been Robert Yates), are now only touched on in graduate school seminars.[7]

In the more than two centuries since the Philadelphia convention, interpretations of the Constitution have changed, sometimes radically, and the manner in which Americans have viewed the document is to a great extent a parallel of the manner in which the nation has viewed both itself and the role of slavery in its history.

The Constitution exists as both a legal and a political document. Its legal role was largely defined by two landmark rulings of John Marshall's Supreme Court. The first, *Marbury v. Madison* in 1803, established the right of the Court to rule on the constitutionality of acts of Congress; the second, *McCulloch vs. Maryland,* sixteen years later—with Luther Martin representing Maryland—established once and for all the preeminence of the federal government over the states. (Martin and Maryland lost.) Each of these rulings was justified as an expression of separation of powers and each represented a principle that many of those fifty-five delegates in Philadelphia would have found abhorrent. Ever since the Marshall Court, justices have been interpreting and reinterpreting the Constitution, one Court often taking a view diametrically opposed to that of the previous one.

As a political treatise, the Constitution has been no more clear or straightforward in its interpretation. For the first fifty years after its ratification, the debate became oddly quiescent, America more or less accepting the Constitution on what seemed to be face value. The first real clause-by-clause critical appraisal of the Constitution emanated from an unlikely corner of American society and was ignited by an equally unlikely spark.

Madison died in 1836. Four years later, a three-volume edition of his papers was published, the contents of which he had selected and edited personally. Included were his notes from the Philadelphia convention. As a result, in 1840, Americans finally got a detailed peek into the proceedings. The published version contained omissions and corrections—Madison had revised the notes as an old man—but, by and large, was accepted as an accurate transcript.

Poring over the newly released material, abolitionists were vitriolic in their denunciations. In 1843, William Lloyd Garrison called the Constitution a "covenant with death and an agreement with hell," and proposed that the Northern states secede from the Union. While abolitionism was never more than a fringe movement in America, one abolitionist, George Bancroft, was to provide a bridge from the fiery rhetoric of the Garrisonians to mainstream history.

Born in 1800, Bancroft lived through virtually the entire nineteenth century, and he worked until almost the day of his death in 1891. His father was the first president of the American Unitarian Association, and throughout his life Bancroft remained devoted to the Unitarian principles of individual liberty, personal responsibility, progressive education, and social reform. Also, like most Unitarians, Bancroft saw slavery not only as a moral blight, but as a practical one, sapping the vigor and spirit of innovation from a democratic society.

A remarkably prolific writer, Bancroft produced thousands upon thousands of pages over the course of his long life.[8] In the late 1820s, he began his most famous work and for five decades toiled on what was ultimately to become a ten-volume history of the United States. Then, in 1882, he completed the two-volume *History of the Formation of the Constitution of the United States of America.*

Bancroft was cognizant of slavery, certainly—he spent more time on the question than many modern historians—but his Unitarian optimism got the better of him. Repudiating Garrison, he saw the institution "in a transient form" in 1787. "In the division between northern and southern states," he added, "the criterion was, whether a state retained the power and the will by its inward energy to extricate itself from slavery."[9] The seven northernmost states, in Bancroft's rather rosy view—including his beloved New England—were in the final stages of doing so. Even the four states just to the south, Delaware, Virginia, Maryland, and North Carolina, he felt, were ruled by closet abolitionists, men who hated slavery but were tragically embroiled in the practice by necessity. Only South Carolina and Georgia actually made a continuation of slavery a quid pro quo of union.

That slavery had been an evil forced on the South matched the public statements of a number of Southern delegates to the convention—George Mason had put forth this argument regularly and forcefully—and helped nineteenth- and early-twentieth-century readers square slavery with their otherwise exalted image of the framers. "As long as patriotism remained the principal ingredient of American historical writing, the constitutional convention was regarded as an assemblage of the gods," wrote Gordon Wood.[10] Then, in the early twentieth century, two men produced groundbreaking works: The first marked the end of the romanticized Bancroft era and the second signaled the beginning of quite another.

Max Farrand, a professor of history at Yale, was considered one of the most influential historians of his day. He had majored in biology at Princeton, but switched to history after taking a course with Woodrow Wilson. Among his best friends at the school was Booth Tarkington, whose sentimental novels would eventually make him the most popular writer in America. In 1913, Farrand produced perhaps the most sentimental treatment of the convention of all, a short work called *The Framing of the Constitution*.

As might be expected in a celebration of virtue, Farrand did not give slavery much of a role. "In 1787," he wrote, "slavery was not the important question, it might be said that it was not the moral question that it later became. The proceedings of the federal Convention did not become known until the slavery question had grown into the paramount issue of the day. Men generally were eager to know what the framers of the Constitution had said and done upon this all-absorbing topic. This led to an over-emphasis of the slavery question at the Convention that has persisted until the present day."[11]

Farrand's contribution, however, lay not in original scholarship, but in what has since been called the "model of historical editing."[12] Combining notes of the delegates with subsequent letters, diaries, pamphlets, memoirs, and speeches in the ratifying conventions, Farrand in 1911 published a remarkably complete and scrupulously annotated three-volume work, *Records of the Federal Convention*. (A fourth volume was added in 1937.)[13]

Records made the same basic materials readily available to all. There would be no subsequent discovery that would suddenly change everything—no lost notes of one of the delegates, no forgotten archive, no shoebox full of records found in someone's attic. After Farrand, constitutional interpretation became almost entirely subjective, depending only on which of the available sources historians chose to give the most weight, where they decided to shine the light.[14]

Another book published in 1913 shone its light where none had before, and constitutional interpretation has not been the same since. That year, an Indiana-born, Oxford-trained, radical-socialist history professor at Columbia University named Charles Beard published *An Economic Interpretation of the Constitution of the United States*. In contrast to the optimism of Bancroft and the romanticism of Farrand, Beard advanced the thesis that the Constitution was forged entirely by men concerned not with philosophy or ideology, but only with self-serving economic motives. Beard divided the delegates into those who owned real property—largely debtors—and those whose wealth was in paper or securities, a category he called "personalty"—largely creditors. Working from admittedly incomplete and sketchy data, Beard concluded that those who supported the Constitution did so because the new government would guarantee their wealth and the payment of debts owed to them, while those opposed wanted to stay with the more impotent and forgiving Articles of Confederation. Although Beard was a Quaker, a group that had always ferociously (although nonviolently) opposed slavery, he had little to say on the subject. In fact, Beard seemed confused as to whether to classify slaves as property or personalty.

Portraying America's Founding Fathers as grasping profiteers made Beard a reviled figure in mainstream academia. After he resigned from Columbia in 1917 to protest the university's refusal to reappoint several professors who opposed American involvement in World War I, he never received another university appointment.[15]

Although Beard readily admitted that the work was "fragmentary" and "designed to suggest new lines of historical research rather than to treat the subject in an exhaustive fashion," his analysis stood relatively unchallenged for more than forty years, and stuck in the craws of conventional historians for every minute of that time. Finally, in 1956, Beard was seriously challenged when a professor at Michigan State University, Robert E. Brown, published a rigorous critical analysis titled *Charles Beard and the Constitution*. Two years later, a young researcher in Wisconsin named Forrest McDonald published *We the People: The Economic Origins of the Constitution,* and Beard's edifice collapsed.

McDonald, as conservative as Beard was radical—he was a state chairman for Barry Goldwater in 1964 and has been a prominent contributor to both *The National Review* and the Heritage Foundation—confronted Beard on his own ground and demolished his arguments. Where Beard was superficial, McDonald was meticulous; where Beard generalized, McDonald was specific; where Beard droned, McDonald wrote with wit and panache. He exposed Beard's simple division into real property and paper assets as simplistic, misleading, and often just plain wrong. After *We the People,* only the most radical New Leftists ever took Beard seriously again.

McDonald's treatment of slavery was also more nuanced, dividing slaveholders into three categories: those to whom slaves were an auxiliary labor supply; those whose livelihoods were based on slavery, but to whom slaves' economic value was questionable; and those to whom slavery was both practical and necessary.[16] Still, McDonald was unwilling to ascribe root cause to the needs of slaveholders, allowing slavery to be one of those facets of early American life that existed but did not seem to matter all that much.

In recent years, constitutional analysis has evolved beyond both Beard and McDonald. Practical realities are often substantially ignored, and the delegates in Philadelphia are now often portrayed as little more than repositories for political philosophy. Constitutional scholarship has become, therefore, predominantly a study of ideas and, with the document itself a product of theory, the great compromises become simply the willingness of the nation's leading citizens to moderate differing abstract points of view to achieve a higher end.

In most contemporary chronicles, a small number of cerebral delegates—Madison, Hamilton, Franklin, or even the recently resurrected Gouverneur Morris—are portrayed as having produced virtually the entire document among themselves. Men such as Charles Cotesworth Pinckney have evaporated into little more than footnotes to the proceedings. Slavery has no real place in such a construction and, as a result, has once again been relegated to a minor determinant or none at all.[17]

The major question in constitutional scholarship, still unresolved, is whether the convention was a meeting guided by philosophy and political theory, with a nod to practical exigencies, or one of hardheaded practicality where self-interest was justified by lofty argument.

Edmund Wilson, in his transcendent *To the Finland Station*, devoted his first chapters to the extraordinary nineteenth-century French historian Jules Michelet. Before Michelet, history had been "a series of biographies of great men," and Michelet saw a need to "clear the gods and heroes away." Michelet, according to Wilson, was one of the first in his field to "grasp fully . . . the *organic* character of human society and the importance of reintegrating through history the various forces and factors which actually compose human life."[18]

Nothing could be more true of constitutional history. The story of the forging of the Constitution is as much a study of the forces and factors that comprised American life as it is a stringing together of the political theories of Madison, Hamilton, and Franklin. Many of those forces are no different than those we experience today—a desire for security, economic self-interest, opportunity for personal enrichment, and protection of a way of life. Two of the most dominant forces in the America of 1787, however, are no longer present. The first was a relentless drive to expand the nation's borders; the second was the institution of human slavery. Each bore heavily on the other.

It is crucial to an understanding of the events in Philadelphia that those who participated in the debates not be deified, demonized, or seen merely as extensions of ideas. These were fully formed human beings with virtues, frailties, aspirations, jealousies, and aims both petty and grandiose. They could be alternately sophisticated or naïve, manipulative or gullible. The degree to which Americans can know these men, appreciate how they saw themselves in their surroundings, walk in the door with them in May 1787, is the degree to which they can understand how and why their Constitution was created as it was.

"Michelet," Wilson added, "always shows [remarkable men] in relation to the social group that has molded them and whose feelings they are finding expression for, whose needs they are attempting to satisfy."[19] The men who came to Philadelphia that summer of 1787 operated overwhelmingly not as disinterested philosophers but as pragmatic advocates for the interests of their states, their regions, and their distinctly disparate social systems. That they did so, that they were interested in practicalities and not theory, enabled them to draft a Constitution that worked in the very real world in which they lived.

The convention itself is generally depicted as, if not a monolithic event, at least as one in which the same members were dominant throughout, none more so than Madison. But the tone of the debates changed drastically during the four months. They may have begun with discussions of theories of government, but theory was abandoned as negotiations became increasingly serious and specific. As the weeks wore on and the proceedings tended more and more to practical politics, slavery came progressively to the fore, until, at the end of August, it drove a wedge into the convention that almost wrecked the entire affair. With the shift in mood came a shift in the men who wielded real power.

This narrative will focus primarily on four of those men. Two owned slaves; two did not. Two were wealthy; two were not. Three signed the finished Constitution; one refused. The three who signed—Oliver Ellsworth and Roger Sherman of Connecticut, and John Rutledge of South Carolina—had arrived in Philadelphia in May as dubious nationalists, fully expecting to oppose any plan that placed too much power in the central government. The one who refused—George Mason of Virginia—had arrived as an enthusiast for a more dominant central government. When the meeting adjourned on September 17, each of these four had reversed his position and slavery was in large part responsible. The reasons for the change in attitudes underscore the essential dynamic of the Philadelphia convention.

2. RELUCTANT NATION:
THE ARTICLES OF CONFEDERATION

𝒯he seeds of the struggle for sectional supremacy that would dominate the Philadelphia convention were sown decades earlier, when three distinct societies grew up in the colonies, each largely determined by the role of slavery in the labor force. Sectionalism did not percolate in earnest, however, until the early 1780s, during the first feeble efforts to forge a single, cohesive nation.

Few countries have emerged with less enthusiasm for unity than the United States. From the Stamp Act Congress in 1765 until the delegates convened in Philadelphia twenty-two years later, most Americans bore primary allegiance to the state within which they lived, and the notion of abandoning that identity to be part of a larger whole was preposterous.

Even during the Revolution, when there was grudging acknowledgment of the need for some cooperative authority to help manage and support the war effort, parochial considerations overwhelmed nationalism. In 1775, Benjamin Franklin drafted a proposal to form a national government and presented it to the Continental Congress. It was studiously ignored. A few months later, Silas Deane submitted another version, and Connecticut's congressional delegation offered a third, both proposals suffering the same fate as Franklin's.[1]

Finally, at the same time as a committee was formed to draft a declaration of independence, John Dickinson of Pennsylvania[2] was asked to head another committee to establish some ground rules for a new central government. The plan he presented in June 1776, which he called "Articles of Confederation," was more to Congress' liking than Franklin's or Deane's, but only after seventeen months and two major revisions was a final, much weaker draft offered to Congress in November 1777.[3] Even so, "The debates . . . over the formation of the Confederation were essentially involved with state interests . . . only the debates over representation . . . touched on the nature of union and the problem of sovereignty, and even here the polemics were tied

John Dickinson

closely to individual state interests."[4] Nationalists, such as John Adams and James Wilson, cried in the wilderness that "we are not so many states; we are one large state."[5]

Drafted in war, Dickinson's plan was concerned primarily with establishing a workable mechanism for mutual defense. Avoiding any hint of a transfer of autonomy, he called the new compact a "League of Friendship," in which, "Each Colony shall retain and enjoy as much of its present Laws, Rights and Customs, as it may think fit, and reserves to itself the sole and exclusive Regulation and Government of its internal police, in all matters that shall not interfere with the Articles of this Confederation." The final version made this clause even stronger. "Each state retains its sovereignty, freedom, and independence, and every Power, Jurisdiction and right, which is not by this confederation expressly delegated to the United States, in Congress assembled."

There were other differences between Dickinson's first draft and the final version, some of which presaged divisions in Philadelphia a decade later. Article XI of the draft read, "All Charges of Wars and all other Expences that shall be incurred for the common Defence, or general Welfare, and allowed by the United States assembled, shall be defrayed out of a common Treasury, which shall be supplied by the several Colonies in Proportion to the Number of Inhabitants of every Age, Sex and Quality, except Indians not paying Taxes."

The southern states were furious—the clause made no distinction between slaves and white men. Slaves were property, not people, and Dickinson's lack of awareness was offensive. At the same time, southerners refused to be taxed on their slaves. If population were to determine apportionment of taxes, they insisted, white people alone should be counted; if it were property, land and improvements should be the basis.

In the middle of a conflict that was then being fought largely in their part of the country, northerners were none too eager to engage in extensive discourse as to the sociopolitical status of slaves, and so, setting the pattern for the debates to come, northern congressmen gave slaveowners their way. The final, tortuous version read, "All charges of war, and all other expences that shall be incurred for the common defence or general welfare, and allowed by the united states in congress assembled, shall be defrayed out of a common treasury, which shall be supplied by the several states in proportion to the value of all land within each state, granted to or surveyed for any Person, as such land and the buildings and improvements thereon shall be estimated according to such mode as the united states in congress assembled, shall from time to time direct and appoint." Unlike simply counting people, however, assessing the value of property could be subjective to the point of meaninglessness.*

To further appease the southerners, one other clause was inserted: "If any Person guilty of, or charged with treason, felony, or other high misdemeanor in any state, shall flee from Justice, and be found in any of the united states, he shall, upon demand of the Governor or executive power of the state from which he fled, be delivered up and removed to the state having jurisdiction of his offence." Thus, even if slaves were lucky enough to successfully escape bondage, they could no longer find sanctuary anywhere in the new nation. And so, the fugitive slave clause was born.

The revised Articles of Confederation were presented to the states for approval. As they considered the plan in 1779, Washington was desperately trying to hold the Continental army together. The great victory at Saratoga aside, defeat seemed inevitable without a concerted effort across the entire Union. Nonetheless, ratification stalled.

States with claims to western territories—Massachusetts, Connecticut, the Carolinas, Georgia, and especially Virginia—wanted to retain their western lands as state domain (although overlapping claims often left unclear which state

---

*To add to the difficulties, the power to borrow money was kept substantially broader than the power to raise it—according to the Articles, the government could apportion taxes but not impose them.

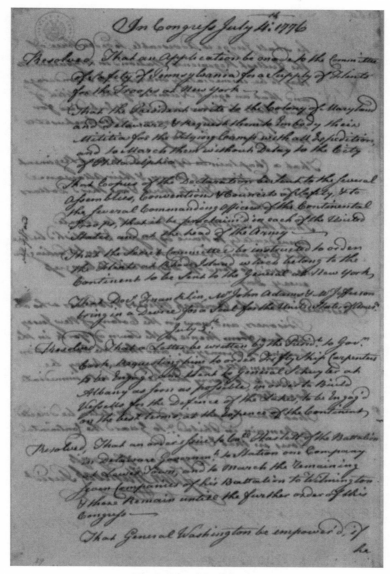

The Articles of Confederation

owned what), while states with no claims, such as Maryland, New York, and Rhode Island, bigheartedly viewed western territories as the property of all.[6] The landed states countered that the landless states were only interested in opening the West for speculation, a charge with more than a dollop of truth in it.

At first, the landless states refused to ratify the Articles, but one by one they came around, until, by late 1779, every state had agreed to the Articles, except Maryland. Maryland would not budge. Its legislature issued a statement that insisted "the back lands ... if secured by the blood and treasure of all, ought in reason, justice and policy, to be considered a common stock, to be parceled out by Congress into free, convenient, and independent Governments." This lofty sentiment was somewhat undercut when Maryland wished to exempt from joint ownership any territory staked out by its own speculators.[7]

Since universal suspicion of authority had given each state a veto power over adoption—unanimous approval was required to put this league of friendship into effect—Maryland found itself in an enviable bargaining position: It could hold out for the absolute best deal.

What Maryland wanted was for the landed states, especially Virginia, to cede their territorial claims in the West to the nation as a whole, so that Maryland speculators might have an equal shot at the riches. Only after Virginia agreed to do just that (and Maryland decided that it needed the strength of a national government to ward off a feared attack by Benedict Arnold on Chesapeake Bay) did Maryland agree to "rise above their principles" and provide the last link to confederation on March 1, 1781. Maryland's principles were further compromised when Virginia included a clause that expressly nullified Maryland's land claims. Still, the United States of America (as Dickinson had termed the nation in his draft) was finally a country. "Thus in the last, and most brilliant period of the war, while Greene was leading Cornwallis on his fatal chase across North Carolina, the confederation proposed at the time of the Declaration of Independence was finally consummated."[8]

Once the Articles had been ratified, the Congress of the new United States moved with uncharacteristic speed to establish ministries of war, finance, and foreign affairs. Unfortunately, Congress picked a particularly unsuitable man to head each of the three.

Robert Morris, while an obvious choice for superintendent of finance, was also a man for whom the term "conflict of interest" might well have been coined. Possessed of perhaps the most astute economic sense in the entire nation, he had kept the country afloat during the war through a series of the same sort of book-juggling maneuvers that would eventually break him and send him to debtors' prison and a penniless death. From the first, many suspected

Morris would look upon his new post more as an opportunity for personal gain than as a sacred trust from a nation in need.*

As superintendent for foreign affairs, Congress tapped Robert Livingston, an able man with a distinguished career ahead of him—he would eventually swear in President Washington in 1789—but who in 1781 was a close associate of Morris and could therefore be expected to use his office to fashion deals with foreign governments more in the interests of speculators than of the new nation. He left the foreign affairs ministry less than a year later, before he had a chance to prove his detractors correct; still, no one mourned his departure.

But by far the worst choice was for secretary at war, where, astoundingly, Congress elected the utterly incompetent Benjamin Lincoln. Lincoln's most noteworthy achievement had come in South Carolina, where he had allowed his entire army to be captured after a bungled attempt to break the siege at Charleston. His only military success was still six years away, and that would be over a bunch of poorly organized farmers in Massachusetts, one of whom was named Shays.

The nation could ill afford such blunders since, even after the Treaty of Paris of 1783 ended the war, threats to the survival of the United States had in no way disappeared. Regardless of the treaty's specific stipulations, British troops remained lodged in New York and British forts continued to dot American territories in the Northwest. What's more, Britain closed its West Indian ports to American produce while continuing to sell its goods to Americans who craved them, thereby deepening the economic crisis. Protests by John Adams, the new ambassador to England, were barely acknowledged.

Relations with other European nations were equally inauspicious. The Spanish feared the growing American presence on the east side of the Mississippi and renewed their threats to close New Orleans to American commerce. Even France, whose support for the fledgling democracy had been crucial in preventing Washington's army from being annihilated, began to make commercial and diplomatic demands as if the new nation were now a part of its empire.

The domestic situation was none too buoyant either. The nation was worse than broke, with a crushing war debt that not even Robert Morris could figure

---

*Morris resigned in disgust three years later when Congress continued to refuse to provide any workable method for raising money. Anticipating the howls from his enemies that he had profiteered, he requested an official inquiry. A committee was appointed, headed by Jefferson and including Roger Sherman, which issued a report clearing Morris of chicanery and attesting to the "great advantages" to the nation of having had his services.

how to pay off, since Congress had no real means to raise money. Lots of men who had bled in the revolution had not only been unpaid and dismissed by the government they fought to establish, but had returned home to find their farms ruined or seized for back taxes. The country may have been called the "United States," but its thirteen members lived under thirteen different constitutions,[9] with thirteen different ways to value money, thirteen different rules of commerce, and thirteen views on how all the problems of the nation should be solved.

The Articles of Confederation both reflected this entropy and was the perfect vehicle for encouraging it. Under the Articles, the nation lacked both an executive and a court system. Members of Congress were appointed each year by state legislatures without popular vote or referendum, each state required to appoint between two and seven delegates. The body itself, "organized as a debating society," often foundered in rhetoric, with "no authority whatever to enforce its recommendations."[10] It voted officially by state and unofficially by region. As nine states were needed to pass any measure of significance, either New England or the South could—and often did—block any proposal not to its liking. As a result, the only pieces of meaningful legislation that ground through Congress were those few that the members of each section, sometimes mistakenly, had decided would benefit them rather than their adversaries to the north or south.

With its impotence increasingly apparent, the government of the United States steadily receded as a seat of real power. After a time, Congress rarely had enough members present to even propose legislation, let alone enough votes to get a measure through. Republicans like Patrick Henry grew bored with the central government and nationalists like Hamilton, Madison, and Dickinson were discouraged by it.

European nations smelled weakness and sensed opportunity. In 1783, Spain finally made good on its threat and closed the port of New Orleans. The closure did not affect New England shippers very much or interfere with British goods arriving at ports in Massachusetts or South Carolina, but it threatened to strangle the settlers living west of the Alleghenies, who were not likely to haul their goods over the mountains to bring them to market. If residents in what was to become Kentucky and Tennessee could not use the Mississippi, they would starve.[11]

In 1785, Congress instructed its new superintendent of foreign affairs, John Jay, to negotiate a deal with the Spaniards.[12] Jay had been charged with a similar task five years earlier and had traveled to Madrid as minister to Spain, only to return empty-handed. This time, however, Madrid came to America in the person of a special emissary named Diego de Gardoqui, who arrived early in 1786.

Gardoqui was as charming and urbane as most Americans were considered rustic. He immediately set upon the intense, hardworking, humorless Jay, employing a flanking action that went through Jay's adored wife. Mrs. Jay, according to Gardoqui, "likes to be catered to and even more to receive presents." He added, "A skillful hand which knows how to take advantage of favorable opportunities, and how to give dinners, and above all to entertain with good wine, may profit without appearing to pursue them." And so, the Spaniard proceeded to escort Mrs. Jay to affair after affair, bestowing compliments and foisting gifts upon both husband and wife. When time allowed, he and Jay (whom he had called "a very self-centered man") negotiated for rights to the most important trading route in North America.[13]

In the deal they agreed to, the United States would cede all its claims to the Mississippi for thirty years in return for gaining access to Spanish ports in Europe and the New World, particularly Havana. For all Gardoqui's ministrations, Jay had negotiated an agreement that was not at all bad for America, or, to be precise, for a part of America—the Atlantic states. American claims to the Mississippi had been hazy to begin with, so Jay may well have simply given up something to which the country had no right anyway. Trade in Havana, on the other hand, would be a boon to New England shippers. For the South and particularly the settlers in the Southwest, however, the proposed treaty looked like a sellout.

Since Jay had been sent into the negotiations with specific instructions from Congress *not* to surrender use of the Mississippi, he was forced to go back and ask for permission to change his authorization. He pushed hard for his treaty. "It appears to me," he said in a speech to Congress in August, "that a proper commercial treaty with Spain would be of more importance to the United States, than any they have formed or can form with any other nation."[14] Jay continued, "At a time when other nations are showing us no extraordinary marks of respect, the court of Spain is even courting our friendship by strong marks, not only of polite and friendly attention, but by offering us favors not common for her to hold out or bestow; for I consider the terms she proposes as far more advantageous, than any to be found in her commercial treaties with other nations."[15]

The southerners were, to say the least, unmoved. In a rare show of attendance, when the vote was taken as to whether or not to change Jay's authorization, all five southern states were present and each voted no, successfully thwarting seven of the eight northern states present and voting in the affirmative. The settlers in the southwestern territories, who had no official representation, were even more livid, threatening to secede, or march on New Orleans, or march on Congress, or align themselves with Spain, or even with England, if the treaty were approved.

Thus, in a waste of Spanish expense money, the Jay–Gardoqui agreement was defeated.[16] Two years later, the Spanish relented and allowed American commerce on the Mississippi to use New Orleans on payment of a duty. The deepened scars of distrust between North and South were not so easily removed, however.

The Mississippi was not the only territorial issue. An ineffectual Congress encouraged bickering over borders. After the war formally ended, Virginia and Maryland quickly resumed their feud. Maryland, still smarting from the abuse it had received at being the last holdout, struck the first blow. According to the charter granted in 1632 by King Charles I to Cecilius Calvert, 2nd Lord Baltimore, the new colony of Maryland extended up Chesapeake Bay to the mouth of the Potomac, and then westward, following the river "from shore to shore." In other words, the boundary between Maryland and Virginia was not in the middle of the Potomac, but on the bank of the Virginia side. Maryland owned the entire river.*

In 1784, Maryland threatened to close the Potomac to Virginia. Virginia retaliated by threatening to close the mouth of Chesapeake Bay, which lay within its charter. If Maryland could not enter the bay and Virginia could not navigate the river, commerce would cease, this at the same time that commerce had also virtually ceased on the Mississippi. For once, cool heads prevailed and the two states chose diplomacy over confrontation.

There was a legal impediment to an agreement, however. The Articles of Confederation expressly stated that "No two or more States shall enter into any treaty, confederation or alliance whatever between them, without the consent of the United States in Congress assembled." Nonetheless, like the separate nations that they thought they still were, Maryland and Virginia decided to negotiate a private treaty. A meeting was arranged in Annapolis and representing Virginia was none other than George Washington himself.

Washington had emerged as the most prominent nationalist in the country, and he had long seen the Potomac, not the Mississippi, as the route to open the West. Navigation of the Potomac would prove a boon to Virginia, and Washington was abetted in his aims most notably by his friend and one-time mentor George Mason and the young political philosopher James Madison.

---

*As it does today.

Although the Annapolis conference did not finalize a treaty, the Virginians and Marylanders did agree to manage the Chesapeake-Potomac waterway through a joint entity they called the Patowmack Company. Although each state was to buy a block of stock, shares in the company were also made available to private investors. Washington, an inveterate speculator, immediately bought stock. Mutual financial interest had been a good first step, and Madison secured another meeting to be held the following March.

Washington, who had a financial stake in the outcome, recused himself from official involvement, but did offer to host the second meeting at Mount Vernon, where delegates from the two states sat down on March 25, 1785. Washington unofficially but regularly dropped in on the proceedings. On March 28, both states signed a wide-ranging agreement that came to be called the "Mount Vernon Compact"—"compact" since treaties between states were illegal. Not only did both states promise to respect the navigation rights of the other, but they established the jurisdictions of each state and recommended formulas for tariffs and currency exchange.*

Although Congress had been informed of the meetings, only after the agreement was signed did the parties seek official congressional approval. With its application to Congress to form a compact, Maryland had added additional stipulations, "that currencies should be regulated; that duties and imposts should be the same in both states; that commissioners should be appointed to regulate commerce; that Delaware and Pennsylvania should be notified and requested to join with Virginia and Maryland."

In this clause, Madison saw a chance to proceed with a more ambitious plan. He had been trying for some time to convince the Virginia assembly to press Congress into expanding its control over interstate commerce and trade with foreign nations. He used the success at Mount Vernon as a demonstration of the benefits of cooperation, which he said would increase trade and profits for all.

After months of cajoling, the Virginia assembly passed a resolution in January 1786, inviting the other twelve states to send delegates to a special meeting to discuss commercial issues at Annapolis in September.[17] The opening session of what came to be called the Annapolis convention was scheduled for September 11, 1786. That turned out to be just after the Jay-Gardoqui debacle, so Madison had heightened hopes that commerce was a sufficiently hot topic to attract interest.

---

*The Mount Vernon Compact aside, the issue has never been settled. In 2003, Maryland petitioned the Supreme Court to prevent Virginia from drawing water from the Potomac for its suburbs, citing the 1632 charter.

Ever fastidious, Madison arrived a week early (a tactic he would also employ in Philadelphia the following year), took rooms at a local inn, and sketched out a plan. Instead of the national conference he was hoping for, however, only eleven other men showed up, representing but four other states. Maryland, which had offered its own Senate chamber as the location for the meetings, did not even bother to appoint delegates, nor did Connecticut, South Carolina, or Georgia. Massachusetts, New Hampshire, North Carolina, and Rhode Island claimed to have appointed delegates but no one from any of these states ever appeared.[18]

Instead of disaster, however, Madison once more saw opportunity. There may have been a shortage in the quantity of delegates, but no lack of quality. His eleven colleagues were all ardent nationalists and included not only Edmund Randolph from his own state, but also Alexander Hamilton from New York and John Dickinson of Delaware, two of the best minds and most powerful personalities in the country. Madison knew that the towering spirit of Washington was with him as well, so as soon as his fellow delegates started to drift in, Madison began to plot. He initiated informal strategy sessions trying to divine a way to derive maximum benefit from the sparse turnout.

With so few states present, dealing with rules for national commerce or any other substantive issue was pointless. As the delegates wrote in their report later, "Your Commissioners did not conceive it advisable to proceed on the business of their mission, under the Circumstance of so partial and defective a representation."[19] If they were to be denied the small, however, Madison and his fellow conspirators would take on the large. They determined to use this meeting as the beginning of an effort to change the very structure of the government.

Madison, Hamilton, and Dickinson had each soldiered on through the early 1780s, fruitlessly extolling the virtues of nationalism. For five years they had waited for an opportunity. Hamilton had written in 1782, "There is something . . . diminutive and contemptible in the prospect of a number of petty States, with the appearance only of union, jarring, jealous and, perverse . . . fluctuating and unhappy at home, weak and insignificant by their dissensions in the eyes of other nations."[20] Since the states had agreed to try to find solutions to a mutual problem, these men were ready.

They wanted a justification that would allow them to produce a report going far beyond commerce, and they found it in the instructions to the New Jersey delegation, an irony considering the events to come. Hamilton noted

Alexander Hamilton

in the convention's report that New Jersey had expanded the mandate to its delegates, "empowering their Commissioners, 'to consider how far a uniform system in their commercial regulations and other important matters, might be necessary to the common interest and permanent harmony of the several States.'" They were to try and produce a formula that "would enable the United States in Congress assembled, [to] effectually provide for the exigencies of the Union." In other words, as Hamilton read it, New Jersey was willing to redraft the Articles of Confederation.

By the time the commission officially convened, the business had already been all but concluded. The first day's proceedings were confined to unanimously electing Dickinson as chairman, sitting through a reading of the commissioners' credentials, and then unanimously agreeing to appoint a committee to prepare a draft report to be presented to the legislatures of the five states in attendance. When that was done, the meeting was adjourned.

On Wednesday, the committee produced its report (which Hamilton also wrote), handed out copies to be read overnight, and then adjourned once more. On Thursday, "the meeting resumed the consideration of the draft of the Report, and after some time spent therein, and amendments made, the same was unanimously agreed to." Hamilton's report, signed by all twelve members and transmitted to the legislatures of only the five participating states, stated that "there are important defects in the system of the Federal Government... that ... from the embarrassments which characterize the present State of our national affairs, foreign and domestic ... may reasonably be supposed to merit a deliberate and candid discussion, in some mode, which will unite the Sentiments and Councils of all the States." Hamilton went on, "Your Commissioners submit an opinion, that the Idea of extending the powers of their Deputies, to other objects, than those of Commerce, which has been adopted by the State of New Jersey, was an improvement on the original plan, and will deserve to be incorporated into that of a future Convention." Leaving nothing to chance, the report even specified a time and place for the convention—the second Monday of the following May in Philadelphia.

Yet, for all their machinations, nothing in the commission's charter compelled any of the states to attend a Philadelphia convention. Eight of the states had not even received the report, although Dickinson did present it to the denuded Congress on September 20, 1786. The call for a second convention could easily have backfired. "By the fall of 1786, it could no longer be safely assumed that time lay on the side of reform. Sectional rifts in Congress over commercial policy and navigation of the Mississippi had exposed fault lines along which the Union might divide ... while the idea that the Union might devolve into regional confederacies still seemed incredible, events since 1783 had called into question the very idea of a national interest."[21]

The nationalists needed help in order to move members of the various states to consider giving up power and authority to a central government. In the second half of 1786, they got it from a band of farmers, ne'er-do-wells, and army veterans in western Massachusetts.

3. RABBLE IN BLACK AND WHITE: INSURRECTION

*A*s was true in many of the former colonies, Massachusetts had turned into two de facto states. On the Atlantic coast lay Boston and the prosperous, cosmopolitan, mercantile East, where shippers like John Hancock and James Bowdoin grew wealthier by the day. Inland, away from the ports, was the agrarian West, where gruff, laconic, debt-ridden farmers were regularly hauled into court to be deprived of their land or sent to prison.

Not surprisingly, the two groups did not much like each other. The Bostonians found the westerners to be loutish, not worthy of a say in the state's affairs. By a happy coincidence, the westerners *had* very little say in the state's affairs. The westerners, on the other hand, looked on Boston as a den of iniquity, populated by rich, overfed merchants living off the exorbitant taxes, state fees, and repossessed property of patriotic farmers and army veterans. The westerners were particularly incensed at court costs and lawyers' fees, which were so high that honest patriots found it almost impossible to access the legal system to protect their rights. In addition to lowering taxes, eliminating court fees, and suspending foreclosure of mortgages, the answer, they insisted, lay in the old debtors' standby—paper money.[1]

In Boston, Governor James Bowdoin—he and Hancock handed the governorship back and forth for the entire decade—made some token gestures offering debt relief, but stopped short of the institutional reform the westerners wanted. He certainly had no intention of issuing paper money, which was tantamount to writing down debts to, at best, a dime on the dollar.

Lacking a legitimate channel through which to press their point of view, in June 1786, an ad hoc group of angry farmers, many of them veterans, showed up in Taunton and, borrowing a prerevolutionary tactic, blocked the local court, demanding that the judges, clerks, tax collectors, and lawyers pack up and go home. Since a number of the farmers had brought guns with them, the judges and lawyers agreed. Similar protests followed and spread across western Massachusetts throughout the summer. The court shutdowns were soon accompanied by county conventions, after which the locals sent petitions to Boston demanding a redress of grievances.

On August 29, a slightly more organized group of farmers marched on the Court of Common Pleas at Northampton and threatened the judges and administrators with unnamed consequences if they convened. This court, which, like the others, was set to hear a number of cases that could have landed some local farmers in debtors' prison, also decided to suspend operations.

Bowdoin continued to take a low-key approach, hoping the protests would blow over as the cooler weather set in. Just to be on the safe side, however, he and his fellow merchants—creditors all—opted to bankroll an army to be kept in reserve in case the upheaval did not subside of its own accord.

Out in the provinces, realizing that they had struck on a useful idea, the protestors decided that impeding the judicial process was just the start, and took aim at reforming, if not overthrowing, the state government in Boston. The angry corps of farmers and veterans dubbed themselves "Regulators," shouldered arms, and, possibly backed by impenitent Tories, began drilling in the countryside. One of the Regulators was a forty-year-old former captain in the Continental army named Daniel Shays. Shays had a distinguished war record, having fought at Lexington, Bunker Hill, and Saratoga, but he never actually "led" anyone, and why the movement came to be named for him remains a mystery.

In September 1786, the "Shays Men," as many called themselves, forced the state supreme court at Springfield to adjourn. The movement began to gather steam as the leaves fell and Bowdoin responded by offering amnesty to any rebel who laid down his arms by January 1, 1787. Few did, so Bowdoin approached Benjamin Lincoln—essentially unemployed since leaving the war ministry in 1784—and offered him command of an army of 4,400 men to lead against the rebels. Lincoln, who was by this time speculating heavily in land in Maine, jumped at the chance. To raise additional money for the army, Lincoln, who was friendly with most of the wealthy merchants, "went immediately to a club of the first characters in Boston, who met that night, and suggested to them the importance of their becoming loaners of a part of their property if they wished to secure the remainder." Lincoln, who was described as "very persuasive," had no trouble raising the funds and soon had his army, many of whose officers were either wealthy merchants or their sons, heading west.[2]

With Lincoln on the march, the Regulators decided to supplement their stock of antiquated weaponry by raiding the arsenal in Springfield. They reached the city on January 25, 1787, before Lincoln's troops could cut them off. Unfortunately for the Shays Men, a militia brigade under General William Shepard was guarding the arsenal and opened fire on the rebels with cannon. Evidently, all that marching and drilling in the hills had not achieved the desired effect, because the Regulators immediately took flight, leaving four dead and twenty wounded. Once clear of Springfield, they found themselves pursued by Lincoln, who caught up with them at Petersham, where they were roundly defeated. Lincoln kept after the remains of the ragtag band, completing a mop-up operation in Sheffield on February 27.[3] Shays himself beat a path to Vermont, a safe haven since it had not yet joined the Union and was technically a foreign country.[4]

All things considered, Shays' Rebellion did not amount to very much. The Regulators has been easily routed, order had been restored, and the authority of the state government reaffirmed. Nothing about this abortive uprising should have instilled fear in anyone. That it did was in no small part the work of Henry Knox.

Knox was perhaps the most unlikely hero of the Revolution. With no formal education or military training, the grossly overweight bookseller was appointed as Washington's commander of artillery when he was only twenty-five years old.[5] He proved to be expert at both tactics and logistics, possessing an instinctive understanding not only of how to place and use artillery in battle but also of how to move heavy cannons long distances in a short time. After Lincoln had resigned the post, Knox was made secretary at war by Congress, a position he would reprise during Washington's first term.*

In late 1786, Knox heard rumors that the British were planning to incite a counterrevolution and that Tories in western Massachusetts had recruited and armed thousands of disaffected farmers and war veterans to seize the arsenal at Springfield and then march on Boston. The British were plotting to provoke an Indian uprising as well. Knox instantly wrote a letter to Washington presenting this wholly uncorroborated story as fact, adding some embellishment of his own in case Washington did not appreciate the gravity of the situation.

Not only was the number of Shays Men drastically inflated from perhaps fifteen hundred to fifteen thousand, but, according to Knox, the rebels wanted to impose a kind of pre-Marxian communism on the United States. "They see the weakness of government," he wrote, "and they feel at once their own poverty, compared to the opulent, and their own force, and they are determined to make use of the latter in order to remedy the former. Their creed is that the

---

*After ratification the title was changed to secretary *of* war.

property of the U.S. has been protected from the confiscations of Britain by the joint exertions of all, and therefore should be the common property of all."[6]

Knox's letter eventually enjoyed wide distribution in Congress and state legislatures. Thus, as news that Shays' Rebellion had been crushed filtered south, it became not the revolt of a thousand or so undisciplined farmers who had bolted at the first cannon blast, but an uprising of fifteen thousand determined anarchists.

If this sort of insurrection against life and especially property could happen in Massachusetts, it could happen anywhere. A single state might not have sufficient resources to quell such an uprising. Perhaps a stronger national government was not such a bad idea after all. For southerners, an even more dire specter had been raised.

What if the insurgents had been *slaves*?

Fear of black rebellion among planters was deep and long-standing.[7] It began in the first years that African slaves were brought ashore, but in 1739, an incident of unprecedented ferocity caught every slaveowner in its grip.

Shortly after midnight on Sunday, September 9, about twenty miles from Charles Town, South Carolina, a group of about twenty slaves, led by an Angolan called Jemmy, slipped away from their plantations and met up at a bridge over the Stono River. Hugging the banks, they proceeded to Hutchenson's store, where they broke in and stole guns and ammunition. In the process, the slaves murdered Hutchenson and his clerk, cutting off their heads and depositing them on the front steps. The slaves then left the river and moved south, "in a Daring manner out of the Province, killing all they met and burning several Houses as they passed along the Road," according to a report the following month to the Board of Trade by William Bull, lieutenant governor of the colony.[8] By the time the sun rose, at least ten white Carolinians were dead.

The runaways recruited other slaves they encountered on the way and by noon more than one hundred had joined the group. The rebels continued to kill any whites who were unfortunate enough to be in their path to Florida and freedom. The Spanish in Saint Augustine, either because of humanitarian concerns or, more likely, to nettle the English with whom they were at war, were well-known for offering safe haven to any escaping slaves who could make it there.

Early in the afternoon, the rebels were spotted by a party of five men on horseback, who galloped off before the runaways could bring them down. One of the men happened to be Lieutenant Governor Bull. One can only imagine Bull's reaction at encountering a band of one hundred blacks carrying guns and machetes on a South Carolina road. He immediately spread the alarm and marshaled a militia. Soon an equal number of armed white men was pursuing the rebels.

That afternoon, after a twenty-mile march, Jemmy's band stopped in a field near the Edisto River for the night. They had killed more than twenty white men, women, and children. Bull's militia came upon the camp at about four o'clock and rode in firing. The rebels fired back but the whites had better weapons and better training. Fourteen of the slaves were killed and others captured and summarily executed. The remainder escaped into the woods as the whites returned to send out a broader alarm.

South Carolina went on what was described as a "war footing" and commenced the hunt for the remaining slaves.[9] Every white male in the colony was armed, and checkpoints were established at ferry crossings. Members of the local Chickasaw and Catawba tribes were offered a bounty for every black they caught.

Within a week, as many as sixty of the rebels had been killed or executed, thirty in one skirmish. Their heads were also cut off, and then left on pikes on the side of the road for other slaves to see. A few escaped again, only to be hunted down and executed over the coming weeks. One man managed to elude capture for three years, until he was finally betrayed by other runaways, after which he was captured and hanged.

The Stono Rebellion, as it came to be called, was the largest slave uprising in the North American colonies before independence, and it had a profound impact on slaveholders for decades afterward. The effects were still being felt when the delegates met in Philadelphia. In the short term, it caused South Carolina to place a prohibitive duty on slave imports, although rice economics soon overwhelmed that idea. Far more significantly, the following year, after authorities uncovered another plot involving more than two hundred slaves, the colony passed a slave code called the Negro Act. It eliminated whatever small freedom slaves had enjoyed and placed severe restrictions on their conduct, their activities, what implements they could carry, what they could do with their free time, and even the way they could dress.

What the slave code could not do was lessen the fears of white southerners. Having spent decades justifying slavery as the natural domination of a civilized race over a savage one—"translating a set of human beings from a bad country to a better," as Rawlins Lowndes later put it—they were now forced to live with their own propaganda. Fear of uprisings by frenzied, barbaric blacks grew exponentially and wildly out of proportion to actual events.

Stono aside, most "rebellions" involved two to four slaves, whose interest was escape, not fomenting revolution. The larger, significant uprisings of Denmark Vesey and Nat Turner were still the better part of a century away. There were numerous incidents of slaves who were driven to violence by the barbarity of their treatment, but they hardly amounted to rebellion.[10] Overall, in fact, the colonial period in British North America was notable for the quiescence of its slave population.

To justify their fears, however, slaveowners of the southern colonies needed to look no further than the West Indies, where the conditions on the sugar plantations were far worse than even in the rice fields of South Carolina, and slave revolts were more common and far more deadly. They also knew of the famous Maroon uprising in Jamaica, where an enslaved Coramantee warrior named Cudjo led an uprising that lasted an incredible forty years, and resulted in the British governor signing a peace treaty in 1738 that ceded part of the island to the rebels.

One danger that the West Indian slaveowners did not have to face was having slaves freed by other white men. That was reserved for the five southern colonies in mainland North America, who saw themselves facing increasingly hostile neighbors to the north. As northerners either outlawed slavery or phased it out,* southerners were convinced that their northern neighbors intended to compel them, either by financial pressure or force, to do the same.[11] At best, the northern colonies might easily come to offer the same safe haven to escaping slaves as the Spanish in Florida, thus further encouraging murderous runaways who might then seek freedom in either direction.

Or perhaps foreigners would free the slaves. During the French and Indian War, Lieutenant Governor Robert Dinwiddie of Virginia, when informed of French victories in the Ohio territory, which supposedly had created rumblings among the slaves, wrote that "the villainy of Negroes on any emergency of government is what I always feared." Five days later, he ordered military commanders to "leave a proper number of soldiers in each county to protect it from the combinations of negro slaves, who have been very audacious since the defeat on the Ohio. These poor creatures imagine the French will give them their freedom."[12]

---

*In 1780, the Massachusetts constitution abolished slavery and Pennsylvania passed a law of gradual abolition. Connecticut and Rhode Island passed gradual emancipation laws in 1784; New Hampshire in 1792; New York in 1799; and New Jersey in 1804. Vermont had outlawed slavery in 1777, while it was still a territory.

As Madison would later note in the *Federalist*, belying his enduring reputation as a nonracist southerner, "An unhappy species of population abounds in some of the states who, during the calm of the regular government, are sunk below the level of men; but, who, in the tempestuous scenes of civil violence, may emerge into the human character, and give a superiority of strength to any party with which they may associate themselves."[13]

When the Revolution came, the fear of imposed emancipation was transferred to the British. "On September, 26 [1775] Edward Rutledge [of South Carolina] moved that Washington be instructed 'to discharge all the Negroes as well as Slaves as Freemen in his Army.' Rutledge was worried about the example that armed black men would furnish for South Carolina's numerous slaves. False rumors of an impending British-instigated slave insurrection had touched off a panic in the colony in May and June 1775."[14]

Rutledge was not alone. Two days before in Philadelphia, Archibald Bullock and John Houstoun, two congressional delegates from Georgia, spent the evening with John Adams. Adams reported that "These Gentlemen gave a melancholy Account of the State of Georgia and S. Carolina. They said that if 1000 regular Troops should land in Georgia and their commander be provided with Arms and Cloaths enough, and proclaim Freedom to all the Negroes who would join his camp, 20,000 Negroes would join it from the two Provinces in a fortnight. The Negroes have a wonderfull Art of communicating Intelligence among themselves. It will run severall hundreds of Miles in a Week or Fortnight."[15]

That Rutledge turned out to be right likely gave him scant comfort. During the war in the South, British forces freed more than twenty-five thousand slaves, promising them permanent freedom if they helped defeat their masters. A few eventually escaped, but almost all of the rest were killed or recaptured, or died of disease.

Southerners often put slave control on a higher level than defeating the enemy. In April 1776, as Washington was desperate to strengthen the Continental army in an effort to repel the expected land-sea assault by England, Major-General Charles Lee pestered Congress with a series of panicked letters about controlling the slaves. The last of these, to Robert Morris, urged that three or four regiments be kept in Virginia to protect against a slave uprising.[16]

Fear of slave rebellion had a practical impact on the war. In 1779, South Carolina reported that it was unable to use its militia effectively against the British because it was needed as a home guard to prevent rebellion and flight among the slaves. Perpetuation of slavery united Whigs and Tories. "When the war came, South Carolina had to deal with large numbers of barbaric Africans.

The most influential citizens, whether 'patriot' or 'loyalist,' were determined to preserve the existing industrial and social order as a necessary condition of life in the district, no matter which system of government and allegiance should prevail."[17] In fact, when Bullock and Houstoun were warning Adams of the danger of a slave uprising in South Carolina, they noted that "their only Security in this, that all the Kings Friends . . . have large Plantations and Property in Negroes. So that the Slaves of the Tories would be lost as well as those of the Whiggs."[18]

The combination of Shays' Rebellion (or at least Henry Knox's version of it) and the ongoing fear of slave revolts turned out to be the lever that Madison, Dickinson, and Hamilton needed to generate interest in a meeting of all the states. On February 21, 1787, six months after it had received Dickinson's report from Annapolis, and one month after the Springfield raid, Congress endorsed the commission's recommendation that a national convention be called in Philadelphia that May to consider changes to the Articles of Confederation.

4. TAMING THE WEST: THE OHIO COMPANY OF VIRGINIA

*T*he Jay-Gardoqui affair had exposed the nation's deepest rift, one that could cleave the United States between North and South. The rift was not new. For four decades, before even the most ferocious patriot contemplated independence, the forces that later combusted in New York had been building in the ports of New England, the tidewater of Virginia, the swamps of South Carolina, and, perhaps most of all, in the vast untamed frontier that stretched to the Mississippi and beyond.

This was in no way lost on the delegates to the Constitutional Convention. Not one of them came to Philadelphia believing that he was there to create a new government—or reform an old one—only for the benefit of thirteen states on the Atlantic. Roger Sherman would say on July 14, 1787, that "we are providing for our posterity, for our children & our grand Children, who would be as likely to be citizens of new Western States, as of the old States."[1]

The United States was exploding westward. Elbridge Gerry called it "a rage for emigration from the Eastern States to the Western Country."[2] Frontier expansion was the future, with fertile land for new farms and new farmers, rivers to carry goods across a larger and more prosperous nation, lumber and furs, minerals and trade. If managed deftly, all this would create wealth for the country and profits for shippers, merchants, and manufacturers, to say nothing of those who owned the land itself.

After Virginia did so in 1781, a number of other states had ceded much or all of their Western land claims to the federal government. As a result of congressional land ordinances in 1784 and 1785, almost everyone understood that this territory, which stretched to the Mississippi from just north of the Gulf of Mexico

MAP USED IN THE LONDON REPRINT

all the way to Canada, would spawn new states. The only questions were: How many states would there be? What form would they take? How were they to be admitted? Would they be equal partners with the existing thirteen? And, most important, whose interests would they support? Would they be planter or farmer, merchant or artisan, and, most vitally, slave states or free?

Thus, the Constitutional Convention became simply an extension of the ongoing sectional struggle, a dispute that had begun to fester in the late 1740s, when land consortiums began to lay claim to millions of acres in the West. These partnerships first petitioned the crown, and then, after independence, called on the new government to legitimize old claims or authorize new ones. The fortunes of two very different land companies, each of which called itself the Ohio Company—one slave, one free; one southern aristocrat, one northern presbyter—would be key in determining that victor.

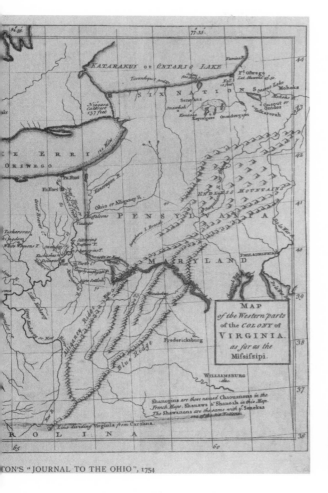

"Map of the Western parts of the Colony of Virginia as far as the Mississippi," used in the London reprint of George Washington's "Journal to the Ohio," 1754

The first of these, the Ohio Company of Virginia, began operation in 1748. Citing the wording of the royal patent for Virginia, which granted the colony territory stretching "from sea to sea" (although no one had any idea how far that would turn out to be), Thomas Lee petitioned the acting governor, Sir William Gooch, for a grant of two hundred thousand acres in the Ohio Territory, which at the time stretched from the western boundaries of the various states—principally Pennsylvania—to the Mississippi. In return for the grant, the company promised to survey the land, build roads, and populate the terrain with two hundred settlers—who would pay for it, of course—at one thousand acres each. To protect these settlers, the company pledged to clear a road into the territory, and then build and man a fort, all at its own expense.

Lee's group consisted of wealthy planters like himself, most of whom inhabited the tidewater region of Virginia—the so-called Northern Neck—rich

accessible land that began on Chesapeake Bay and ran north between the Potomac and Rappahannock Rivers. This was Virginia's old money, families that
had been in the colony for three and four generations. In addition to Thomas Lee,
the group included Augustine and Lawrence Washington; William Fairfax,
brother of Lord Fairfax, the largest landowner in the colony; a number of Mer-
cers; and Robert Carter, the grandson of the legendary Robert "King" Carter,
who had forged a sprawling empire of land and slaves in the early 1700s.
Within two years, three of Thomas Lee's sons, including Richard Henry, and
the Washingtons' half-brother George would join the group, as would a prosperous and ambitious young planter named George Mason IV. Mason had inherited thousands of acres and married into thousands more. He was made
treasurer soon after his entry in 1750.

For the members of the Ohio Company, acquisition of new land in the
West was intimately intertwined with tobacco and slavery. Tobacco, the source
of the great fortunes amassed by the Virginia planters, was also their bane, a
crop that was notorious for decimating the land. "The voracious plants sucked
nutrients; the often violent rains gullied the bare earth around them. Three
successive years in tobacco finished a field . . . its eroded subsoil, henceforth
known as 'old field,' was abandoned to a straggle of scrub pine while the process was repeated in another newly opened clearing."[3]

Soil exhaustion could easily have been controlled by prudent land management, but allowing fields to lie fallow was not an option open to Virginia
planters. They had too many slaves and, just as tobacco sucked nutrients from
soil, slaves sucked capital from their owners. Slaveholders were forced to undertake a large, ongoing investment in their workforce, providing food, lodging,
clothing, and even medical care from birth until death. As a slave's productiv-
ity did not really begin until young adulthood, a planter could invest upwards
of ten to twelve years in a slave before a return could be expected. If slaves died
or, even worse, were incapacitated before their most productive years were
completed, the planter's return on investment shrank still further. On the
other end, a slave's productive years ended early, so the planter's investment
had to continue even after the life of the asset was exhausted.[4]

Oversupply was an ongoing problem. Tobacco was grown in a pleasant climate under generally tolerable working conditions, so mortality was relatively
low. Unlike those who employed free labor, slaveowners did not have the option of firing unproductive workers. When planters found themselves with
more slaves than they needed, the only alternative was to try to find a way to
sell off the excess. But with their fellow planters just as overstocked, not much
of a market existed. With unproductive slaves, there was no market at all.

Nor was redirecting capital into other ventures an alternative. Most Virginia planters did not have any excess capital anyway, nor did they have any interest in industry or commerce. The best the overstocked planter could hope for was to train slaves to perform new tasks, but even here the options were limited. "The institution of slavery caused the exportation of wealth from the prosperous districts for the purchase of recruits to the labor supply, and excluded or discouraged most of the population from sharing or endeavoring to share in large scale industrial affairs. This fixed the community in a rut, deprived it of the great benefits of industrial diversification, and kept the whole community in the state of commercial dependence on the North and Europe like that of any normal colony on the mother country."[5]

With so much of the available resources going to support—or control—the workforce, a more measured approach to planting was out of the question. Instead, the tobacco planters were compelled to work their land harder and harder to generate larger crops to offset costs. "Planters bought fresh lands and more slaves to make more tobacco, and with the profits they bought more and more slaves to make more tobacco with which to buy yet more land and slaves. . . . The process involved a heavy export of wealth in the acquisition of every new laborer. . . . [T]he southern planter, as a rule, invested all his profits in a fictitious form of wealth, and never accumulated a surplus for any other sort of investment."[6]

The resemblance of tobacco farming to modern strip-mining is unmistakable. "[Virginians] devastated natural vegetation to clear a patch of land, planted tobacco on the patch for six or seven years, then abandoned it unprotected to the elements while they moved on to destroy new patches."[7] Gouverneur Morris was appalled during his first trip to Virginia at the vast stretches of scrub pine, all that was left of previously productive farmland.

Not surprisingly, therefore, planters looked to the fertile Ohio Territory as a solution to their problems, a "new injection of fertile land to replace the soil wasted by tobacco production."[8] Although most of the Ohio Company speculators expected to turn a profit through resale of some of the land to immigrants, acquisition of the Ohio lands represented an extension—and a protection—of their way of life.

Picking just the right tract was critical and so, although he was not a Virginian, not wealthy, not a planter, and owned no slaves, Thomas "Big Spoon" Cresap was immediately offered a share by the Ohio Company. Cresap lived in Old Town, a settlement that he had personally carved out of the wilderness on the Maryland side of the Potomac, just east of the Alleghenies at the western edge of civilization. He was a renowned trader, frontiersman, and braggart, a crack shot and ferocious fighter, and perhaps the most colorful character in all of North America. He had been reviled as the "Maryland Monster" during border disputes with Pennsylvania in the 1730s, and in 1748, almost seventy years old, lived in a fortress he had built himself that doubled as a trading post. His youngest son, Michael, had built a similar structure nearby.[9]

Loved and feared by the local tribes, Thomas Cresap was known to every Indian and white man from Canada to the Carolinas. Cresap had acquired his nickname for the pot of meat stew that simmered constantly on his stove for the gratification of any Native American who happened to chance by. No Virginian—not a Lee, not a Mercer, not a Washington—who ventured west did so without a stop at Old Town. No one was more suitable to help choose a spot for the Ohio Company's claim than Thomas Cresap.

Choice was vital since the land that the company had set its eyes on was not simply there for the taking. The Iroquois, Miamis, Wyandots, Cherokees, and other local tribes would have to grant approval, to say nothing of the French, who thought little of charters issued by English kings and considered the western territory theirs. The Cresaps notwithstanding, the French, who respected Native American traditions quite a bit more than the English, had generally better relations with the tribes. Still, since the costs of surveying, personnel, and construction were all to be borne by the investors—the twenty shares of the company were subscribed at a hefty £200 each—Lee and his fellows anticipated quick approval from Governor Gooch.

But Sir William turned them down. Saying that he wished to avoid trouble with the tribes and the French, he flatly rejected the company's application.

This was not a group of men accustomed to being refused anything, especially since Sir William had just granted a rival consortium, the Loyal Company, a grant of eight hundred thousand acres south of the Ohio, in what is now Kentucky. That grant was pure speculation, not even requiring any settlement or forts. To make matters more galling, the Loyal Company was largely made up of nouveaux riches like Peter Jefferson from the western end of the state. The suspicion at once arose that Sir William's interests might not be exactly arm's length, and the Ohio Company dispatched Lawrence Washington to London to have him overruled.

Washington made the rounds and, after he granted unpaid shares in the new company to men of influence such as Robert Dinwiddie and the Duke of Bedford, the king himself saw fit to grant the company's charter. The Ohio Company could claim one hundred thousand acres immediately and the second one hundred thousand after the first hundred colonists were settled and the fort was built. Also, by the time Lawrence Washington returned to Virginia, Sir

William Gooch had been ordered replaced as acting governor by Thomas Lee, and Washington was made head of the Ohio Company.

In 1749, Lawrence Washington sent his half-brother, seventeen-year-old George, to Old Town to do some preliminary scouting for a suitable access route into the Ohio Territory. The younger Washington, although having spent the previous two years honing his craft surveying the millions of acres in Virginia that had been granted to Lord Fairfax, was not enough of a frontiersman to venture very far and so, the next year the company hired Christopher Gist.

Gist is one of the great forgotten figures of the American frontier, a man whose achievements rivaled those of his neighbor, Daniel Boone. Gist's job was to survey along the Ohio River from its headwaters near Shannopin's Town in Pennsylvania (now Pittsburgh) eight hundred miles into Kentucky, to current-day Louisville. In a six-month trek begun from Old Town in November 1750, he covered about two-thirds of the distance, mapping the entire Ohio countryside as he went.[10] The following winter, Gist completed a similar survey on the south side of the Ohio, mapping most of what is today West Virginia. In addition to providing detailed descriptions of the landscape, Gist also traded with the indigenous tribes, thus paving the way for peaceful settlement. With Gist's surveys in hand, the Ohio Company decided to exercise its mandate in the territory near Shannopin's Town, south and east of the Ohio, an excellent tract that unfortunately was also claimed by Pennsylvania and by the French crown. The company began to clear a road north from western Virginia up toward their claim.

In February 1751, Thomas Lee died and was replaced by Robert Dinwiddie, one of the men Lawrence Washington had enticed into the Ohio Company in England. Later that same year, Lawrence Washington contracted tuberculosis. He sailed to Barbados with his half-brother to try to cure the disease, the only time in his life that George Washington would be out of North America. The trip was a disaster. George was struck with smallpox and, although he recovered, his teeth fell out and he probably lost the ability to have children. Lawrence recovered but he died in Virginia the following year. Following his death, the Ohio Company did not elect another head. Instead, most of the responsibilities fell to the recently appointed twenty-seven-year-old treasurer, George Mason.

A crisis soon developed. By this time, the road had been completed, and Gist and Cresap were spreading trinkets around in the Ohio Company's name and meeting with tribal chiefs. The French, however, had no intention of sitting passively by and allowing a swarm of Englishmen to claim their territory. By 1753, Marquis Duquesne, the French commander in Quebec, had dispatched almost two thousand experienced soldiers to post claims to the land

and establish a string of forts. (Pennsylvania, none too thrilled as well, confined itself to a series of diplomatic protests.)

In November, Lieutenant Governor Dinwiddie sent Gist and George Washington at the head of a delegation of six to tell the French that they were trespassing and demand that they leave immediately. The French commander at the floridly named Fort Le Boeuf received Washington politely, but after reading Dinwiddie's letter, told him to leave immediately and that he would arrest any English settlers entering the Ohio country. Washington and his party trudged back to Virginia, dodging bullets and nearly drowning in a half-frozen river.

The Ohio Company was not through, however. The following year Washington returned, this time without Gist but with a company of militia. (Officially, the militia should not have been used to support what was in fact a piece of private enterprise, but Dinwiddie was wearing two hats.) By the time Washington arrived at the forks of the Ohio, the French had almost completed a more formidable Fort Duquesne. When they heard that Englishmen were moving their way, they sent out a scouting party. Washington attacked the sleeping French on May 28, 1754, killing their commander and sending the rest scurrying for the fort. Washington then decided to build a fort of his own, which he dubbed Fort Necessity. The French commander at Fort Duquesne sent out a much larger force of soldiers and Native Americans to attack Fort Necessity, where on July 3 they soundly defeated the hopelessly overmatched Washington, capturing or killing his entire force. Washington and the other survivors were paroled and once again sent slogging back to Virginia.

For most men, a minor battle in a colonial backwater would have caused less than a ripple in world politics, but George Washington was not a man destined to be involved in small things. The battle at Fort Necessity between the Ohio Company and France ignited a clash between Virginia and France, and then a full-scale colonial war between England and France. The fighting spread across Europe and Asia, through Russia, Germany, Sweden, India, and even Africa. Called the French and Indian War in America and the Seven Years War everywhere else, the conflict cost many thousands of lives, millions of pounds, brought on the Stamp Act, and shaped the future of three continents. Only twenty-two years old, George Washington had helped ignite the first world war.

For the next nine years, as France and England fought for control of North America, the Ohio Company waited, having nothing to show for its efforts except expenditures that exceeded £10,000. War in the Ohio country was particularly difficult since most of the Native Americans supported the French.[11] Only after the French were defeated on the Plains of Abraham above Montreal in 1759 did the future of the Ohio Territory no longer seem in doubt. The following year, George Mason joined four other members of the Ohio Company in a letter to fellow member Lieutenant Governor Dinwiddie:

> As we expect a peace next winter, and have no doubt North America will be secured to the British government and liberty will then be granted to his Majesty's subjects in these colonies to settle on the lands on the Ohio, we the committee of the Ohio Company think it a proper time as soon as peace is concluded to apply for a grant of the lands intended us by his Majesty's instructions to Sir William Gooch, and have for that purpose sent over a petition to his Majesty and a large and full state of our case . . . let us beg you will please to exert yourself in getting us a patent . . . on the best terms possible . . . for the government here . . . from jealousy or some other cause have ever sought to disappoint us in every design we could form to settle and improve the lands. We will agree to any reasonable consideration of such a deed from England."[12]

Also in anticipation of victory, members of the company had been buying up land as individuals, both within the current boundaries of the colony as well as in the unsettled territory to the west. While the Ohio Company's patent never exceeded the original two hundred thousand acres, many references indicate that the claims were actually for five hundred thousand acres or more, encompassing the total holdings claimed by the company's membership as well as the specific patent granted to the corporation. Most of the private purchases were south of the Ohio and west of the territory to which Pennsylvania had a claim, in present-day West Virginia and Kentucky. No one was more fond of buying land than George Mason. He acquired land by all means available, and, by the war's end, personally owned thousands of acres in the West.[13]

When the French were defeated and the Treaty of Paris in 1763 ceded all of France's North American territory east of the Mississippi, except New Orleans, to England, the Ohio Company investors seemed certain to finally achieve their aims.* But the optimism of Mason and his colleagues proved premature. Fearing a swarm of English settlers now that their French allies were no longer there to prevent it, Pontiac, chief of the Ottawas, led an alliance of Ohio-area tribes against the English in an uprising that became know as Pontiac's War. Although it amounted to little more than a series of skirmishes that the British would easily put down a year later, the prospect of continued troubles in the West, with its concomitant drain on a treasury already facing bankruptcy from almost a decade of world war, was not something London would risk.

---

*New Orleans was ceded to Spain, which eventually led to the Jay-Gardoqui affair.

Even before Pontiac was subdued, the British government issued the Proclamation of 1763, forbidding English colonists from settling west of the Appalachians, which included the land that the Ohio Company had spent £10,000 trying to develop. Although those with existing claims were specifically exempt, the Ohio Company had yet to settle any pioneers or establish formal title. Worse for the Virginians, as part of the terms of surrender in 1764, the tribes that had supported Pontiac were forced to cede some tribal lands as reparations to the "suffering traders," as they were called, whose goods and property had been allegedly destroyed. Pennsylvania, whose western boundary had always been a matter of conjecture, insisted that its traders had been more ill-used than those of Virginia and therefore the forfeited territory should be theirs. If the crown agreed, Pennsylvania would extend its boundaries well past the Alleghenies and swallow up the Ohio Company's one hundred thousand acres.

In 1768, a group of Pennsylvania speculators, including Benjamin Franklin's son William, formed a land consortium and put in a claim for an even larger stretch of territory, eventually three million acres, on both sides of the Ohio. Originally calling it the Traders Company (for the "suffering traders"), then the Indiana Company, the Pennsylvanians ultimately settled on Vandalia Company and, availing themselves of Benjamin Franklin's influence in London, claimed that the land was for a fourteenth colony, to be called Vandalia, in honor of Queen Charlotte's German lineage.

The Virginians were livid, none more so than George Mason. The Proclamation of 1763 had radicalized him—he wrote his first political paper in response to the decision—and he spent the next years furiously but fruitlessly trying to persuade or goad London into reversing its decision. But the Virginians were so inept in London that their own representative, James Mercer, ended up being bought off with Vandalia Company shares. With Benjamin Franklin making Pennsylvania's case while Mason fumed in Virginia, the crown ruled in Vandalia's favor in 1770, thus formally terminating the Ohio Company's claim.[14]

Although Virginia did not relinquish its claims north of the Ohio—and in fact maintained a titular claim to the entire territory up to what is now Wisconsin until 1781—with the 1770 decision, Virginia's northern boundary was effectively limited by the Ohio River.[15] Even worse for the frustrated Virginians, the Proclamation of 1763 was roundly ignored and more than thirty thousand new settlers poured over the mountains in the next five years. Fort Duquesne became Fort Pitt, the West was open, and the land that Christopher Gist had recommended became every bit as valuable as he thought it would, with the investors in the Ohio Company receiving not one shilling for their foresight.

PART II

Four Architects

5. SORCERER'S APPRENTICE:
VIRGINIA AND THE UPPER SOUTH

*V*irginia was pivotal for any plan of union. The state split the country geographically, was the home of the most important political figures of the day, and provided political and economic transition between northern commercial interests and the Carolina rice planters. And, if Virginia was the fulcrum of the United States, George Mason IV was very much the fulcrum of Virginia.

From the early 1750s, while he was still in his twenties, Mason had wielded vast power and influence in almost every aspect of Virginia life. One of Washington's closest friends and confidants, George Mason was among the wealthiest men in the state, sought after socially and politically, and universally respected for his democratic vision and as a champion of individual rights.

Mason was both comfortable in this role and believed it was warranted by birth and lineage. A product of the unique development of the Upper South, he never doubted his identity as an aristocrat. He spent much of his adult life working, writing, philosophizing, dispensing largesse to the community and wisdom to his fellows, all while rarely venturing from his baronial estate, Gunston Hall. Other than some youthful visits across the Potomac to neighboring Maryland, his journey to the convention in Philadelphia was his first trip out of Virginia.

The Virginia tobacco nobility was a product of the plantation economy, which in Virginia was originally created not through slavery, but by the convergence of a number of other factors, including unrest in England, the promise of America, disease, and opportunistic second marriages.

While the early settlers in Virginia had to contend with hostile terrain and sometimes hostile tribes, by the middle of the seventeenth century a thriving colony had developed. The coastline had been cleared and pacified, permanent settlements were expanding, and fortunes were being made growing staple crops, especially tobacco. As a result, by the 1650s, Virginia had come to look substantially more appealing to many royalists than an England dominated by Oliver Cromwell, his puritans, and the tyranny of republican government. There was also a chance to stand out. "Englishmen with spare cash came to Virginia also because the prestige and power that a man could expect in Virginia was comparatively much greater than he was likely to attain in England, where men of landed wealth and gentle birth abounded."[1] Two such men, Gerard Fowke and George Mason I, both of George Mason IV's great-grandfathers, arrived from the midlands in England sometime around 1650.

Once in America, the new pioneers, having taken advantage of the cheap and plentiful land, had to cultivate a labor source to work their estates. They naturally looked to the mother country to supply their needs and were pleased to discover a surfeit of willing recruits. America was already acquiring a reputation as a place to get rich, and the only way that Englishmen without spare cash could avail themselves of those opportunities was to indenture themselves for a term of years to one of the wealthier planters in exchange for passage from England. When their term expired, they would hopefully have saved enough to buy land of their own. Plantations were thus initially staffed almost exclusively by white servants.

But for all its opportunity, Virginia was still the frontier, and the dual hazards of violence and disease took the lives of master and servant alike. Men, who did the fighting and the clearing, were more susceptible to these perils than women, and Virginia soon became the home of a good many widows, some of them quite wealthy. A few of these women returned to England, but the prospects for remarriage there were less favorable than in America, where fresh crops of eager young unmarried men of good birth arrived every year.

Mergers, both of the heart and the pocketbook, were the natural result. "The fortunes gathered by those early immigrants during the deadly first half century were not necessarily lost or dispersed. Capital still accumulated in the hands of widows and joined in profitable wedlock the sums that well-heeled immigrants brought with them. [The wealthy families] not only shared the spoils of office among themselves, but also by well-planned marriages shared the savings gathered by their predecessors..."[2] Wealthy widows thereby became a key factor in centralizing wealth, a consolidation that caused plantations to grow and introduced economies of scale, which in turn accentuated the need for a different kind of labor.

That slaves became those laborers was due largely to the elimination of disease and violence. African slaves had been in Virginia since the 1620s, but, since one owned a slave for life instead of for only four or five years, they were about twice the price of white servants. Given the high mortality rate of those early years, Africans were thus initially seen as an uneconomic investment for field work. As conditions improved, the economics changed, but only if one had the money—or the credit—to pay. Slaves still cost substantially more than servants, two or three times as much for a "seasoned man or woman." African slaves were thus a luxury item at first, available only to a man who could avail himself of economies of scale. Only after Africans began to supplant the white workforce, since they could be made to work harder and longer, did they become the labor of choice for any planter who could scrape together the cash.[3]

Large plantations manned with slave labor soon overpowered smaller ones staffed by whites, which gave the slaveowner the wherewithal to buy more and more of the surrounding land and squeeze out smaller farmers. Unable to compete, the farmers were often forced either to become tenants of plantation owners or to migrate westward and attempt to establish some independence from the plantation system by reverting to subsistence farming. This further increased the stranglehold of the plantation on all but the frontier regions and intensified the animosity between coastal planters and backcountry farmers that was present throughout the South. In addition, since slaves were property, any of their children legally belonged to the owner, thus turning slaves into much more of a self-perpetuating investment than term-servants.

There was one more advantage. Once slavery was entrenched, it "offered incomparable advantages in keeping labor docile,"[4] since the punishments regularly inflicted on African slaves would never have been allowed for white servants. Robert "King" Carter, for example, one of the early land barons, successfully petitioned a court to be allowed to chop off the toes of one of his slaves who had tried to run off.

Brutality was not an aspect of the slave system that Virginians publicized. They worked hard at perpetuating the notion that slavery was, at its core, a benign institution. Robert Beverley in his *History and Present State of Virginia*, published in 1705, went so far as to assert, "Slaves are not worked near so hard, nor so many Hours in a Day, as the Husbandmen and Day-Labourers in England."[5] What Beverley failed to mention was that, unlike day laborers in England, slaves who were deemed difficult could be lashed to death or dismembered, all within the bounds of both the law and accepted rules of proper behavior.

Slaves on a tobacco plantation

Virginia planters put such effort into propagandizing slavery because it had become the foundation of the social structure. "Along the Potomac and Rappahannock, and the lesser rivers and creeks that emptied into them, most of the riparian lands consolidated into major plantations. The larger owners supplied both the county leadership and the ranking personalities of the colony. On this basis, the English class society reproduced itself."[6]

Thus, for Virginians, in the early eighteenth century, the plantation became the American version of the sprawling English estate. The planter who owned it evolved into a self-appointed manor lord, dispensing justice and munificence to his subjects, which included not only his slaves, but also the poorer tenant farmers around him, and anyone else less wealthy who happened by. A Virginia clergyman named Devereux Jarratt wrote in the 1780s, "We were accustomed to look upon gentle folks as beings of a superior order. For my part I was quite shy of them, and kept off at a humble distance. A periwig in those days was a distinguishing badge of gentlefolk, and when I saw a man riding the road, near our house with a wig on, it would so alarm my fears and give me such a disagreeable feeling, that I daresay I would run off as if for my life."[7]

As the slave system took hold, so did the indebtedness that would haunt Virginia. "The planters in Virginia were more eager to buy slaves than to pay for them ... By 1705 the Virginia Assembly was so disturbed by the rising indebtedness that it tried to slow down the traffic ... but by then the conversion to slave labor had already been made ... Between 1708 and 1750 Virginia recorded the entry of 38,418 slaves into the colony."[8] The surprising cost of slave upkeep, however, did little to discourage Virginians from increasing their holdings. Slaves were property, property was wealth, and a man was judged by how much he owned. As such, slaves, at least at first, were encouraged to breed, like cattle, sheep, or hogs. By the time of the Philadelphia convention, Virginians had been so successful in breeding their human property that the slave population had overtaken that of whites.[9] While not yet in the majority, slave populations in the other tobacco states, Maryland and North Carolina, were also approaching critical levels. These states imposed tariffs and temporary bans, and sometimes resorted to desperate measures to stop further importation of Africans.[10]

The lords in England did not mind the Virginians' pretensions to aristocracy as long as they continued to ship tobacco eastward and used the proceeds to buy English goods for the return voyage. They even enhanced the aristocratic mood by bestowing honors and titles on the Virginia gentry, one of which was an appointment as county lieutenant. Named by the royal governor, the recipient was granted the title "colonel," a title and position equivalent to those that existed in English shires. George Mason I was so named in the 1670s. He passed it down to his son, George Mason II, in the 1680s, who in turn passed it to his son, George Mason III, in 1709.[11] The office seems to have become an anachronism before George Mason IV could claim it, but he nonetheless insisted on being addressed as "Colonel Mason" for most of his life.

In 1725, George Mason IV was therefore born into a mature aristocracy and was groomed from the start to take his place among the Virginia elite. Mason's father died when he was a boy, drowning in a ferry mishap on the Potomac, when his son was only ten. Young Mason fell under the guardianship of a pragmatic uncle, John Mercer, a graduate of Trinity College in Dublin, who had come to the colonies to make a success of himself in business, then married a planter's daughter, Catherine Mason, George IV's aunt. Mercer was an astute businessman and multiplied his wife's already impressive holdings.

As he grew more successful, Mercer developed an interest in the law. Although he became a highly successful attorney, he was not so much interested in practical applications but rather in history and philosophy. Mercer amassed one of the finest private libraries in the colony, more than 1,500 volumes, mostly history, classical studies, and legal theory. In true Virginia tradition, he went into debt to do it.

As George Mason IV approached manhood, his uncle's library was an immense resource. It was in no way obligatory for well-born Virginia youth to be sent to England for an education. Most received early instruction from private tutors and then were sent either to the College of William and Mary, like Jefferson and Edmund Randolph, or, like Madison, to Princeton, then called the College of New Jersey. Mason did not attend college at all, but was instead tutored exclusively by Mercer, who provided him with a classical education equal or superior to that of most of his peers.

When he reached his majority, Mason set himself to expanding his assets. After buying up property in the newly incorporated city of Alexandria and joining the Ohio Company, he married sixteen-year-old Ann Eilbeck, the daughter of a prosperous Maryland planter with extensive holdings on the Virginia side of the Potomac. Soon after his marriage in 1750, Mason and his bride moved to one of the family's estates, located on a peninsula called Dogue's Neck. One of the couple's neighbors was eighteen-year-old George Washington, who had just inherited a plantation after the death of his half-brother Lawrence. Washington and Mason became friends, the self-assured Mason also becoming something of a mentor to the younger man.

Almost immediately, Mason imported a master builder and architect named William Buckland to complete a palatial mansion on 550 acres in Dogue's Neck, about twenty miles south of Washington, D.C., that would become known as Gunston Hall. Buckland, who arrived from England on a four-year indenture, combined the styles of the great English architects Christopher Wren and Inigo Jones with a modernist vision to create a classical plantation home, notable for its intricate interior carvings, five-sided entranceway, arches, porches, and series of gardens. While the wealthiest planters often lived in palatial homes, for one of them to undertake the building of such a home while still in his mid-twenties was highly unusual.[12]

Gunston Hall took more than five years to complete, but once it was built, it became the center of Mason's world for the rest of his life. Except for reluctant trips to the capital at Williamsburg, Mason almost never left Dogue's Neck. He had little need to do so. With Mason's hundreds of slaves seeing to every chore and need, Gunston Hall was completely self-sufficient.

Mason's son John described life at his father's plantation: "It was very much the practice with gentlemen of landed and slave estates . . . to so organize them as to have considerable resources within themselves; to employ and pay but few tradesmen and to buy little or none of the coarse stuffs and materials used by them, and this practice became stronger and more general during the long period of the Revolutionary War which in great measure cut off the means of supply from elsewhere. Thus my father had among his slaves carpenters, coopers, sawyers, blacksmiths, tanners, curriers, shoemakers, spinners, weavers and knitters, and even a distiller."[13] Luxury goods, however, had to be purchased from England. "The master's wines and broadcloth were imported from abroad with the silk dresses and jewels of the mistress."[14] Furniture, fabric, books, and other finery came from the continent as well, brought across the Atlantic, more often than not, by New England shippers.

The result was not surprising. "The gentlefolk in their wigs, with their humble white neighbors bowing down before them, their white indentured servants and negro slaves, had every temptation to pride and arrogance."[15]

Through most of the 1750s, with the exception of his activities with the Ohio Company, Mason's involvement in political affairs was casual, restricted to the types of immediate local issues in which every man of great means was expected to participate. He was elected to the House of Burgesses in 1759, and during the French and Indian War was charged with providing logistical assistance in obtaining supplies for Virginia's troops.[16] At about this time he began to insist on being addressed as "Colonel," although he would never don a uniform or participate in a single battle.[17]

Mason's paper protesting George III's Proclamation of 1763 prohibiting western expansion was his first foray into politics, but his real political career began on December 23, 1765. Outraged by the Stamp Act, like most of his fellow Americans, he tried to both avoid and undermine the hated legislation. Mason's December broadside contained a strategy for allowing courts to function in property actions while avoiding issuing or accepting any documents that would require stamps. This tract, Mason's first important public paper, began not with a denunciation of the Stamp Act, but with an attack on slavery. "The policy of encouraging the Importation of free People & discouraging that of Slaves has never been duly considered in this colony," he wrote, "or we should not at this Day see one Half of our best Lands in most Parts of the Country remain unsettled & the other cultivated with Slaves; not to mention the ill Effect such a Practice has upon the Morals & Manners of our People. One of the first Signs of the Decay, & perhaps the primary Cause of the Destruction of the most flourishing Government that ever existed was the Introduction of Great Numbers of Slaves—an Evil very pathetically described by Roman Historians."[18]

George Mason

This passage was the first of many instances in the coming years in which Mason would issue scathing condemnations of slavery.[19] In 1773, he ratcheted up his rhetoric still further in a landmark paper, *Extracts from the Virginia Charters, with Some Remarks Upon Them.* "That slow Poison, [slavery] . . . is daily contaminating the Minds & Morals of our People. Every Gentleman here is born a petty Tyrant. Practiced in Acts of Despotism & Cruelty, we become callous to the Dictates of Humanity, & all the finer feelings of the Soul. Taught to regard a part of our own Species in the most abject & contemptible Degree below us, we lose that Idea of the dignity of Man which the Hand of Nature had implanted in us, for great & useful purposes. Habituated from our Infancy to trample upon the Rights of Human Nature, every generous, every liberal Sentiment, if not extinguished, is enfeebled in our Minds. And in such an infernal School are to be educated our future Legislators & Rulers."[20]

Mason's denunciations of slavery struck a surprisingly receptive chord with his fellow planters. In the coming decades, Virginia slaveowners would often complain that they found themselves enmeshed in a system that they loathed, but felt was too dangerous to public welfare to end. Jefferson was later to famously assert that reliance on slavery was like trying to hold "a wolf by the ears." Slavery had been forced on southern planters by Britain, the argument went, and the mother country's voracious appetite for the fruits of slavery—tobacco, rice, and indigo—perpetuated the detestable institution. One can almost imagine groups of Virginia planters sitting in the grand parlors of the manor houses that were built by slaves, eating food that was grown, cooked, and served by slaves, drinking fine wine that was poured by slaves, and speaking with complete conviction and sincerity about the evils of the system.

But Mason was not so much an apologist as a visionary. He was not opposed to slavery on ethical grounds—this was no William Lloyd Garrison—but rather because he saw that reliance on slavery was undermining the social fabric of Virginia. As Mason well knew, by the 1770s, protecting slavery had become more than an exercise in convenience for Virginia planters. For these men, slavery was their life. It shaped their politics, their economics, and, most important, their view of themselves. But Mason also realized that the chains forged by slavery had come to bind the owners as much as the slaves. The seemingly geometric expansion of the slave population threatened to overwhelm Virginia, and Mason was one of the few planters who foresaw that, in order to survive, Virginia would have to find a solution to its slave problem.

If opposition to slavery was as deep-rooted as most historians have contended, a man as clever as Mason would have proposed the most obvious and least painful method to phase it out—simply prohibit the institution in newly settled lands. Yet not once did he ever suggest that slavery be prohibited anywhere.[21] Quite the contrary—Mason fully expected slavery to spread throughout the Southwest and viewed this eventuality as a fortuitous means by which Virginia could rid itself of its oversupply of slaves.

As practical as Mason's analysis of slavery might have been, there was no doubt of his idealism when it came to questions of individual freedom and democratic government, at least for men such as himself. In April 1775, in *Remarks on Annual Elections,* he wrote, "We came equal into this world, and equal shall we go out of it. All men are by nature born equally free and independent . . . In all our associations; in all our agreements let us never lose sight of this fundamental maxim—that all power was originally lodged in, and consequently is derived from, the people. We should wear it as a breastplate, and buckle it on as our armour."[22]

Although Mason almost never held public office—he declined to run for a seat in the House of Burgesses more than once and also declined to serve in the Continental Congress—perhaps no one save Washington more influenced the course of his state's history. In 1769, he drew up Virginia's nonimportation statutes, which Washington then presented to the Virginia assembly.[23]

In 1776, Mason wrote the first draft of the Virginia constitution and is generally acknowledged as the author of the Virginia Declaration of Rights. He claimed to be at any rate, writing to his cousin George Mercer in 1778, "to show you that I have not been an idle spectator of this great contest . . . I enclose you a copy of the first draught of the declaration of rights just as it was drawn and presented by me." (Edmund Randolph, however, asserted that the declaration was actually written by Patrick Henry.)

Even with all of these activities, and despite the great changes brewing around him, what occupied Mason the most, where he put his greatest energies, was his long-standing obsession with the Ohio Company.

After being bested by Franklin in "Vandalia," Mason had been forced to turn his attention elsewhere. In 1773, he engaged a young frontiersman named George Rogers Clark to find an alternate tract for the Ohio Company's claim. To Mason's delight, Clark did just that, locating almost eight hundred thousand acres in what is now West Virginia that were, if anything, superior to the acreage that the company had lost. In a long letter to Robert Carter, Mason noted that the new acreage was "clear of . . . the Vandalia Company's claim . . . equal to any land on this continent, being exceeding rich and level." He complained to Carter, however, that the £650 bill for surveying, which was supposed to be paid by the members, was due but that most of his colleagues had not yet come through. "It is unreasonable," he complained, "that I should advance the remainder." Mason was upset that "upon the credit of the Ohio Company, and the particular promises of several of its members to advance £50 sterling each, I agreed to make myself liable for the charges of this survey, and am now liable to suffer for it."[24]

As events in the colonies were reaching a crisis, Mason could not understand why his fervor for land speculation was not always shared by other Virginians. In March 1775, one month before Lexington and Concord, he wrote to Washington, "The inattention of our Assembly to so grand an object, as the right of this colony to the Western lands is inexcusable, and the confusion it will introduce will be endless."[25]

At the outset of the war, Mason refused appointment to the Virginia Committee of Public Safety because of continued bouts of "ill health," most likely recurring bouts with his old nemesis gout, although he corresponded regularly with Washington and threw his weight as a private citizen behind the Revolution. As an agent for the committee, he procured supplies and arranged shipping. But even as the fighting began in Massachusetts, he had in no way abandoned his attempts to secure Clark's newly surveyed acreage for the Ohio Company.

His reaction to Maryland's demands that states cede their western lands as a condition of ratification of the Articles of Confederation was typically personal. Mason was convinced that Maryland's mulishness was specifically aimed at denying the Ohio Company its claims. In April 1779, he wrote to Richard Henry Lee "that the secret and true cause of the great opposition to Virginia's title to her chartered territory [Virginia and the Ohio Company being as one in the same] was the great Indian purchase between the Obache and Illinois Rivers, made in the year 1773 or 1774, in which Governor Johnston and several of the leading men of Maryland are concerned with Lord Dunmore, Governor Tryon, and many other noblemen and gentlemen of Great Britain."[26]

But most of Mason's antipathy was reserved for the Pennsylvanians. At his prompting, the Virginia legislature had declared before the war that all purchases by the "Indiana Company" (essentially the same crew as the Vandalia Company) were void, a resolution with no teeth whatsoever since those decisions were being made in London. Once the the crown was out of the picture, Virginia was free to fight it out with Pennsylvania in Congress. With Franklin back on American soil, however, Congress seemed no more amenable to Virginia's claims than had been Parliament or the king.

In December 1779, while Washington prepared for another brutal winter, Mason drafted a *Remonstrance of the General Assembly of Virginia to the Delegates of the United American States in Congress Assembled* that stated, "The General Assembly of Virginia cannot avoid expressing their surprise and concern, upon the information that Congress had received and countenanced petitions from certain persons styling themselves the Vandalia and Indiana Companies, asserting claims to lands in defiance of the civil authority, jurisdiction and laws of this commonwealth, and offering to erect a separate government within the territory thereof. Should Congress assume a jurisdiction [by the Pennsylvanians] . . . it would be a violation of public faith . . . and establish in Congress a power which . . . must degenerate into an intolerable despotism." Mason went on to assert that in its petition, Virginia was protecting not only its own claims, but those of the very Marylanders he had denounced in his letter to Richard Henry Lee.[27]

Eventually, dealing with Pennsylvanians, Marylanders, and Northerners became too much, and Mason threw up his hands. In 1781, he announced that he was retiring from public life.

Retirement did not, however, lessen his influence. As an intimate of Washington and a figure of respect up and down the Northern Neck, Mason continued to be sought out on matters affecting the state. When it seemed certain that the Ohio Company would not succeed in gaining control of any significant western territory, Mason backed a growing movement to cede all western lands to the Confederation, advocating like Jefferson the division of this land into new states. This would at least get Congress (and Franklin) out of the picture.

But the fight was already over. By the war's end, the Ohio Company of Virginia existed only on paper, and would not even have had that distinction had not Mason continued to maintain it.[28]

By May 1787, the sixty-two-year-old Mason was still a preeminent figure in Virginia politics, one of the most respected advocates for the tobacco planters of Virginia, but the doddering Franklin was no longer a force on the national scene. As Mason contemplated his first visit north, he may have wondered who his new adversaries might be. There was no shortage of possibilities—the delegate list was filled with men of national reputation, important men from important commercial states, such as Gouverneur Morris and Robert Morris from Pennsylvania, Alexander Hamilton from New York, and Elbridge Gerry and Rufus King from Massachusetts. While the northerners would indeed prove treacherous, a fellow slaveholder, a man whose background was in many ways the mirror of Mason's own, would most prove to be Virginia's undoing.

6. GOLD IN THE SWAMPS: SOUTH CAROLINA, RICE, AND THE LOWER SOUTH

$\mathcal{U}$pon arriving in New York in 1765, South Carolina's John Rutledge, who had been educated in England, wrote to his mother, "This is my first trip to a foreign country."[1]

Unlike the self-contained aristocracy of Virginia, the men that South Carolina sent to Philadelphia—Rutledge, the Pinckneys, and Pierce Butler—were almost more British than the British. They saw themselves as English gentry, behaved like English gentry, and Butler even reminded his fellow delegates that he was the only member of the convention who had actually descended from English gentry.[2] All four were planters who had trained in the law and each played a pivotal role in Philadelphia. But the undisputed leader of the delegation was Rutledge. Perhaps the nation's most successful lawyer—he hadn't lost a case in court in twenty-six years—Rutledge had also risen to be South Carolina's most powerful and respected political figure. During the Revolution, he had been granted such sweeping powers to guide the state through the war that he had become known as the "Old Dictator" or "Dictator John," attaining this position through a combination of talent, attitude, and some extremely adroit marketing by his uncle.[3]

The Old Dictator's saga began around 1730, when an appealing but non-descript young man with a law degree from the University of Dublin named Andrew Rutledge arrived in Charles Town, South Carolina.* Although he had no money and no discernible pedigree, within a year Rutledge had succeeded in charming his way into the tightly knit, generations-old Charles Town social elite, so much so as to get himself elected to the South Carolina assembly.[4]

---

*"Charles Town" did not officially become "Charleston" until after the Revolution.

In early 1732, Rutledge was retained to prosecute a lawsuit by the immensely wealthy Colonel Hugh Hext. Hext was in his mid-sixties at that time, with a beautiful second wife in her twenties who had borne him an adored seven-year-old daughter, Sarah. Rutledge won the suit, and Hext invited him to dinner in gratitude. A few months later, Colonel Hext died, and a few months after that Andrew Rutledge married his widow.

According to the terms of the colonel's will, however, the widow was only to receive income from the estate during her lifetime. When she died, the estate passed not to any new husband, but to Sarah, who would take possession on either her twenty-first birthday or her marriage, whichever came first. What's more, the colonel's brother Thomas, a widower with no heirs, had left his entire, quite substantial estate to Sarah as well, as had another uncle. Little Sarah Hext was thus poised to become one of the richest women in South Carolina.

Seeing an opportunity, Andrew Rutledge undertook a search for his brother John, a ship's doctor, some years younger but with equal charm. John had never been to America, and it took Andrew two years to track him down and bring him to Charles Town. When Dr. John, as he became known, finally arrived, he moved in with his brother and was introduced to Andrew's stepdaughter.

Romance blossomed and, on Christmas Day 1738, Sarah Hext, just turned fourteen, married twenty-five-year-old John Rutledge. A little more or less than nine months later, their first son was born, also named John for his father.[5] Six children followed in quick succession, the youngest, Edward, destined for no small measure of distinction of his own.

Dr. John's rollicking early life had rendered him susceptible to both alcohol and disease, the former of which he could now readily afford with the latter an inevitable result. The day after his twelfth wedding anniversary, December 26, 1750, John Rutledge I died at age thirty-seven. His eldest son, John II, was eleven, but would not lack a father for long, as Uncle Andrew moved in as surrogate to his brother's children, just as John Mercer had done for the children of George Mason III. From the first, young Rutledge showed no interest whatever in the classics, poetry, or history, but demonstrated a strong mathematical mind and both fascination and aptitude for his uncle's profession, the law. While John Mercer was a theoretician, however, Andrew Rutledge favored the practical application of the discipline.

Law was a respected gentleman's calling in genteel Charles Town, the most culturally British city in America. "It was said that if a man who had been to England appeared on the streets of Boston or Philadelphia he would be pointed out and people would turn to look at him, whereas the only man people would turn to look at in Charles Town was the one who had not been to England."[6]

Charles Town was also the wealthiest city in America, with at least four men whose fortunes exceeded any in the North. Pretenders to gentry as they were, the South Carolina "first families"—the Manigaults, the Laurenses, and the Pinckneys—lived by a code that was almost a caricature of the British upper classes.[7] Men did no manual labor, did not speak badly of women, and always kept their word. They did not smoke or utter profanities. (Drinking, however, often in copious amounts, was permitted.) The best families had country plantations set on thousands of acres and large, three-story houses surrounded by walled gardens in Charles Town's best neighborhoods. They ate from fine china, drank from crystal, had been to Oxford or Cambridge for their educations, and dressed in the latest London fashions.

And, of course, they all owned slaves—lots and lots of slaves. Planters had game cooks, vegetable cooks, servers, butlers, coachmen, footmen, maids of every type, houseboys, body servants (who were allowed to sleep on the floor at the foot of the master's bed), and, in the country, lowly field hands. Almost every manual task, from candlemaking to smithing, was performed by a slave. In the low country near the Atlantic coast where the plantations were clustered, the black population was at least double and, in some sections, six times that of whites. In Georgetown parish, up the coast from Charles Town, slaves made up an incredible 90 percent of the population when the Revolution began.[8] Charles Town itself was the low country's hub, and in the townhouses there was a strict rule that only between ten and twenty slaves should be kept. More than twenty and the owner risked the sin of ostentation; less than ten, the greater sin of poverty.

For all their affluence, proper South Carolina gentlemen almost never handled cash. Everything was done on credit, barter, by bank draft, or, most often, on a handshake. The only time a gentleman put his hand in his pocket was in a tavern. But the system was as merciless as it was genteel. A deterioration of fortune, a whiff of economic downturn, and a family could be excised from society like a dead limb sawed off a tree. The South Carolina elite were so snobbishly arrogant that even British aristocrats found them insufferable.

The font of this baronial lifestyle was the rice trade, "South Carolina gold." For a time, indigo complemented and even briefly outstripped rice as a source of riches for the planters, but rice was king. And the engine for both crops was slaves.

Several versions exist of how rice cultivation was introduced into South Carolina, the most ironic of which is that it was by the slaves themselves, whose experience with the crop in their native Africa was seized on by white planters. However it began, when rice was introduced in the 1690s, it provided a long-sought solution for assuring the prosperity of a colony whose terrain seemed unsuited for cultivating anything else.[9]

From the first, planters realized that no white person could be made to undertake the rigors of rice growing. Even Native Americans, who initially made up much of the slave population before the large-scale importation of Africans, and who were accustomed to the climate and the swamps, were not up to the task and died off too quickly to be cost-effective.* Rice only began to be profitable when an army of blacks was imported from Africa and the planters switched from dry land planting to damming the freshwater swamps that dotted the land near the coast. Rawlins Lowndes knew from whence he spoke when he declared, "Without negroes, this state is one of the most contemptible in the Union . . . that whilst there remained one acre of swamp-land in South Carolina, he should raise his voice against restricting the importation of negroes. Negroes were our wealth, our only natural resource."

Working a swamp into a rice field was killing work. Once the boundaries were laid out, slaves, working thigh deep in standing water infested with leeches, snakes, and mosquitoes, cut down trees and vegetation, and then hauled it up on dry land for burning. Trenches were dug through the mud that surrounded the cleared swamp, and floodgates were built to drain off excess water. Eventually, a grid of canals and banks was constructed and the rice could be planted in about six inches of water.

Cultivation was no easier. Seeds were required to be treated so that they would not simply wash away, after which they were pressed into the ooze. Growing season was late spring until early fall and fields required constant maintenance—weeding and hoeing—all done in the increasingly fetid marshland in midsummer. Finally, in early September, when the temperature still often exceeded ninety degrees, the stalks were cut with sickles, and then bound and stacked for curing. Chaff was separated with mortar and pestle and the rice was then placed in standard-sized barrels and sent to Charles Town for export.

In addition to its other dubious attributes, rice was heavy and hard to work, so slaves who toiled in the rice fields alternated bending for long periods

---

*Captured members of Native American tribes also knew the terrain well enough to successfully escape at the first opportunity. Africans, completely disoriented in a new continent, could be kept in line much more easily.

and lifting heavy loads. Fatigue, standing water, humidity, and mosquitoes combined to make malaria and yellow fever constant companions.

Many historians—and not just those from the South—have since argued that because planters had invested an excessive proportion of their capital in slaves, they were unlikely to risk that investment through mistreatment. Most slaves, they argue, were well fed and housed, even given the same medical care as whites, all so as not to squander a planter's most important asset. In addition, many slaves enjoyed some small autonomy through the implementation of the "task system": A specific amount of work was required during the course of a day, after which the slaves' time was their own.

Actual witnesses saw things quite differently. A European visitor to a rice plantation wrote, "If ever a work could be imagined peculiarly unwholesome, and even fatal to health, it must be standing like the Negroes, ankle and even mid-leg deep in the water, which floats on oozy mud; and exposed all the time to a burning sun which makes the very air they breathe hotter than the human blood; and these poor wretches are then in a furnace of stinking, putrid effluvia; a more horrible employment can hardly be imagined."[10] Life expectancy in such conditions was often less than three years. What's more, overseers, who were paid according to production, usually harbored aspirations of

Slaves in a rice field

ownership. The only way to raise the capital to buy land was to raise the output of the plantations they managed, an unlikely incentive for humane treatment. It was more expedient and cheaper to work older slaves to death and
replace them with younger, healthier imports, than to provide food, medicine,
and shorter working hours.[11]

As the rice profits rolled in, more and more slaves were needed and, by
1730, two-thirds of South Carolina's population was black. In the 1750s, a
system of "tidal flooding" was developed, which allowed the natural flow of
tides to wash through the rivers near the coast, creating even greater
economies of scale. The labor intensity of rice cultivation coupled with the
truncated life expectancy of the slaves led to a further increase in imports. By
1775, South Carolina had brought in nearly sixty thousand additional
slaves.[12]

Due to a series of wars in Europe, rice exports stagnated in the 1740s,
so the introduction of indigo as a staple crop late in the decade provided a
second profit base to South Carolina planters.* Indigo, the source of the
brilliant blue dye then prized in Europe, also promised to vastly improve
the working conditions for South Carolina slaves. The crop was grown on
dry land, not in swamps, and producing cakes of dye from the plant leaves
was specialized and meticulous work in contrast to the brute force of rice
cultivation.

The process required a number of specific operations, and each needed to
be performed at a precise time and in an exacting manner to ensure the best
quality dyestuff. After harvesting, the plants were placed in a series of three
adjoining vats. The plants were immersed in the first vat until they oxidized
(the planters thought they had merely rotted). When the resulting liquid
had reached the right consistency and odor, it was transferred to the second
vat where it was aerated by being agitated with paddles. At this point, the
liquid was still clear. Eventually, the solution turned blue, although that part
of the process could be speeded up with the addition of limewater, again at
precisely the right moment and in the correct amount. The blue liquid was

---

*The development of indigo as a cash crop was largely enabled by General Pinckney's mother,
Eliza Lucas Pinckney, one of the most remarkable women in colonial America. Left in charge of
three plantations and her ailing mother when she was just sixteen, she succeeded not only in
keeping the properties afloat, but also in perfecting a method of cultivating indigo in the
swampy Carolina tidewater. By the time she married the general's father, yet another Charles
Pinckney, she was the best-known woman in the Carolinas, and when she died in 1793, George
Washington himself asked to be one of her pallbearers.

drained into the third vat, where it sat until a muddy substance settled to the bottom. After the remaining liquid was drained off, the semisolid remainder was placed in linen bags to drain further, and then placed in boxes to form into cakes, which were dried in sheds away from any direct sunlight. When fully dried, the cakes were cut into cubes and packed into barrels for shipment. Failure in any of these steps would result in either an inferior product or none at all.

Unfortunately for the South Carolina planters, more than three hundred varieties of indigo existed, some yielding a richer dye than others. American indigo was inferior to the variety grown in India and the West Indies, and at first promoting demand was difficult. With the onset of the French and Indian War, however, West Indian indigo became much harder to come by and South Carolina indigo was used in its place. The British even put a bounty on the crop, thus increasing profits to the planters. When the war ended in 1763, demand for rice exploded, so in the decade leading up to the Revolution, South Carolina planters grew richer than ever before. Rice and indigo became such a source of wealth that almost every successful professional man in the low country supplemented his income by planting.

South Carolina indigo continued to sell until the onset of the Revolution, despite its inferior reputation. War, however, was indigo's ruin. The bounty disappeared as did the British market. Other markets proved impossible to develop, and by the time the convention convened in Philadelphia, indigo production had virtually disappeared and rice had once again taken its place as the financial wellspring of the low country planters. Slaves who had cultivated indigo were sent back into the swamps to die.*

Andrew Rutledge died in 1755, when his nephew John was sixteen. Two years later, John Rutledge sailed for England and Oxford. When he returned in 1761, possessed of a law degree and acceptance at the London bar, the Hext fortune had nearly been squandered. Dr. John had made a series of disastrous business decisions, the full impact of which had not been felt until after his eldest son had begun his studies in England. Plantations had been leased or sold for a fraction of

---

*South Carolina planters constantly sought a second crop but could not grow anything cheaply enough and in sufficient quantity in the lowlands until the 1790s, when a Yankee named Eli Whitney figured out how to separate cotton seeds from cotton fiber and the continuation of both prosperity and slavery was assured.

their worth, and others had been run into the ground by incompetent management. The family's expenses had been so inflated that their resources were inadequate to maintain the obligatory planter's lifestyle and the family had sunk into
debt, so much so that the Rutledges' very survival lay in the hands of the great
commodity and slave merchant Henry Laurens. Had Laurens refused to extend
Sarah Rutledge more credit, their plight would have become public and the family ruined.

Rutledge persuaded Laurens to extend the family credit one more time,
and then used the money to throw an enormous party for the first families.
There, he announced that he intended to run for a seat in the General Assembly and unseat one of the current members, a shocking breach of etiquette.
Still, after a furious house-to-house campaign, John Rutledge was elected. The
position didn't pay, but since South Carolina law stated that assembly members were immune from lawsuits, the family's precarious financial position was
temporarily stabilized.

Rutledge had returned from England with a reputation as a spellbinding
orator with a penetrating legal mind, so he assumed he could recoup the family's wealth simply by nailing up his shingle. But, like just about everything
else in Charles Town, the law was a private club, and none of the highly successful attorneys, men like Charles Pinckney,* were about to cede any of their
business to a young upstart. Henry Laurens threw Rutledge a crumb or two,
but these cases paid next to nothing.[13] Even Rutledge's great optimism had begun to erode when a young woman named Mary Cooke walked into his office
with a breach of promise case. It was the first unsolicited business that Rutledge had attracted, although such cases were considered unseemly and were
generally settled privately and quietly.

But Rutledge saw an opportunity. The prospective defendant was one
William Lennox, who, with his brother, had opened a retail emporium in
Charles Town. Their establishment sold not just one commodity, like everyone
else's, but a variety of goods, "America's first department store."[14] As a result,
the Lennox brothers had begun to take business away from Henry Laurens and
the other more specialized merchants.

So, instead of burying the case, Rutledge brought it to court, with the young
plaintiff testifying against her alleged betrothed, the sort of testimony never before heard in a Charles Town courtroom. The jury members, all prominent citizens, including Henry Laurens, listened transfixed. When Rutledge forced Lennox

*This Charles Pickney was the general's uncle.

to admit during cross-examination that he had, indeed, proposed to the young woman, the verdict was assured.

Not only did Rutledge garner a hefty fee, but the case made him a celebrity and catapulted him into the top tier of Charles Town lawyers. Within two years, still just twenty-four years old, he was the most active, the most successful, and the highest-paid lawyer in South Carolina. Rutledge began to amass a personal fortune, buying thousands of acres of land and hundreds of slaves. His political influence increased with his landholdings. In 1765, when Massachusetts proposed a meeting of all the states in response to the Stamp Act, South Carolina was the only state south of Maryland to agree and the twenty-five-year-old Rutledge was chosen as one of its three delegates. In New York, the "foreign country," Rutledge headed the committee of the Stamp Act Congress that drafted a letter to the House of Lords requesting repeal. Rutledge did not especially enjoy working with Yankees, but the experience would serve him well throughout his career.

Rutledge returned to South Carolina a respected man of national politics. He resumed his law practice and his investments, took charge of his brothers' education, and managed the family interests. He served as a member of the South Carolina assembly and briefly as the state's attorney general. Then, in 1774, both he and his younger brother Edward were appointed to the Continental Congress.

Rutledge traveled to Philadelphia confident that he could wield the same influence nationally as he had done in his home state. But not all his new colleagues were taken with the young lawyer from South Carolina. John Adams, for example, noted that "his Appearance is not very promising. There is no Keenness in his Eye. No Depth in his Countenance. Nothing of the profound, sagacious, brilliant, or sparkling in his first Appearance."[15] As to Rutledge's luminescence as an orator, Adams noted that "he dodges his head too [referring also to Edward] rather disagreeably, and both of them Spout out their Language in a rough and rapid Torrent, but without much Force or Effect."[16] Patrick Henry, Adams noted later, had a "horrid opinion" of Rutledge, whose ideas "would ruin the Cause of America."[17]

Part of this antipathy certainly stemmed from the fact that, like Benjamin Franklin, Rutledge was a reluctant revolutionary. Feeling almost English himself, he constantly sought a middle ground, some means to attain the autonomy the more radical colonists sought within the existing system. As the crisis deepened, Rutledge, like Franklin, was pulled along in its wake, hoping all the while that some accommodation could be reached.

During Rutledge's tenure in Congress, when compromise clearly was not going to be possible, Rutledge still did not abandon hope. He seconded the nomination of Washington to head the army, and then met with him privately to express the hope that, even in the face of military action, the colonies could somehow reconcile with Britain. During the latter half of 1775, Rutledge shuttled back and forth between home and Congress, until in early 1776 he came home to stay. Reluctantly, he accepted an appointment to chair a committee that would draft a state constitution to enact provisions for self-rule. The constitution was adopted in March and soon afterward, John Rutledge was elected as the first president of South Carolina.

With his brother Edward back in Philadelphia, preparing to become the youngest signer of the Declaration of Independence, Rutledge faced an immediate crisis. The British under Henry Clinton had a flotilla just outside Charles Town harbor, poised to invade the city. Ignoring General Charles Lee's advice that the still unfinished fort on Sullivan's Island at the mouth of the harbor be abandoned to prevent British ships from slaughtering its defenders, on June 28, 1776, Rutledge wrote a note to General William Moultrie, who had command

John Rutledge

on the island. "General Lee wishes you to evacuate the fort. You will not do it without an order from me. I would sooner cut off my hand than write one. JOHN RUTLEDGE."[18]

Moultrie held, the British withdrew, and Charles Town and South Carolina were saved. This was, however, only a temporary reprieve: South Carolina would be ravaged during the later years of the war.

In December 1779, Henry Clinton once again sailed for South Carolina. In early February of the next year, the General Assembly passed a resolution "herewith delegating to John Rutledge . . . power to do everything that to him . . . appears necessary to the public good."[19] Excepting summary execution, Rutledge, by then Dictator John, had unquestioned authority.

His initial reign would be short. Clinton, and his deputy, Charles, Lord Cornwallis, arrived on February 11, 1780, this time opposed by the hapless Benjamin Lincoln. Clinton soon outflanked Lincoln and imposed a full blockade of the city. Hobbling around with gout, Lincoln allowed his army to be cut off, and then on May 8 rebuffed Clinton's demand for surrender. Clinton opened fire on the town the next day, destroying much of the waterfront. After three days of bombardment, Lincoln surrendered anyway, losing his entire army in the process, the largest single loss of men and materiel in the entire war. Rutledge did not wait around for the final act, rushing out of town in late April.

With Charles Town in their hands, the British proceeded to confiscate virtually all of Rutledge's property, as well as that of the Pinckneys and the rest of the planter aristocracy. During the next year, until Cornwallis began his futile chase of Nathanael Greene's army that would culminate in defeat at Yorktown, the British occupiers looted, burned, and destroyed almost everything they could not use or steal. Slaves were a particularly inviting target. At the end of the war, there were thirty thousand fewer slaves in South Carolina than at the beginning.[20] Rutledge never recouped the fortune that he lost to the British army.

Carolinians had begun the war in debt and ended it in even greater debt. To make matters worse, much of the money was owed to the same British merchants they had dealt with extensively before the Revolution. After the war, in a fever to rebuild, many of the planters borrowed heavily to buy slaves.

By early 1787, rice exports had recovered sufficiently to give the planters some hope that they might regain their former wealth, but not enough to create the kind of profits that could get them out of debt. This was perhaps the worst position of all. Not quite rich and not quite poor, South Carolina planters became obsessed with hanging on to what they had left, all the while hoping that rice and slavery would return them to past glory. Had their staple crop collapsed entirely, they might have been forced to examine alternatives to the agrarian slave economy. As it was, they came to Philadelphia thinking not of the possibilities of the future, but dwelling on the splendor of the past.

7. THE VALUE OF A DOLLAR: CONNECTICUT

*T*he three delegates who represented Connecticut at the Constitutional Convention have been referred to as the "spokesmen for *realpolitik*."[1] Each was a lawyer who had entered politics, two of whom, Oliver Ellsworth and William Samuel Johnson, were the most successful in the state. The third, Roger Sherman, while not making much of a mark in the courtroom, had become a man of vast influence in both state and national politics. While Johnson was an active participant in the proceedings, Ellsworth and Sherman would have the most profound impact on the final product.

Connecticut sent its delegation to Philadelphia with some definite objectives in mind. Despite possessing a coastline with more than one hundred miles of harbors, many of which lay at the mouths of navigable rivers, Connecticut imported very little, instead acquiring most of its foreign goods by way of Rhode Island or New York. Still, Connecticut had begun to build ships after the Revolution—New Haven alone expanded its commercial fleet from one sloop in 1783 to sixty-one vessels in 1787—and only a shortsighted businessman would have been unaware of the potential of Connecticut's ports, particularly as the country expanded westward.[2] So, while Connecticut might have been in favor of a strong central government that could regulate commerce while it was forced to rely on others, it would also have favored a weaker government that could not limit its own tariffs as time went on—unless, of course, it could have the happy confluence of a strong government that favored states involved in maritime commerce.

Of a more immediate nature, internal security was a pressing need— Shays' Rebellion, after all, had been fought a good deal closer to Hartford than to Boston. "People at Large are more ripe for a Revolt against Government than I conceive our Rulers are generally apprized of," wrote Benjamin Gale in 1787.[3] A central government pledged to aid individual states in suppressing insurrections therefore also held great appeal to Connecticut. In order to attain just the right mix of strength, weakness, and perspective from any new government, Connecticut's delegates came to Philadelphia prepared to deal.

Oliver Ellsworth was that most determined and indefatigable of antagonists—the self-made man.

Born in 1745, the son and grandson of subsistence farmers, Ellsworth had a boyhood so humble and bleak that it would qualify as New England caricature if it were not true. His hometown of Windsor, north of Hartford, boasted only one carriage, and most people ate their food from trenchers, crude wooden plates. Calvinism was as severe as the endless winters, manners simple to coarse, and humor, frill, and finery unknown.[4] Oliver's father wanted his son to have something better, and that meant the ministry, so he scraped together enough money to send the boy to a tutor, and from there borrowed to send him to Yale in 1762.

Yale and the young Ellsworth did not mix, however, and he left after his sophomore year. According to legend, he was expelled for a series of student pranks and protests, but that story is so at odds with everything in Ellsworth's persona and future behavior, that this might well have been wishful thinking by his supporters.[5] In any event, he journeyed south to attend Princeton. Eleven of the fifty-five delegates in Philadelphia were to attend the same school at roughly the same time, and one of Ellsworth's classmates (in a class of thirty-one) was a self-assured and opinionated Maryland boy named Luther Martin.

Ellsworth at the time was neither. He lacked sufficient experience or sophistication to forge opinions, and he had neither the wealth nor the breeding to project an aura of self-assurance. What he did have, however, was bulldog tenacity and directness, both of which were assets at Princeton, then every bit as Calvinist as northern Connecticut. Later in life, when asked the secret of his success by a young lawyer, Ellsworth issued this assessment of his adolescence. "Sir, after I left college I took a deliberate survey of my understanding. I felt that I was weak—that I had no imagination and but little knowledge or culture. I then resolved on this course of study: to take up a single subject at a time, and to cling to that with an attention so undivided that if a cannon were fired in my ears I should still cling to my subject. That, sir, is my secret."[6]

In his junior year, Ellsworth organized a debating society, which proved to be his introduction to political discourse. He particularly took aim at the

Stamp Act, but even went as far as to question the relationship of the colonies to the British crown. He found to his surprise that, lack of imagination notwithstanding, preparation and attention to detail could often overcome a florid and dramatic presentation, and that he could influence the way others thought.

After graduation in 1767, he returned home to Windsor, in debt and prepared to accede to his father's wishes and become a minister. But Ellsworth realized that he had become much more drawn to the persuasion of argument than the persuasion of Scripture, and taking on himself as his first client, convinced his father to allow him to follow the law. There were no law schools in Connecticut, so he embarked on a course of individual study. Four years later, he was admitted to the bar, and during that time he was forced to teach school to survive financially.

Ellsworth's law career in hardscrabble Connecticut did not begin well. Although "the people of Connecticut were thought to be peculiarly and perversely litigious," few of those litigious citizens came Ellsworth's way. In his first three years as an attorney, his fees totaled only three pounds.[7] When he had to appear in court, he was forced to walk to Hartford and back, a twenty-mile round-trip. As his prospects diminished, Ellsworth tried to pay off his debts by selling his only asset, some timberland that he had acquired either by inheritance or gift. When there were no takers, Ellsworth chopped down the trees himself, and then sold the timber in Hartford.[8]

Things began to brighten in 1772 when Ellsworth married sixteen-year-old Abigail Wolcott, the not especially attractive daughter of a wealthy Connecticut businessman. He had gone to the Wolcott home to court Abigail's older sister, but once there, had quickly altered his plans. Although he began his married life working his father's farm to supplement his still scant legal fees, the following year, doubtless through the Wolcott connection, Ellsworth found himself a member of the Connecticut General Assembly. One year after that, he had established himself as a highly successful and sought-after attorney. In 1775, he gave up the farm and moved to Hartford, where his law practice boomed. His son-in-law reported that Ellsworth generally handled between a thousand and fifteen hundred cases at a time. "It is doubtful if in the entire history of the Connecticut bar any other lawyer has ever in so short a time accumulated so great a practice."[9]

Ellsworth's courtroom manner was a pure extension of self. Years later, after he had been elevated to the bench, John Trumbull, Connecticut's resident wit, noted that "when Judge Ellsworth rose, the Jury soon began to drop their heads, and winking, looked up through their eyebrows, while the thunders of his eloquence seemed to drive every idea into their skulls in spite of them."[10]

But despite Ellsworth's uninspired technique, he found that clients were interested in a lawyer who could win, and win Ellsworth did. The days of financial hardship were over as the fees rolled in. As soon as he made a dollar, Ellsworth tried to turn it into two. He speculated in local real estate, bought stock in the Hartford Bank, invested in a mill, and lent money. Eventually, he built a large house in Windsor, but no matter how successful he became, the memory of his early subsistence existence was never far off. While he did not live simply, he made it a point to conceal from his servants how wealthy he had become.

During the Revolution, although he was a member of the local militia, Ellsworth did not participate in the fighting, but was active politically on both the state and national level. In Connecticut, he was first appointed to the five-member Committee of the Pay Table, which controlled dispersal of state funds, and then to the Council of Safety, which oversaw the state's entire war effort. But his most significant activity was as a member of the Continental Congress.

In Congress, Ellsworth developed two relationships in particular that would prove significant in his role in Philadelphia. The first was with a fellow citizen of Connecticut, Roger Sherman, after whom Ellsworth later said he had modeled his character. The second was more adversarial. Until his appointment to Congress, the provincial Ellsworth had rarely met citizens of neighboring New York, let alone from the far-flung reaches of the colonies. As bickering over funding the war and running a new country increased, sectional divisions became more pronounced. Ellsworth found himself increasingly locking horns with a man who in the future would be both opponent and ally.

"Ellsworth stood with his New England colleagues, sometimes clearly opposing the interests of South Carolina and other Southern states, which were now championed in Congress by John Rutledge."[11] Ellsworth had likely never met someone whom he could not overcome with steamroller persistence, but Rutledge was as immovable in protecting the values of the South as Ellsworth was in championing those of New England.

While most of Congress' business was centered on holding the country and the army together, there were other measures that were debated, which, while trivial, gave some hint of the sectional differences that posed a constant potential for disunion. Opposed by delegates from the South, Ellsworth voted for resolutions condemning gambling, horse racing, and attending plays, "proclaiming the necessity of a very strict morality among a people fallen on such evil times."[12]

After the war, Ellsworth, by then one of the most prominent citizens in

Oliver Ellsworth

the state, returned to his posts on the governor's council and as Connecticut state attorney, but soon relinquished both when he was appointed to the bench. He also returned to speculating in anything that might make him money, and during that period there were few investments more tempting than Continental paper. The fledgling government had issued bonds and notes throughout the war in a desperate attempt to raise funds, but now these securities were selling for around ten cents on the dollar. If the new nation descended into a loose Swiss-type confederation of thirteen separate republics, or even failed altogether, the securities would likely be worthless. If, on the other hand, a strong national government developed, it would almost certainly be forced to meet these obligations. Thus, anyone dabbling in Continental paper—as Ellsworth did—was also casting a vote for nationalism.*

---

*On the other hand, any man who invested in shipping—as Ellsworth also did—was casting a vote for regionalism.

Still, while Ellsworth always fought tenaciously to protect his interests, he was also a man of unshakable integrity, and promoting nationalism merely for personal gain would have been unthinkable. There was never a whiff of scandal in his business or personal affairs, or even an intimation of conflict of interest. Given his own path to respectability, however, he was motivated to protect a way of life, a path of opportunity for others, rather than merely to amass wealth. He would encounter similar sentiments in Philadelphia among southern planters, in particular his old congressional adversary, John Rutledge, although the ways of life that they sought to protect were far different.

The Oliver Ellsworth who arrived in Philadelphia had acquired a worldliness and sophistication from his years in Congress and on the bench, and was financially secure and comfortably at ease with his success. His sense of practicality had, if anything, increased, and he was convinced that politics and law often needed to coexist.[13]

William Pierce of Georgia, one of his fellow delegates, described him as follows: "Mr. Elsworth [*sic*] is a Judge of the Supreme Court in Connecticut;—he is a Gentleman of a clear, deep, and copious understanding; eloquent, and connected in public debate; and always attentive to his duty. He is very happy in a reply, and choice in selecting such parts of his adversary's arguments as he finds make the strongest impressions,—in order to take off the force of them, so as to admit the power of his own. Mr. Elsworth is about 37 years of age, a Man much respected for his integrity, and venerated for his abilities."[14]

Colonel Pierce described Roger Sherman as well.

> Mr. Sherman exhibits the oddest shaped character I ever remember to have met with. He is awkward, un-meaning, and unaccountably strange in his manner. But in his train of thinking there is something regular, deep, and comprehensive; yet the oddity of his address, the vulgarisms that accompany his public speaking, and that strange new England cant which runs through his public as well as his private speaking make everything that is connected with him grotesque and laughable;—and yet he deserves infinite praise,—no Man has a better Heart or a clearer Head. If he cannot embellish he can furnish thoughts that are wise and useful. He is an able politician, and extremely artful in accomplishing any particular object; it is remarked that he seldom fails. I am told he sits on the Bench

in Connecticut, and is very correct in the discharge of his Judicial functions. In the early part of his life he was a Shoe-maker;—but despising the lowness of his condition, he turned Almanack maker, and so progressed upwards to a Judge. He has been several years a Member of Congress, and discharged the duties of his Office with honor and credit to himself, and advantage to the State he represented. He is about 60.[15]

Roger Sherman was actually sixty-six when he went to Philadelphia, the oldest delegate at the convention except for Benjamin Franklin. His profession was generally given as "politician," although the contemporary sense of that word would hardly define him. He was shambling, stiff-jointed, physically unattractive, and, by all accounts, an utterly dreadful speaker. He took no care whatsoever with his dress or appearance, nor did he exhibit any skill at conciliation or dissembling. John Adams described him as "Rigid as Starched Linen."[16]

On the other hand, as Pierce also pointed out, Sherman's reasoning was always sound, his views plain, and his allegiances trustworthy. He was elected or appointed to position after position because he was, without doubt, what other politicians claimed to be—an unshakably honest man.

The most fitting word to describe Roger Sherman is "sober." He did not drink, disapproved of those who did, felt a Calvinist God on his shoulder at every moment, and conducted his business and personal affairs with absolute gravity. His portrait shows a rumpled, solemn, stern man, an image that renders Ellsworth devil-may-care by comparison. As a birthday greeting, Sherman wrote to his beloved wife Rebecca in May 1770:

> *This is your birthday. Mine was the 30th of last month. May we so number our days as to apply our Hearts to wisdom: that is, true Religion. Psalm 90:12.*
>
> *I remain affectionately yours,*
> *Roger Sherman*

Sherman was born in Massachusetts in 1721, the third of seven children, and spent most of his early life in Stoughton, about twenty miles south of Boston. Never poor, never rich, the Shermans were a solid, industrious family. His father William split his time between farming and cobbling. William believed in both the spiritual and practical so, in addition to teaching Roger both his trades, he sent him to the new town school to learn to read, write, and gain instruction in the Puritan interpretation of the Bible. The school was surprisingly good for the times, and Roger came away with a basic knowledge of poetry and history, and a smattering of Latin as well. From there, the boy proceeded on his own, carrying books everywhere, even on his house-to-house rounds as a shoemaker. He developed a particular skill for mathematics. His inquisitiveness came to the attention of the local pastor, a Harvard-trained protégé of Increase and Cotton Mather, and his education proceeded further.

In 1743, after William Sr. died, the Sherman family followed the eldest son, William Jr., and relocated to New Milford, Connecticut. Here again, Roger initially farmed and supplemented his living by cobbling. Soon, however, his mathematical bent resulted in an appointment as a local surveyor. He began to buy land and became a half-partner with his brother in a general store. Most of the Shermans' business worked on barter, but in 1752, when a Connecticut law required that merchants accept depreciated Connecticut paper money, Sherman issued his first political paper, a pamphlet protesting the rule.

In 1750, Sherman began producing almanacs. Almanacs—a combination newspaper, weather forecast, planting guide, and humor magazine—were popular at the time, second only to the Bible.[17] Sherman's almanac, as might be expected, excelled in the factual, the inspirational (sometimes in verse), and the moral, but fell somewhat short on humor. There was such a paucity of frivolity that Sherman asked his publisher to supplement the material before publication. The publisher complied but, unfortunately, decided to spice up the issue by including anecdotes that were, for the time, mildly bawdy. Sherman was so incensed when he found out that he insisted that his letters of protest and disavowal be printed in the *New York Gazette*.

With fees from surveying, sales of the almanac, income from the store, and an expanding asset base from purchases of land, Roger Sherman built himself into a one-man Puritan capitalist testament to the glory of God. Eventually, at the suggestion of a neighbor, he decided to add the study of law to his repertoire, an exercise that he undertook, as had Ellsworth, on his own. Although he was admitted to the bar in 1754, he rarely practiced but soon entered local politics.

Like the man himself, Sherman's political success was steady and inexorable. He became a selectman, a justice of the peace, a county justice, a member of the Connecticut General Assembly, a member of the local school committee, a deacon of his church, and treasurer of its building fund. In 1760, Sherman's wife Elizabeth died after giving birth to her seventh child in nine years, and the following year he left New Milford for New Haven.

Sherman prospered in New Haven even more than he had in New Milford. Within five years, he had remarried, owned two stores instead of one, was named treasurer of Yale, was appointed a justice of the local superior court, and served in both houses of the colonial assembly.

When the Stamp Act was passed in 1765, Sherman was one of the first to insist that Parliament had no legal right to enact measures pertaining to the colonies, yet when emotions began to rise, Sherman called for moderation. He voiced public disapproval of the Sons of Liberty, finding their radicalism distasteful. Instead of being branded a loyalist for his refusal to join public demonstrations, however, Sherman's prestige grew, and eventually he was designated to represent Connecticut in the first Continental Congress. Never an ardent nationalist, his focus was always on reform and orderly change. Still, in 1774 he wrote that "no laws bind the people but such as they consent to be governed by," predating Jefferson's similar assertion by two years.[18]

After his death, found among his papers was a plan for government reform that was either written just before or in the early days of the Philadelphia convention. It reveals that Sherman, like Ellsworth, did not go to Philadelphia with the aim of overturning the Articles of Confederation, but simply to augment the powers of Congress to include (not surprisingly) control over foreign and interstate commerce, the power to levy and collect taxes, the establishment of a supreme national tribunal, and to make laws passed by Congress binding on the states. Other than denying individual states the right to issue bills of credit—which would certainly have included paper money—Sherman was an unlikely proponent of a radical new Constitution.

Yet, according to John Adams, Sherman's early vision, while remaining essentially republican, foresaw the Great Compromise of which he and Ellsworth were to be the authors. "We ought not to vote according to Numbers," Sherman said on August 1, 1776. "We are Representatives of States not Individuals . . . The Vote should be taken two Ways. Call the Colonies and call the Individuals, and have a Majority of both."[19]

Despite his quirky demeanor, Sherman became one of the most respected voices in Congress, thought of as a man who would consider a problem objectively, then render a thoughtful and honest judgment. He served on the committee to create the Articles of Confederation and was one of the five members chosen to draft the Declaration of Independence. His influence was no less in his home state. Concurrent with his tenure in Congress, Sherman served on the Governor's Council, was a sitting judge, and was the mayor of New Haven. In 1783, he was one of two men chosen to redraft Connecticut's legal code.

Roger Sherman

As Sherman's influence grew, however, his fortune shrank. He had "invested almost all his property in the revolutionary cause, and he was almost ruined by the depreciation of his securities after the war."[20] In addition, two of his sons turned out to be failures in business, William losing the store in New Milford, which was sold for nonpayment of taxes in 1786. Sherman's financial situation became so precarious that on more than one occasion he was forced to write plaintive letters to Connecticut's governor asking for back pay so that he might avoid complete collapse. By early 1787, his financial position had stabilized, although he was dependent on the redemption of his securities for recovery.

As the convention began, Connecticut, commercially squeezed between Massachusetts and New York, should have been a classic "small state." Other than Maryland (and Rhode Island, which refused to send anyone at all), Connecticut was the last state to appoint delegates, waiting until mid-May to even take up the question. When the General Assembly finally appointed a delegation, it consisted of two men who were considered moderate republicans, Ellsworth and William Samuel Johnson, and one rabid republican, Erastus Wolcott.[21] When Wolcott declined to serve, Sherman was appointed in his place.

In a letter dated June 3, 1787, during the early days of the convention, a Connecticut archnationalist, Jeremiah Wadsworth, wrote to his friend, Massachusetts delegate Rufus King, to warn him about Sherman. "I am satisfied with the [delegation]—except Sherman, who, I am told, is disposed to patch up the old scheme of Government . . . he is as cunning as the Devil, and if you attack him, you ought to know him well; he is not easily managed, but if he suspects you are trying to take him in, you might as well catch an Eel by the tail."[22]

PART III

Supreme Law of the Land

8. PHILADELPHIA: THE CONVENTION BEGINS

*A*s he had done the year before in Annapolis, Madison arrived quietly in Philadelphia ten days early, the first out-of-state delegate to make an appearance. He checked into Mary House's Boarding House, the most elegant in town. Mary House, a widow, also owned the famed Indian Queen Tavern, a block and a half away.*

Washington arrived a week later. He rode into the city escorted by senior officers and regular soldiers of the old Continental army, who had been joined by civilians on horseback. As he proceeded through the streets, church bells throughout the city pealed forth in his honor.[1] He too had originally taken rooms at Mary House's, but had been persuaded by Robert Morris to instead be his guest for the duration of his stay.

At the time of the convention, Philadelphia was the nation's largest city, with about forty thousand residents. It had been devastated during the British occupation and, in 1787, was just beginning to recover from the effects. As in New York, the British had quartered troops and horses in public buildings and many still reeked of human and animal waste. Smashed windows had not yet been repaired and broken pavement turned the streets to muddy swamps after even a moderate rainfall.[2] Mindful of the momentous gathering to be held at the State House, city officials had sand poured on Chestnut Street so that the arriving delegates would not have to walk through ankle-deep muck.

Philadelphia was also the most diverse city in the nation. Quakers, German Lutherans, Catholics, Presbyterians, Anglicans, Native Americans, and a small, thriving Jewish population mixed freely. There was an active

---

*About 20 percent of all the taverns in Philadelphia were run by women, as widows were given preference in obtaining licenses.

antislavery society, known as the Pennsylvania Society for Promoting the Abolition of Slavery and the Relief of Free Negroes Held in Bondage, which drafted a letter to the convention on May 23, 1787, urging an end to the slave trade.[3] Its president was Benjamin Franklin. The letter was also published in local newspapers.

Despite Philadelphia's diversity, the class system was in full bloom. Five percent of its citizens owned 50 percent of the wealth, while at least half the city lived in poverty. Public services, except in the wealthiest sections, were virtually nonexistent. Rotting garbage and animal carcasses lay festering about, especially in the boisterous waterfront section, aptly named Helltown. The Quaker influence notwithstanding, drunkenness, brawling, disease, and prostitution were rampant.

Despite this, Philadelphia's intellectual tradition was strong and its populace, along with Boston's, was perhaps the most politically astute in the United States. In 1784, the *Pennsylvania Packet* had become the first daily newspaper in the country, and the city had two other newspapers that were published at least twice weekly. Philadelphians prided themselves on civic awareness and

The State House in
Philadelphia

were eager to follow the coming events closely. This eagerness, as much as any other factor, prompted the delegates to keep the proceedings secret.

Pennsylvania had its delegation substantially in place, since all but one of its eight appointees lived in the city. The men were an odd mix. As far as the public was concerned, the leader was the renowned Franklin, who, at eighty-one, was, in one historian's words, "approaching senility."[4]* The real force behind Pennsylvania's delegates, however, was a man who, after the opening session, would not utter a word during the entire four months, Washington's host, the notorious former superintendent of finance, Robert Morris.

The son of a Scottish nail maker, Morris had crossed the Atlantic without a cent at age thirteen in 1747, and then used a sparkling financial mind to become, at least on paper, the wealthiest man in America. With his assistant, Gouverneur Morris, to whom he was not related, Robert Morris almost single-handedly kept America afloat during the war by finagling accounts, begging loans, wheedling credit, and eventually pledging his own fortune as collateral. Robert Morris fiercely favored a national government largely because it would provide one central location for a speculator to co-opt, cajole, and bribe potential associates to gain financial and regulatory advantage.[5]

Another of the Pennsylvania delegates, James Wilson, was one of the great legal theorists at the convention, and also happened to be Robert Morris's attorney. He was generally assumed to speak for Morris, especially if the matter might somehow concern money. Wilson, who had also been born in Scotland, slipstreamed behind Morris's speculations and ultimately suffered the same fate. By 1790, he was penniless and heavily in debt. He was appointed to the Supreme Court in 1789 but eventually could not hear cases in a number of states for fear of being thrown into debtors' prison.[6]

Robert Morris's old assistant, Gouverneur Morris, although appointed by Pennsylvania, was actually a New Yorker, raised on a sprawling estate still called the Morrisania section of the Southeast Bronx in New York City. He arrived soon after Madison and stayed at Mrs. Dailey's Boarding House, also one of the nicest in Philadelphia.

Imperious and sarcastic, Gouverneur Morris was a fourth-generation aristocrat, and thus one of the few delegates with a pedigree to match the Southerners'.

---

*Other commentators were not so extreme, describing Franklin as frail but mentally alert. The truth seems to lie somewhere in between. At times, Franklin made insightful and incisive comments during the course of the debate; at other times he meandered or inserted minutiae into the proceedings. He had also taken to writing speeches that he wanted inserted into the record (even though there was no official record).

His older brother had been a signer of the Declaration of Independence. Over six feet tall, with a peg leg from a carriage accident, he was an intimate of Washington's and one of those rare men who was a match for him physically.

He was also a study in contradictions. One of the strongest antislavery delegates, he came from a family of slaveowners—there were still twenty thousand slaves in New York at the time of the convention.[7] Known as a committed democrat, Morris nonetheless had contempt for the common man. One of the most cerebral of the delegates, he was a notorious womanizer who had once, during the revolution, absented himself for two weeks at a crucial moment because he could not resist a woman's charms. He encouraged the story that he had actually lost his leg after jumping from a balcony to escape an irate husband.

On May 14, 1787, the scheduled start date, only Pennsylvania and Virginia were represented. Although many states had appointed delegates, Madison must have wondered if the Philadelphia convention would suffer the same fate as the one in Annapolis. Rather than conduct any business, Washington, Madison, and the Pennsylvanians adjourned. Almost two weeks would pass before the delegates convened again.

The next day Edmund Randolph arrived. Only thirty-four, Randolph was governor of Virginia. A member of a distinguished family that descended from Pocahontas, he had been an aide to Washington at twenty-two and a member of the Continental Congress by the time he was twenty-five. Although he had inherited a large estate with more than one hundred slaves, Randolph was so strapped for cash that he had been forced to borrow money from his brother-in-law to travel to Richmond after he was elected governor. He checked into Mary House's and immediately began to meet with Madison to draw up a strategy for the weeks to come.

Two days later, Rutledge, Charles Pinckney, and Mason arrived. Mason took a room at the Indian Queen, and was pleasantly surprised at the low prices. "In this City the Living is Cheap," he wrote to his son. "We are very well accommodated, & have a good room to ourselves, & are charged only 25s. Penslva. Curr[enc]y a Day, including our Servants and Horses, exclusive of Club in Liquor, & extra Charges." Despite the low cost, he added, "I hope I shall be able to defray my Expences with my public Allowance."[8] Soon after his arrival, Mason joined the daily meetings of Virginia delegates.[9]

Rutledge, rather than rent, became a guest of James Wilson, where the two powerful lawyers "began to lay plans for 'managing' the convention." Wilson had already spoken with Madison and with the two Morrises. Rutledge was doing some additional conspiring of his own "and his would be far more effective."[10] Many of the arrangements and accommodations that later seemed to spring spontaneously from the debates had likely been first discussed in these early days, before the convention had its first full session.

Charles Pinckney, who took rooms at an undisclosed inn, was considered something of a boy genius. Born in 1757, he was just reaching the age where he would ordinarily have been sent to Oxford when the political situation deteriorated just before the Revolution and he was kept home. He never seemed to get over it. As a result of not going to England, Pinckney lacked the seasoning of his cousin, the general, and, perhaps in compensation, became outspoken, impetuous, and egotistical, even by the standards of his fellow southerners.

The day after the southerners arrived, Alexander Hamilton reached Philadelphia from New York. A single-minded nationalist, Hamilton was something of a northern Charles Pinckney—arrogant, impatient, and brilliant. He also took rooms at Mrs. Dailey's. When Hamilton, Gouverneur Morris, and another guest, Massachusetts's Elbridge Gerry, were all present, Mrs. Dailey's would have been one of the liveliest places in Philadelphia. The other two members of New York's delegation, Robert Yates and John Lansing, both committed to opposing anything but a modest revision of the Articles, arrived soon afterward.*

A number of delegates drifted in over the next two weeks. Three members of the Delaware delegation arrived, with instructions that they could only support a revision of the Articles and had to refuse to back any plan that altered the by-state voting formula. Ironically, the most important member of Delaware's delegation was a nationalist, John Dickinson, one of the Annapolis triumvirate. In deteriorating health, Dickinson did not arrive until the third session on May 29, just in time for the presentation of the Virginia Plan.

Connecticut's representatives did not arrive until the end of May. Roger Sherman and Oliver Ellsworth took rooms at the somewhat out-of-the-way Mrs. Marshall's Boarding House. A good hike from the State House, Mrs. Marshall's was within easy walking distance of the City Tavern, where delegates often met after hours, although Sherman himself, of course, did not imbibe.

---

*As a result, when Lansing and Yates were present, New York voted as a "small" state. Both left early in July. Hamilton, who thought it wrong that a single man should represent a state, would not cast a ballot on his own so, for the last two and a half months of the convention, New York did not vote at all.

The Massachusetts contingent also arrived late, except for Rufus King, who rode down from New York. King was a shopkeeper's son who scrimped to go through law school, married an affluent shipper's daughter, and then moved to the city to become one of the major stockholders in the Bank of New York and a leading figure in New York society. Nathaniel Gorham, the son of a packet-boat captain who had amassed a sizable fortune privateering during the war, but had less success after it, arrived at about the same time as Ellsworth and Sherman. He saw the chance of rebuilding his fortune in the free movement of merchant vessels. Elbridge Gerry came to town the day after Gorham and stayed with friends while he awaited the arrival of his wife, after which he moved to Mrs. Dailey's. Quirky and utterly unpredictable, he was the son of a prosperous merchant and shipper, who took over the family business and invested heavily in western lands. His wife, Ann, whom he revered, was beautiful and about thirty years his junior.[11]

Early in June, William Blount of North Carolina journeyed from New York as a replacement for the state's governor, who declined to attend. Blount was to play no role in the proceedings, but was nonetheless a fascinating character. Dark and good looking, he had amassed millions of acres speculating in what was to become Tennessee.[12] Also in June, also as a replacement, Luther Martin came to Philadelphia. In a category of his own, dismissed by many as a drunken buffoon, Martin was an enormously successful lawyer who would serve as Maryland's attorney general for thirty years. Possessed of as keen a mind and as sharp a wit as any of the delegates in Philadelphia, and a ferocious defender of the rights of individual states, Martin was also one of the few delegates whose moral opposition to slavery could not be tempered by economic necessity.

By May 25, a sufficient number of delegates had arrived for the convention to actually begin. Before the session was called to order, the nationalists had already outflanked their opponents. Most of the leading figures who wanted to scrap the Articles and replace them with a strong central government—Hamilton, Madison, Gouverneur Morris, James Wilson, Rutledge, the Pinckneys, and even Mason and Elbridge Gerry—were there. Washington, quickly and unanimously called to the chair, also favored a radical overhaul of the existing arrangement.[13]

Some of the important states' rights proponents were present as well, but of these, only William Paterson of New Jersey could have been considered a heavy-weight.[14] The lack of urgency exhibited by the republicans is understandable—there was, after all, little reason to believe that the Philadelphia convention would have any more success than the Annapolis convention, or even the sessions of the enfeebled Congress. Still, this left a vacuum that the nationalists—especially Madison, who had waited years for this opportunity and had come prepared after months of study and research with a detailed plan for a strong new national government—were all too willing to fill.[15]

To open the session of May 29, Madison did precisely that.

9. JUNE: THE COLLOQUIUM

*D*ubbed the Virginia Plan, it was presented to the convention by Edmund Randolph. Although disingenuously called a "revision," the plan dispensed with the Articles entirely and replaced them with a government divided into legislative, executive, and judicial branches. The legislature would consist of two houses. Other details of just how the different branches were to be constituted or how their members chosen were generally left vague, and the specific powers of each branch were only loosely defined. Still, by delivering an authoritative plan up front, Madison and the nationalists had succeeded in seizing the agenda.

Of the fifteen articles in the plan, the first simply set out the goals of "common defence, security of liberty and general welfare."[1] The second article, the most important and the most significant in departure from the Articles, set the rule for apportionment, reading "that the rights of suffrage in the National Legislature ought to be proportioned to the Quotas of contribution, or to the number of free inhabitants, as the one or the other rule may seem best in different cases." So, while "free persons" would explicitly exclude slaves from apportionment, "quotas of contribution"[2] would implicitly count slaves in full, thereby setting the boundaries for the debates to come.[3]

Also on May 29, not to be outdone, Charles Pinckney presented a plan of his own, which was evidently quite a bit more detailed than the Virginia Plan, agreeing in principle with the major points and containing, if we are to believe its author, many provisions that were later adopted by the convention. Unlike Randolph, Pinckney never got to read his plan into the record, or even to have it inserted later. It seemed, in fact, to have been given short shrift by the delegates, perhaps as a result of the outspoken, impossibly brash Pinckney's unfortunate decision to pretend he was only twenty-four.[4]

For the next month, the delegates launched into a series of debates that were called "one of the most brilliant displays of learning in political theory ever shown in a deliberative assembly."[5] These June debates, more than any other factor, garnered the framers the well-deserved reputation of being perhaps the most sophisticated political philosophers of the day. This was certainly the high-water mark of Madison's efforts.[6]

Because the delegates were bound neither by tradition (there was none), nor by loyalty to their leaders (they were the leaders), and not even by a social or cultural imperative (a recent work claims that their very provincialism allowed their creativity to blossom[7]), the range and depth of the discussions was astonishing. Practical politics mixed with theory in a manner never heard before. There has likely been no other four-week period in history when the nature of power, of a citizen's relation to government, of the search for the best means by which humankind might govern itself has been so carefully, exhaustively, and eloquently examined.

Not every delegate was a Pericles, certainly, and not all the debates were memorable. Every delegate was entitled to speak twice on a question, which often led to extensive haggling over the definition of a word, or the parsing of a clause, or the insertion of some piece of minutia. The issue of remuneration of the executive and legislators, for example—whether they should be paid, how much, and by whom—took the better part of three days, with the issue debated largely on philosophical rather than practical grounds. Still, when the delegates focused on meatier issues, the debates soared.

If the June debates were notable for their radiance, they were equally notable for their civility. Provisions that one would think would cause the most bitter and divisive argument were discussed only in the most lofty and sanitized fashion, and some of the most controversial ideas were accepted without discussion into the plan. No one sniped, no one was sarcastic, no one threatened to walk out. There was passion in the content of the speeches but, by and large, delegates behaved with the utmost graciousness and deference to their opponents. Hypocrisies that would later be held up and skewered were tolerated with equanimity in those early weeks.[8]

The reason that these early debates could be conducted with such civility is that they were almost entirely devoted to where power *should* reside rather than to where power *would* reside. This distinction was both the greatest strength and the greatest weakness of this phase of the convention—strength because it allowed the delegates to use their education, intellects, and experiences to range into the ether of political theory; weakness because almost nothing was resolved.

Big states, small states; debtors, creditors; slaveholders, merchants—representatives of every faction present maneuvered to set guidelines for further discussion, to create boundaries within which the new government would fall. Every delegate seemed to know that nothing said in June bound them in any way to a final decision later on. Every question agreed to in principle in that first month of debate reappeared, often biliously, later in the proceedings. When specifics finally began to intrude into the debates, especially the practical questions of how power was to be distributed, when actual control of the government was at stake, harmony proved harder to come by.

Slavery was dealt with in the same collegial manner as every other contentious issue. The day after Randolph read Madison's Virginia Plan into the record, Madison himself suggested a significant change. "Observing that the words 'or to the number of free inhabitants,' might occasion debates which would divert the Committee from the general question whether the principle of representation should be changed, [he] moved that they might be struck out."[9] That would have left "quotas of contribution," as the only means of apportioning representation, which meant a full counting of slaves.

Rufus King immediately—but civilly—pointed out that the North had no intention of counting slaves in full, and Madison retreated, admitting the "propriety" of King's observation, simply noting "that some better rule ought to be found." Hamilton then went the other way and moved that "quotas of contribution" be struck out, leaving "free inhabitants" as the only standard of apportionment. That would not do either, and the initial skirmish ended when a motion by Randolph and Madison to postpone the question was agreed to.[10]

There were other hints of the acerbic mood to come. On June 11, Roger Sherman opened the proceedings with a proposal that "the proportion of suffrage in the 1st branch [of the legislature] should be according to the respective numbers of free inhabitants; and that in the second branch or Senate, each State should have one vote and no more."[11]* This compromise, at least structurally, was how the large state/small state divide would be closed, and Sherman was certainly addressing those delegates who did not want to give up the equal vote that each state enjoyed under the Articles. It did nothing to resolve the dispute over distribution of seats in the lower house, since Sherman tried to end-run the question of counting slaves by choosing the more restrictive pole of the Virginia Plan, as Hamilton had done to rebut Madison on May 30.

---

*This, of course, is often called the Great Compromise or the Connecticut Compromise, which Sherman and Ellsworth came up with in the evenings at Mrs. Marshall's Boarding House.

But no one was going to end-run Rutledge. He immediately made a proposal of his own, returning to Madison's suggestion that "the proportion of suffrage in the 1st branch should be according to quotas of contribution. The justice of this rule could not be contested." Rutledge's fellow South Carolinian Pierce Butler, the brocaded aristocrat, immediately agreed, "adding that money was power; and that the States ought to have weight in the Govt.—in proportion to their wealth."

The setting of the extremes by Madison and Hamilton on May 30, and then by Sherman and Rutledge two weeks later, makes clear that the debates over how slaves would figure in apportionment to the legislature had little to do with a "compromise over taxation and representation as historians have traditionally claimed," and had everything to do with whether slaves would be counted in full, not counted at all, or counted in some compromise formula yet to be determined.[12] That Sherman was on the other side of the issue from Rutledge on slavery would stand in contrast to a far more accommodating relationship later on.

The skirmish lines on representation having been reestablished with no give perceived on either side, Rufus King and James Wilson immediately moved to once more postpone discussion of the issue, stating simply that "the right of suffrage in the first branch of [the] national Legislature ought not to be according to the rule established in the Articles of Confederation, but according to some equitable ratio of representation." Lack of agreement on the meaning of the term *equitable* was lost on no one.

James Wilson tried further to deflect the issue by then taking the floor on Benjamin Franklin's behalf. No longer able to give extended speeches, Franklin had taken to penning monographs, which Wilson then read to the convention. The readings were inevitably lengthy and, by the time Wilson was done, the other delegates had usually forgotten what they had been talking about. After this reading, which was a vague, rambling discourse on sovereignty that simply restated that representation should be according to population or wealth, the delegates gratefully passed Wilson and King's motion to suspend discussion on the nuts and bolts of apportionment by a vote of 7-3.*

---

*Voting was, as in Congress, by state, by majority rule within each delegation. A tie would be recorded as a state being "divided" on the question. Although twelve states participated in the convention, all twelve were never present and voting at the same time. New York, as noted, did not vote from early July on. New Hampshire's delegation, John Langdon and Nicholas Gilman, did not even arrive until the last week in July. As a result, there was a maximum of eleven votes on any measure, with ten votes all that were available during the crucial mid-July debates on apportionment. Abstentions and states "divided" further decreased the total on a number of measures.

But not everyone agreed to allow the debate to once again simply drift away. Rutledge, the dogged advocate, seconded by Butler, proposed "to add to the words 'equitable ratio of representation' at the end of the motion just agreed to, the words 'according to the quotas of contribution.'"[13]

Rutledge's insistence on continuing the debate on including slaves in the calculation for apportionment threatened the entire spirit of camaraderie. Wilson countered and Charles Pinckney* seconded with a proposal to add instead, "in proportion to the whole number of white & other free Citizens & inhabitants of every age sex & condition including those bound to servitude for a term of years and three fifths of all other persons not comprehended in the foregoing description, except Indians not paying taxes, in each State."

Although this was the precise wording that Congress had used in revising the formula for the apportionment of taxes in 1783—which Wilson duly pointed out—this was the first time that anyone had suggested the same formula for representation. Until then, the issue had been moot, because voting was only by state.

Although himself known for opposing slavery, Wilson may simply have been reaching for middle ground, and at that moment came upon the three-fifths formula as something that might be acceptable to everyone.[14] On the other hand, it is equally possible that Wilson did not conveniently pull three-fifths of a rabbit out of his hat, but that this was a compromise that had already been discussed privately. The divisions over slavery had been clearly established and neither side would ever be able to claim total victory. Quite possibly, the two attorneys, Wilson and his housemate Rutledge, had agreed over dinner or brandies one evening that three-fifths would make an excellent plea bargain for slave apportionment.[15]

The eagerness with which most of the delegates embraced a solution to the convention's most intractable division was palpable, but Elbridge Gerry was not ready to concede. "Blacks are property, and are used to the southward as horses and cattle to the northward," he said, "and why should their representation be increased to the southward on account of the number of slaves, than horses or oxen to the north?"[16] Gerry was brushed aside, however, and the motion was agreed to by a 9-2 vote, only New Jersey and Delaware—two states that opposed any apportionment by population—voting against. And

---

*This is the younger Pinckney. Charles Cotesworth Pinckney will henceforth be referred to as "General Pinckney."

so, James Wilson, the democrat from Pennsylvania, introduced the three-fifths rule into the debates that would frame the most sacred document in American history.

For two weeks, the Virginia Plan had been the sole subject of the debate. The "small state" group had been outmaneuvered, reduced to holding actions against Madison, since its delegates had no plan of their own. That changed on June 15, when William Paterson of New Jersey presented a detailed response to Madison and the nationalists.[17]

Under what came to be known as the New Jersey Plan—or the Paterson Plan, after its author—Paterson pointedly retained the by-state voting scheme of the Articles but addressed, much more specifically than had Madison, the most egregious defects in the existing system. Under this plan, Congress would have the power to raise revenue, to tax imports, and to regulate commerce. One revenue-raising measure was the old notion of a state-by-state tax, proportioned according to population, in which Paterson included the "three fifths of all other persons" that had been the theoretical hook on which Wilson had hung his legislative apportionment formula four days earlier. Legislative apportionment had no place in Paterson's plan, obviously, but a second northerner known to oppose slavery had affirmed that a slave was worth three-fifths of a white person.

Little attention was paid to the three-fifths clause at the time; it seemed a useful compromise and there were bigger issues on the table. To the Paterson camp, the proceedings had been hijacked, and amounted to little more than what Luther Martin later called a "conspiracy" to violate the congressional mandate authorizing the convention. To Madison and the Virginia Plan adherents, the obsession of some members of the northern small states to hang on to a failed system of representation was leading to the inevitable collapse of the United States into three or four or thirteen sectional fragments, an outcome that must be prevented at all costs. Deadlock seemed inevitable until Alexander Hamilton helped everyone put the issue into focus.

Three days after the submission of the New Jersey Plan, Hamilton, declaring that he was "obliged . . . to declare himself unfriendly to both plans," weighed in with one of his own, which was, not surprisingly, as extreme in investing power in a central government as was Paterson's in its defense of the status quo. It was a dazzling speech, filled with historical parallels and inexorable logic. Taking the British model as his starting point, monarchy and all,

James Wilson

"the best model the world ever produced," Hamilton spoke for virtually the entire session, and with each sentence he disemboweled the sovereignty of individual states further, at one point suggesting that the state governments be abolished entirely.[18] According to his fellow New Yorker Robert Yates, he said, "I have well considered the subject, and am convinced that no amendment of the confederation can answer the purpose of a good government, so long as State sovereignties do, in any shape, exist."[19]*

Had Hamilton's plan received serious consideration, the small-state contingent might as well have packed up and gone home. Even many of the delegates who favored strengthening the central government sat stunned. This was nationalism run amok.

Suddenly, the Virginia Plan itself looked like a compromise and, for many of the delegates, some fast reconsideration of alternatives was in order. One commentator wrote, "If there was one evening on which a historian would have liked to eavesdrop on the delegates' conversation, it was that of June 18."[20]

---

*The following day, Hamilton claimed that he had been misunderstood and that he had never advocated eliminating states entirely.

The next morning, with the New Jersey Plan "at large before the Committee" and Hamilton's speech lurking in the background, Madison responded. He too spoke for virtually the entire session and he too gave a dazzling speech filled with historical parallels and inexorable logic. When he was done, a vote was taken on a motion by Rufus King to table the New Jersey Plan and use the Virginia Plan alone as the sole basis for discussion, Hamilton's plan being conveniently ignored. The delegates voted 7-3 in favor, with New York, New Jersey, and Delaware against, and Maryland divided. The New Jersey Plan was dead, and with it all hopes of a simple reform of the Articles of Confederation. The convention would then move to achieve that to which Madison and the nationalists had so fervently aspired—a system of self-rule built from a new philosophy, without preconception, the like of which the world had never seen.[21]

For the next week, as the delegates refined and revised the Virginia Plan, supporters of the New Jersey Plan saw their choices reduced to staying in Philadelphia and trying to limit the Virginia Plan's scope or walking out. The second choice would not have been mere spite. If the convention collapsed, they knew, the Articles would be retained in full, each state having an equal vote in Congress as before. Although some, such as Lansing and Yates of New York, did eventually leave, most stayed to see what concessions they might wring from the nationalists. Paterson and his comrades were not without power. Defeat of the New Jersey Plan, the nationalists knew, had achieved nothing—that the states' rights group would not prevail did not necessarily mean that the nationalists would. The most obvious and meaningful compromise the states' rights group sought was an agreement by the nationalists to apportion representation in the second house of the legislature by state.[22]

The issues remained deceptively cosmetic for a time—an agreement to substitute "United States" for "national" so that the opening phrase would read "the Government of the United States ought to consist of a supreme legislative, Executive and Judiciary," and to drop the word "national" from "that the national Legislature ought to consist of two branches." Parts of two days were consumed with cementing the concept of a bicameral legislature, and parts of two others confirming that the first house of the legislature would be elected according to some undecided formula by "the people," and not the state governments. Length of terms for the legislators in the first house was debated at length, as was pay. The second house of the legislature was also discussed. Only an hour or two was devoted to postulating that state legislatures should elect senators, but two days were devoted to arguing over the term of office.

All this housekeeping merely delayed the great question of who would control the government. The big-states/small-states tug-of-war had been out in the open from the beginning, while the more significant—and more venomous—slave-states/free-states clash lurked in the wings and would soon supplant all other conflicts.[23]

Hostilities began in earnest on June 27 with an infamous speech by Luther Martin.

Martin, whose antipathy to central authority dwarfed Paterson's, spoke for the better part of two days. He alternately bored and infuriated his colleagues with references to Sweden, the Swiss confederation, England, France, ancient Greece, and the current situation, in no particular order, but always with volubility and fervor. Madison characterized the speech as "delivered with much diffuseness & considerable vehemence," and Yates wrote that "his arguments were too diffuse, and in many instances desultory . . . to trace him through the whole, or to methodize his ideas into a systematic or argumentative arrangement."[24]

The most damning judgment was rendered by Martin's old Princeton classmate Oliver Ellsworth. In a pamphlet issued the following February, he wrote:

> The day you took your seat must be long remembered by those who were present. . . . You scarcely had time to read the propositions which had been agreed to after the fullest investigation, when without requesting information . . . you opened against them in a speech which held during two days, and which might have continued two months, but for those marks of fatigue and disgust you saw strongly expressed on whichever side of the house you turned your mortified eyes. There needed be no other display to fix your character and the rank of your abilities, which the Convention would have confirmed by the most distinguished silence, had not a certain similarity in genius provoked a sarcastic reply from the pleasant Mr. Gerry.[25]

Other delegates, however, viewed Martin's speech as a necessary antidote to the power politics of the nationalists and welcomed both the speech and its length. Elbridge Gerry actually thought highly of it and wrote that "the speech, if published, would do him great honor."[26] In any case, after Luther Martin finally returned to his seat, the tone of the proceedings had indisputably changed. Madison, with uncharacteristic irritability, said, "Those

*Luther Martin as a
younger man*

gentlemen who oppose the Virginia plan do not sufficiently analyze the sub-ject. Their remarks, in general, are vague and inconclusive."[27] Even the vener-ated Franklin was not immune from the testiness that had entered the chamber. Once again too weak to speak, he had read into the record a speech in which he famously ended by moving that "henceforth prayers imploring the assistance of Heaven, and its blessings on our deliberations, be held in this As-sembly every morning before we proceed to business." Other delegates aban-doned their usual deference to the aging sage and snapped back.

"Mr. Hamilton & several others expressed their apprehensions that how-ever proper such a resolution might have been at the beginning of the conven-tion, it might at this late day, 1. bring on it some disagreeable animadversions. & 2. lead the public to believe that the embarrassments and dissensions within the Convention, had suggested this measure."[28]

By June 30, the convention had sunk into a morass. The two divisions over means of apportionment—population against state, and slave state against free—had not been breached and no side would budge. Madison, however, real-ized that what seemed to be two issues were actually only one. In fact, Georgia, although the least populous state present, consistently voted with the large states, joining South Carolina, North Carolina, and Virginia, while New York, at least when its full three-man delegation was present, voted with the small. Maryland was divided only because Luther Martin was so fanatically opposed to centralized authority.[29]

Madison "contended that the States were divided into different interests not by their difference of size, but by other circumstances; the most material of which resulted partly from climate, but principally from the effects of their having or not having slaves. These two causes concurred in forming the great division of interests in the U. States. It did not lie between the large & small States: It lay between the Northern & Southern, and if any defensive power were necessary, it ought to be mutually given to these two interests."

Madison proposed a solution. "Instead of proportioning the votes of the States in both branches, to their respective numbers of inhabitants computing the slaves in the ratio of 5 to 3, they should be represented in one branch according to the number of free inhabitants only; and in the other according to the whole [number] counting the slaves as if free. By this arrangement the Southern Scale would have the advantage in one House, and the Northern in the other."[30]

No one liked the idea and the convention ignored Madison's motion.* At the next session, on July 2, Ellsworth once again introduced the notion of voting by state in the second house of the legislature, which failed 5-5, with four of the five southern states voting no and Georgia divided. Sherman had introduced what came to be known as the Connecticut Compromise on June 11 and, ever since, either he or Ellsworth had tried repeatedly (and fruitlessly) to have it debated.

Immediately after the vote, however, Charles Pinckney agreed that the question of equal votes in the Senate was a sectional issue, as Madison had asserted, not one of large states against small. "There is a real distinction between the Northern & Southn. interests. N. Carola. S. Carol: & Geo. in their Rice & Indigo had a peculiar interest which might be sacrificed. How then shall the larger States be prevented from administering the Genl. Govt. as they please, without being themselves unduly subjected to the will of the smaller?"[31]

If Madison and Pinckney were correct and all the southern states were "large," then none of them would likely agree to a by-state apportionment in one of the two houses of Congress. With resolution appearing hopeless, General Pinckney moved that one representative from each state be appointed to a committee charged with finding a way to break the deadlock. Although most

---

*This vote can be seen as the beginning of Madison's decline in influence. He was simply far less equipped to succeed in practical negotiations than in propounding a theoretical overview.

of the delegates, including Madison, thought the convention might be past saving—"We are now at a full stop," lamented Sherman—General Pinckney's motion passed 9-2, with only New Jersey and Delaware voting nay. Rutledge, Ellsworth, and Mason were chosen to represent their respective states, although Ellsworth became ill and was replaced by Sherman.

After a recess to celebrate July 4, the committee reported to the convention on July 5 that it had in effect accepted the Connecticut Compromise, allocating votes in the first house one representative for every forty thousand inhabitants and in the second house by state. All money bills would originate in the first house.

Not one delegate spoke in favor of the plan. Even Mason, who had been on the committee, said, "The Report was meant not as specific propositions to be adopted; but merely as a general ground of accommodation. There must be some accommodation on this point, or we shall make little further progress in the work."[32]

The next days were spent haggling over minutiae. Which clause should be taken up and which should be recommitted? In what order should the clauses be debated? Should certain language remain in the report to be voted on at some unknown later date? A question was raised, tabled in favor of another, then resumed when the second question was tabled in favor of the first. Delegates debated over what to debate. The convention sank deeper and deeper into a parliamentary quagmire. Ultimately, the best the convention could do was appoint a committee of five on July 6, which included Rutledge, Gorham, Randolph, King, and Gouverneur Morris—all big-state nationalists—to try to create a workable formula for apportionment from the one-representative-per-forty thousand-inhabitants rule for the first house.

When this committee had completed its work, slavery sprang out of the bottle. Only then did the real debate begin.

10. Slavery by the Numbers: The Mathematics of Legislative Control

*O*n July 9, Gouverneur Morris opened the session with the committee of five's report. It was in two brief sections, the first of which dealt with the present; the second with the future. In the first section, the committee, although it had not been asked to do so, provided a state-by-state apportionment for the proposed lower house. "In the 1st. meeting of the Legislature the 1st. branch thereof consist of 56. members of which Number, N. Hamshire shall have 2. Massts. 7. R. Id. 1. Cont 4. N. Y. 5. N. J. 3. Pa. 8. Del. 1. Md. 4. Va. 9. N. C. 5. S. C. 5. Geo. 2."[1]

The skew of representatives to the South was obvious—slave states had been allotted twenty-five of the fifty-six seats.[2] That was three seats short of half, although the southern states were thought to have just over a third of the free population. Slaves had been slipped into the apportionment—about 60 percent of the slaves—although no actual agreement yet existed to count slaves at all. The three-fifths number had also been only a theoretical proportion, no more binding than any of the other trial balloons that had come and gone over the preceding weeks.

Roger Sherman immediately protested. He "wished to know on what principles or calculations the Report was founded. It did not appear to correspond with any rule of numbers, or of any requisition hitherto adopted by Congs."

Gorham admitted that the committee had taken some liberties with the agreed-upon formula of one representative for every forty thousand inhabitants. "Some provision of this sort was necessary in the outset," he replied candidly. "The number of blacks & whites with some regard to supposed wealth was the general guide." The words might have been uttered by a delegate from Massachusetts, but the sentiment was pure South Carolina. Rutledge had

apparently done his work within the committee well. Gorham added that another objection to the one for forty thousand rule was that it might allow new
states admitted from the western territories to eventually "outvote the Atlantic." These were precisely the sentiments that Gouverneur Morris would
voice repeatedly in the coming days.

When Morris and Rutledge realized that the rest of the delegates were not
going to simply accept the committee's numbers, they issued a joint motion to
table the first section and move on to the second, which provided the legislature the authority to adjust apportionment in the future. The convention
agreed without objection to the motion, but Sherman was not ready to let the
first section go. He moved to recommit the distribution of seats in the first
house to another committee of eleven, one representative per state.

Gouverneur Morris, in a strategic retreat, seconded Sherman's motion,
conceding that "the Report is little more than a guess. The Committee meant
little more than to bring the matter to a point for the consideration of the
House." Randolph, who had also sat on the committee of five, added that he
too had, "disliked the report of the Comte, but had been unwilling to object to
it." Four members of the committee of five had disavowed its report within
minutes of its being presented.

This maneuvering was far too cute for William Paterson. He, like everyone
else, *knew* why the South had received so many seats. "He could," he said, "regard negro slaves in no light but as property. They are not free agents, have no
personal liberty, no faculty of acquiring property, but on the contrary are
themselves property, & like other property entirely at the will of the Master.
Has a man in Virga. a number of votes in proportion to the number of his
slaves? And if Negroes are not represented in the States to which they belong,
why should they be represented in the Genl. Govt . . . He was also agst. such an
indirect encouragemt. of the slave trade; observing that Congs. in their act relating to the change of the 8 art: of Confedn. had been ashamed to use the term
'slaves' & had substituted a description."

In pointing out that slave states were demanding representation for slaves
in the national government, when they specifically refused to grant them equal
status in apportioning their own state legislatures, Paterson had raised an objection that no slaveowner could refute. Of equal significance, the foremost
champion of the "small states," the man for whom the New Jersey Plan was
named, had agreed with Madison, the nationalist, that the most important
question regarding the makeup of the legislature was whether or not to count
slaves.

Madison's plan for a national government had once again been thrust to

William Paterson

the brink. If slaves had been treated only as property, South Carolina and Georgia would most certainly have walked out. (Virginia would have been none too pleased either.) If the South Carolina proposal to count slaves in full had been adopted, the Northern states would have walked out. Madison had no answer, other than to desperately resurrect his proposal that each house of the legislature be based on population, one in which slaves were counted in full, the other in which slaves were not counted at all. The delegates reacted as they had done previously—they ignored him. Butler merely "urged warmly the justice & necessity of regarding wealth in the apportionment of Representation."

At this point Rufus King, although he likely did not know it at the time, framed the terms of two crucial compromises to come. King "had always expected that as the Southern States are the richest, they would not league themselves with the Northn. unless some respect were paid to their superior wealth. If the latter expect those preferential distinctions in Commerce & other advantages which they will derive from the connection they must not expect to receive them without allowing some advantages in return. Eleven out of 13 of the States had agreed to consider Slaves in the apportionment of taxation; and taxation and Representation ought to go together."

The delegates then agreed to recommit apportionment of the lower house to a committee of eleven by a vote of nine to two. Once again Rutledge and Gouverneur Morris were appointed, along with King, Sherman, and Madison.

The new committee's report opened the July 10 session. It had expanded the number of seats from 56 to 65, divided "N. Hamshire by 3. Masts. 8. R. Isl. 1. Cont. 5. N. Y. 6. N. J. 4. Pa. 8. Del. 1. Md. 6. Va. 10. N. C. 5. S. C. 5. Georgia 3."[3]

Although slaves had been included in this formula as well, Rutledge was not going to be satisfied unless the slave states could control their destiny. Immediately following the reading of the report, he moved to reduce New Hampshire from three seats to two, with General Pinckney seconding.[4]

King then pointed out that even counting three-fifths of the slaves, the four southernmost states had a population of about seven hundred thousand and had been allotted twenty-three seats, while the New England states with a population of about eight hundred thousand had been granted but seventeen. King added that "he was fully convinced that the question concerning a difference of interests did not lie where it had hitherto been discussed, between the great & small States; but between the Southern & Eastern. For this reason he had been ready to yield something in the proportion of representatives for the security of the Southern. No principle would justify the giving them a majority." King thus became another in the string of delegates to announce that the real division in the nation was slave state/free state.

General Pinckney, again echoing Rutledge, retorted, "The Report before it was committed was more favorable to the S. States than as it now stands. If they are to form so considerable a minority, and the regulation of trade is to be given to the Genl. Government, they will be nothing more than overseers for the Northern States. He did not expect the S. States to be raised to a majority of representatives, but wished them to have something like an equality." This was the first time regulation of trade had been added to the mix. Commerce would form one side of a crucial compromise at the end of August.

The bickering went back and forth until Gouverneur Morris was forced to lament that he "regretted the turn of the debate. . . . the Southern States have by the report more than their share of representation. Property ought to have its weight, but not all the weight."

The vote on reducing New Hampshire's seats from three to two failed, as did similar motions, all by General Pinckney, to increase the representation of North Carolina, South Carolina, and Georgia by one seat each. The convention decided to accept the apportionment (with slaves included) nine to two, the only nays from South Carolina and Georgia, both still holding out for slaves to be counted in full.

Agreement on the initial makeup of the lower house was the first concrete achievement of the convention in weeks, but before the delegates had time to congratulate themselves, the second section of the committee of five's report was put on the table.

That section, as reported the previous day, read, "But as the present situation of the States may probably alter as well in point of wealth as in the number of their inhabitants, that the Legislature be authorized from time to time to augment ye. number of Representatives. And in case any of the States shall hereafter be divided, or any two or more States united, or any new States created within the limits of the United States, the Legislature shall possess authority to regulate the number of Representatives . . . upon the principles of their wealth and number of inhabitants."

Periodic reapportionment was every bit as vital to the slave states as having slaves counted in apportionment. Unless the delegates could be convinced to count slaves in full—an unlikely prospect at best—no other arrangement could prevent a northern majority in the legislature. The North simply had too many people and too many states. What kept the slaveholders in Philadelphia was the conviction that northern dominance would be temporary. An influx of white settlers and their slaves into the existing southern states and the Southwest territories was anticipated within the next two decades. Once it had occurred, the South could take control.

For the planters, the object became to obtain sufficient controls on governmental authority to protect their interests in the short run, while ensuring that they would be able to take control as soon as the apportionment population turned favorably to the South. If that could be achieved, a strong central government would do just fine, even if the Yankees ran things for a while.* The North simply wanted to retain control, granting concessions where need be, in the hope that, once achieved, legislative dominance might somehow be retained, despite the anticipated population superiority in the South.

And so, a periodic census became a crucial pivot.

The Virginia Plan made no provision for a census or reapportionment, nor was a census mentioned specifically in the committee of five's report. While a census might seem tangential to a plan of domination, it was, it fact, central to the slaveholders' overall plan of attack. The South, with no means of obtaining

---

*Again explaining why tiny Georgia consistently voted with the "large state" bloc.

immediate legislative control under any existing plan of apportionment, was willing to cede short-term power over the government to the North in order to obtain a dominant position as population trended southward. For the southern delegates, then, implementation of a periodic national census, conducted as quickly and as frequently as possible, was vital. They would further insist, of course, that the results be used as a basis for reapportionment of seats in the legislature.

On the other hand, for northern delegates, whose control over the legislature would disappear as the nation's demographics changed, opposition to a national census or, if a census were inevitable, ensuring that it occurred as far down the road and as infrequently as possible, was of equal importance. (The North could achieve the same end by enacting a provision that left the means and timing of the census to the legislature. Since Congress was to be dominated initially by the northerners, a recounting of population might either be put off indefinitely or conducted under rules that would underrepresent the South.)

To both northern and southern delegates, then, the question of the census was intimately tied to slavery, and the two questions would become blurred in debate.

As soon as the vote on apportionment had been completed, Randolph moved "that in order to ascertain the alterations in the population & wealth of the several States [the two criteria specified in section two] the Legislature should be required to cause a census, an estimate to be taken within one year after its first meeting; and every_____years thereafter—and that the Legislre arrange the Representation accordingly." Although Randolph left the number of years between censuses blank, as his later remarks made clear, he intended the period to be very short indeed.

Gouverneur Morris countered for the North. He opposed a census entirely, he said, "as fettering the Legislature too much. Advantage may be taken of it in time of war or the apprehension of it, by new States to extort particular favors." Morris was extremely adept at rationalizing a position, but trying to justify not knowing how many people lived in the United States strained even his capabilities. "If the mode was to be fixed for taking a census, it might certainly be extremely inconvenient," he added, without indicating just what "inconvenient" meant, "and if unfixed the Legislature may use such a mode as will defeat the object: and perpetuate the inequality."

Once he had declared himself an enemy of inequality, he once again proposed an unequal role for any new states from the West. He "dwelt much on the danger of throwing such a preponderancy into the Western Scale, suggesting that in time the Western people wd. outnumber the Atlantic States." Morris said that he "wished therefore to put it in the power of the latter to keep a majority of votes in their own hands."

Finally, addressing southern fears that, without a census, the North would simply keep control of the legislature, even if the South had more people, Morris noted that "it was objected . . . that if the Legislre are left at liberty, they will never readjust the Representation." He then "admitted that this was possible; but he did not think it probable unless the reasons agst a revision of it were very urgent & in this case, it ought not to be done."

Morris made no attempt to explain why a census would "fetter the legislature." As to his call for unity, men like Rutledge would never have succumbed to a transparent ploy that asked the planters to simply trust the North to do the right thing. Nor would the southerners accept an appeal to the Atlantic states to stick together against those interlopers from the West who would try to take advantage of *real* Americans. Predictably, the southern delegates did little more than scoff at Morris's pronouncement and discussion of the census was put off until the next morning.

The next day, July 11, was one of the most important of the entire four months.[5]

As the proceedings opened, Sherman opposed a census, and just as quickly Mason supported one, responding directly to Morris's argument. "According to the present population of America, the Northn. part of it had a right to preponderate, and he could not deny it. But he wished it not to preponderate hereafter when the reason no longer continued. From the nature of man we may be sure, that those who have power in their hands will not give it up while they can retain it . . . If the S. States therefore should have 3/4 of the people of America within their limits, the Northern will hold fast the majority of Representatives. 1/4 will govern the 3/4. The S. States will complain: but they may complain from generation to generation without redress."[6]

Mason then added, anticipating his later rejection of the plan, "Unless some principle . . . which will do justice to [the Southern states] hereafter shall be inserted in the Constitution . . . he must declare he could neither vote for the system here nor support it in his state."

Hugh Williamson of North Carolina agreed with Mason and "was for making it the duty of the Legislature to do what was right & not leaving it at liberty to do or not do it." He followed with a motion that "a census shall be taken of the free white inhabitants and 3/5 ths. of those of other descriptions on the 1st. year after this Government shall have been adopted and every year thereafter; and that the Representation be regulated accordingly."

An annual census that included slaves appealed to Randolph and he suggested filling in the blank in his motion with that interval. He also noted that the first apportionment of sixty-five seats was only a guess and that "it placed the power in the hands of that part of America, which could not always be entitled to it." He added that "this power would not be voluntarily renounced; and that it was consequently the duty of the Convention to secure its renunciation when justice might so require; by some constitutional provisions."

After Randolph had taken his seat, "Mr. Butler & Genl. Pinckney insisted that blacks be included in the rule of Representation, equally with the Whites: and for that purpose moved that the words 'three fifths' be struck out." From the census, the two South Carolinians had turned the debate into a referendum on the apportionment of slaves. The convention would succeed or fail on the outcome.

Elbridge Gerry was quick to assert "that 3/5 of them was to say the least the full proportion that could be admitted," and Gorham pointed out that "this ratio was fixed by Congs. as a rule of taxation."

Gorham, as had Paterson the previous day, asked whether or not the South considered slaves human beings in the same sense as whites. It was a sentiment, he observed, that seemed to shift depending on what measure was being considered. "[When the rule of taxation was adopted] it was urged by the Delegates representing the States having slaves that the blacks were still more inferior to freemen. At present when the ratio of representation is to be established, we are assured that they are equal to freemen. The arguments on ye. former occasion had convinced him that 3/5 was pretty near the just proportion and he should vote according to the same opinion now." Gorham was not himself characterizing slaves as human beings, but simply reminding the southerners of their definition, pointing out they could not have it both ways.

South Carolinians, Butler quickly assured the convention, did not consider blacks equal to whites, simply equally valuable, and that should be the basis of apportionment. He "insisted that the labour of a slave in S. Carola. was as productive & valuable as that of a freeman in Massts., that as wealth was the great means of defence and utility to the Nation they were equally valuable to it with freemen; and that consequently an equal representation ought to be allowed for them in a Government which was instituted principally for the protection of property, and was itself to be supported by property."

But Mason was having none of it. Blacks might have some value, be "useful to the community at large . . . as they raised the value of land, increased the exports & imports ... [so] they ought not to be excluded from the estimate of Representation," but never, ever to be thought of as equal.

Mason's comments were more than a mere disagreement over to just what degree slaves were property. To this point, the planters had spoken with one voice on any issue regarding slavery, but here Mason, for the first time, took a position against his fellow slaveholders, one of the first signs that the slave states might not be a monolithic bloc, that the interests of South Carolina and Virginia might turn out to be quite different.[7] This exchange was a preview of the tripartite division—North, Upper South, and Lower South—that was to become critical in the weeks ahead.

Williamson then returned to Gorham's point and reminded the New Englander that "if the Southn. States contended for the inferiority of blacks to whites when taxation was in view, the Eastern States on the same occasion contended for their equality." The North could not have it both ways either.

This was the great irony in all the debates that led to the three-fifths rule—southerners, who insisted that blacks were property, had to assert that they were at least partly people, and northerners, who regularly denounced the enslavement of their fellow human beings, had to acknowledge blacks as at least partly property.

Williamson concluded that "he did not however either then or now, concur in either extreme, but approved of the ratio of 3/5." So did the convention, at least for the moment. Butler's motion to count blacks equally with whites was defeated 7-3, only South Carolina, Georgia, and Delaware voting in favor.[8]

The rejection of Butler's motion did not end the discussion of how to apportion slaves. With the census in the background—Gouverneur Morris briefly resurrected his "fettering the legislature" argument—debate turned to the issue of apportionment by wealth. Morris asked that "if slaves were to be considered as ... wealth, then why is no other wealth but slaves included?" Morris added that "his great objection was that the number of inhabitants was not a proper standard of wealth."

Morris was on firmer ground here and had homed in on the critical weakness of the planters' argument. Butler and General Pinckney, in using wealth as a stalking-horse for slaves, simply applied a standard to measure wealth that suited that end. But what was the correct standard of determining wealth? Would it be fixed or changing? And, most of all, who would decide?

Wealth could not have been simply equivalent to population—if it were, population alone would have sufficed. If wealth were not defined by population, the only way the planters could have rebutted Morris's question as to why no other form of wealth was included but slaves was to establish that slaves were a unique and extremely pure form of wealth, and they would have had to do so without admitting that slaves were human.

Rutledge first tried to dodge the question, then to work it in through the back door. Although he "contended for the admission of wealth in the estimate by which Representation should be regulated," he claimed that his reason was "the Western States will not be able to contribute in proportion to their numbers; they shd. not therefore be represented in that proportion."[9] Rutledge then returned to the supposed subject of the debate, which had gotten a bit lost, and called for a census to apportion congressional seats "according to the principles of wealth & population."

But Rutledge was not going to slip in apportionment-by-wealth so easily. Sherman thought that population was the best measure of wealth; George Read, one of the Delaware delegates, used Morris's "don't fetter the legislature" argument; James Wilson said that he "considered wealth as an impracticable rule"; and Gorham insisted that there was no way to set a fair standard. Even Madison weighed in, giving a long and scholarly discourse against a proposal that had no chance of passage anyway.

The convention refused even to bring Rutledge's motion to a vote, and the first half of Williamson's motion as to taking a census of the free inhabitants passed easily. The convention then moved to consider the second half of the motion, counting three-fifths of slaves for apportionment. If it passed as a part of the census, it would become de facto part of the formula for representation.

The session was nearing adjournment and only five delegates spoke, all of them northerners and nationalists. They let the slaveholders know that, although three-fifths of their "unique species of property" might be counted for apportionment—and taxation—that was the absolute limit and it was as an accommodation, nothing more. Gorham for example, "recollected that when the proposition of Congs. for changing the 8th. art: of Confedn. was before the Legislature of Massts. the only difficulty then was to satisfy them that the negroes ought not to have been counted equally with whites instead of being counted in the ratio of three fifths only."

Wilson went further still. He "did not well see on what principle the admission of blacks in the proportion of three fifths could be explained. Are they admitted as Citizens? then why are they not admitted on an equality with White Citizens? are they admitted as property? then why is not other property admitted into the computation? These were difficulties however which he thought must be overruled by the necessity of compromise."

Gouverneur Morris saved the most strident response for last. He was "compelled to declare himself reduced to the dilemma of doing injustice to the

Southern States or to human nature, and he must therefore do it to the former."

The vote to count three-fifths of the slaves in the census for the purpose of reapportionment was defeated 6-4. The yeas and nays divided along sectional lines, except that Connecticut voted for the motion, seeing a three-fifths compromise as the only path to general acceptance, and South Carolina, still holding out for full apportionment of slaves, voted against. The convention then easily approved a census during the first year that the legislature sat and a period between censuses at fifteen years. A motion to add the words "at least" before "fifteen years" was defeated.

The final vote of the day was on the entire resolution, each section of which had just been approved. Every state voted no.

11. Sixty Percent of
a Human Being

*J*uly 12, 1787, was an infamous day in the history of America, the date on which the delegates to the Philadelphia convention irrevocably agreed to include the three-fifths clause in the new Constitution. As the record of the previous weeks makes clear, the agreement on how slaves would be counted for apportionment was simply practical politics. Not that the delegates were unaware of the ethical implications of the bargains into which they had entered. John Dickinson wrote in his notes on July 9, "Acting before the World, What will be said of this new principle of founding a Right to govern Freemen on a power derived from Slaves . . . themselves incapable of governing yet giving to others what they have not. The omitting the Word will be regarded as an Endeavour to conceal a principle of which we are ashamed."[1]

Because the issues were so critical, the July 12 session was also among the most contentious since the delegates convened. The opening volley was fired as the session opened, with Gouverneur Morris seeking to exploit the rift between South Carolina and Virginia that had surfaced the day before. With a wink to Rutledge and his colleagues, he "moved to add to the clause empowering the Legislature to vary the Representation according to the principles of wealth & number of inhabts. a 'proviso that taxation shall be in proportion to Representation.' "[2]

The taxation issue was vital. South Carolina rice plantations were immensely profitable and South Carolina slaves, as any planter was quick to point out, were the sole reason for those profits. Virginia slaves, by contrast, were far less productive growing soil-killing tobacco. Morris knew that all four members of the South Carolina delegation would therefore be willing to accept the two-fifths more in tax assessments for the two-fifths more in apportionment that a full counting of slaves would entail. Virginia could not afford that exchange. Mason, in the previous day's session, had made it clear that Virginians would

Gouverneur Morris

not allow themselves to be fully taxed on their 280,000 slaves, although he did not phrase it in those terms. The colonel asserted that he "could not however regard [slaves] as equal to freemen and could not vote for them as such." Mason "added, as worthy of remark, that the Southern States have this peculiar species of property, over & above the other species of property common to all the States."

Butler ignored Mason and sided with Morris. He admitted "the justice of Mr. Govr. Morris's motion," and "contended again that Representation Sd.. be according to the full number of inhabts. including all the blacks."

Mason countered once more, also admitting "the justice of the principle," but added that he "was afraid embarrassments might be occasioned to the Legislature by it." Virginia against South Carolina; Mason against Butler—vying to gain the support of Gouverneur Morris and Pennsylvania. For many of the delegates, watching two of the largest individual slaveholders at the convention competing with compliments for the allegiance of a man whose own comments about slavery—and slaveholders—had never at all been complimentary, must have been fascinating.

Morris, who could wedge himself into the narrowest rhetorical opening, immediately moved to exploit his advantage. He "admitted that some objections lay agst. his motion, but supposed they would be removed by restraining the rule to direct taxation. With regard to indirect taxes on exports & imports & on consumption, the rule would be inapplicable."

Direct taxes—based simply on population—would hit each state proportionally and take in the 280,000 slaves in Virginia. Taxes on imports—on which the planters relied for all the fineries of aristocratic life—and exports—on which they relied even more to give them the wherewithal to purchase those fineries—would encumber the agrarian South, particularly the Lower South, far more than the self-sufficient North. By taking import and export taxes off the table with respect to this provision, Morris was eliminating a possible area of accord between Virginia and South Carolina. But in doing so, he had also for the first time introduced the incendiary notion of export taxes into the debates.

General Pinckney noticed. While he "liked the idea" of representation by wealth and counting slaves in full—"he thought it so just that it could not be objected to"—he was not as keen on an export tax. The general was "alarmed at what had been thrown out concerning the taxing of exports. S. Carola. has in one year exported to the amount of six hundred thousand Sterling all which was the fruit of the labor of her blacks. Will she be represented in proportion to this amount? She will not.* Neither ought she then to be subject to a tax on it. He hoped a clause would be inserted in the system, restraining the Legislature from taxing Exports."

All of this was moot if a census at acceptable intervals were not specifically written into the plan, as General Pinckney well knew. That was what the real fight was about anyway. He "foresaw that if the revision of the census was left to the discretion of the Legislature, it would never be carried into execution. The rule must be fixed, and the execution of it enforced by the Constitution."

Wilson knew the makings of a compromise when he saw one and leapt in to support it. He "approved the principle, but could not see how it could be carried into execution; unless restrained to direct taxation." Morris gave up export taxes, at least for the moment, and appended the motion to read, "provided always that *direct* taxation ought to be proportioned to representation."

---

*She would have, of course, if slaves had been counted in full for apportionment.

It passed without dissent. Export taxes would return to cause substantial problems the next month.

William Davie, a North Carolina lawyer, decided that he had heard enough. "It was high time now to speak out," he exclaimed. He had hardly opened his mouth in seven weeks. "He saw that it was meant by some gentlemen to deprive the Southern States of any share of Representation for their blacks. He was sure that N. Carola. would never confederate on any terms that did not rate them at least as 3/5. If the Eastern States meant therefore to exclude them altogether the business was at an end."

Perhaps Davie had been napping through the previous speeches, but it was certainly an odd moment for that particular outburst. No one had suggested that slaves be counted as less than three-fifths and the distinct possibility remained that they might even be counted equally with whites. Perhaps he thought that any link at all with taxation would force the planters to either spend themselves into bankruptcy meeting their obligations or divest themselves of their slaves. He never did make his point clear. After this speech, William Davie returned to his torpor and his voice was rarely heard again.[3] Still, by introducing the threat that slaveowners would walk out and put an end to the entire convention unless slavery were treated with the proper deference, he managed to sharpen the sectional conflict still further.

With Davie back in his seat, the debates returned to substantive matters, and William Samuel Johnson of Connecticut continued the squeeze of the Upper South. He thought "that [wealth and population] resolved themselves into one . . . He concluded therefore that ye. number of people ought to be established as the rule, and that all descriptions including blacks equally with the whites, ought to fall within the computation."

With momentum in his favor, Gouverneur Morris adopted a more conciliatory tone while reintroducing his stipulation for an indefinite census. "It is in vain for the Eastern States to insist on what the Southn. States will never agree to. It is equally vain for the latter to require what the other States can never admit; and he verily believed the people of Pena. will never agree to a representation of Negroes. What can be desired by these States more than has been already proposed; that the Legislature shall from time to time regulate Representation according to population & wealth."

General Pinckney, while grateful for the sentiment, did not completely trust his new allies from Connecticut and Pennsylvania. He "desired that the rule of wealth should be ascertained and not left to the pleasure of the Legislature; and that property in slaves should not be exposed to danger under a Govt. instituted for the protection of property."

That was perfectly all right with Ellsworth, but counting slaves in full was not. He proposed "that the rule of contribution by direct taxation for the support of the Government of the U. States shall be the number of white inhabitants, and three fifths of every other description in the several States, until some other rule that shall more accurately ascertain the wealth of the several States can be devised and adopted by the Legislature."

Ellsworth's bargain was an agreement to accept three-fifths of the South's slaves for apportionment in return for a rule that the census remain nonspecific. Ellsworth evidently hoped that the Virginians would look more favorably on such a bargain in the face of what Morris and the Carolinians were discussing. But this deal had been rejected before and it was rejected again here. The North, the Virginians knew, would never give up congressional control unless it was forced to, and that could ultimately result in the loss of everything that all the slaveholders had gained at the convention. Randolph responded. "The danger will be revived that the ingenuity of the Legislature may evade or pervert the rule so as to perpetuate the power where it shall be lodged in the first instance."

Randolph then proposed his own version. "In order to ascertain the alterations in Representation that may be required from time to time by changes in the relative circumstances of the States, a census shall be taken within two years from the 1st. meeting of the Genl. Legislature of the U.S., and once within the term of every year afterwards, of all the inhabitants in the manner & according to the ratio recommended by Congress in their resolution of the 18th day of Apl. 1783; (rating the blacks at 3/5 of their number) and, that the Legislature of the U.S. shall arrange the Representation accordingly." As an addendum, he "urged strenuously that express security ought to be provided for including slaves in the ratio of Representation."

Randolph "lamented that such a species of property existed. But as it did exist the holders of it would require this security. It was perceived that the design was entertained by some of excluding slaves altogether; the Legislature therefore ought not to be left at liberty."

Ellsworth, unable to get any further, withdrew his motion and seconded Randolph's, and that, more or less, was that. Wilson, who often functioned as the North's lawyer—as his houseguest Rutledge did for the Lower South—tightened the language by proposing that the clause read "that the representation ought to be proportioned according to direct taxation."

With the matter almost closed, Rufus King took the floor and wondered if the North had not just given up too much. "He must be shortsighted indeed who does not foresee that whenever the Southern States shall be more numerous

Rufus King

than the Northern, they can & will hold a language that will awe them into justice. If they threaten to separate now in case injury shall be done them, will their threats be less urgent or effectual, when force shall back their demands?"

Then King tried once more to gain a quid pro quo from the Lower South for agreeing to count slaves for apportionment. He again asked that rules for the taking of a census remain undefined, urging that southerners acknowledge that "confidence" must be placed "to a certain degree in every Govt." and that such confidence should extend to "periodical readjustment."

Again a Pinckney countered, this time Charles. He "moved to amend Mr. Randolph's motion so as to make 'blacks equal to the whites in the ratio of representation.' This he urged was nothing more than justice. The blacks are the labourers, the peasants of the Southern States . . . It will also be politic with regard to the Northern States, as taxation is to keep pace with Representation."

Given the choice, the North preferred counting slaves as three-fifths with specified rules for a census more desirable than counting them in full without such rules. After rejecting a northern attempt to set the interval between censuses at twenty years, the census passed with ten-year intervals. Pinckney's motion to include the full number of slaves was defeated, with only South Carolina and Georgia voting in the affirmative.

So three-fifths it was and, after that final vote, the convention adjourned for the day.

Just because a compromise had been reached did not mean the sectional division had been dissolved and trust restored. On the next day—Friday the 13th, as it turned out—what began as a housekeeping measure prompted a heated and revealing exchange.

"By common consent," according to Madison, the census provision was once again taken up with the notion of striking out "wealth" from the formula "wealth and number of inhabitants."[4] With the three-fifths formula agreed to, "wealth" was now a superfluous and potentially distracting entry.

Still, in order to compute three-fifths of the slaves, all of them had to be counted. Since South Carolina and Georgia had in no way abandoned their desire to have slaves counted in full, a full census of slaves could lead to mischief down the road. It would have been a singular irony if because of the expected migration to the Southwest, counting three-fifths of the slaves allowed slaveholders in the legislature to vote at some point to count all of them, and even perhaps to eliminate the direct taxation provision in the bargain.

Gouverneur Morris rose to speak. "The Southn. Gentlemen will not be satisfied unless they see the way open to their gaining a majority in the public Councils," he said. "It has been said that N. C., S. C., and Georgia only will in a little time have a majority of the people of America . . . If the Southn. States get the power into their hands, and be joined as they will be with the interior Country, they will inevitably bring on a war with Spain for the Mississippi. He wished to know what security the Northn. & middle States will have agst. this danger.

"There can be no end of demands for security if every particular interest is to be entitled to it. The Eastern States may claim it for their fishery, and for other objects, as the Southn. States claim it for their peculiar objects." If the South could not bend, Morris insisted, "instead of attempting to blend incompatible things, let us at once take a friendly leave of each other."

Pierce Butler replied instantly. The South, he assured the convention, had some concerns of its own. "The security the Southn. States want is that their negroes may not be taken from them, which some gentlemen within or without doors, have a very good mind to do."

In this atmosphere of good fellowship, the motion to strike "wealth" passed 9-0.

12. Balancing Act:
Two Great Compromises

*W*ith the problem of apportionment in the first house solved, the delegates moved on to the seemingly insoluble question of the second house. Ellsworth and Sherman had tried their Connecticut Compromise a number of times with no success, and Madison's suggestion that both houses be based on population, one counting slaves in full, the other not at all, had not even rated debate. Other formulas for proportional representation had likewise been rejected.[1] Apportionment of what would become the Senate was a complex problem because of an overlap of three separate issues: sectional divisions were blurred by both the insistence of small northern states to have an equal voice in the legislature and the uncertain status of potential new states in the West.[2] The question of terms under which new states would be admitted had emerged during the census debates and had become more dominant as the days progressed.

In his rejoinder to Gouverneur Morris at the end of the July 13 session, Butler had said, "It was not supposed that N. C., S. C. & Geo. would have more people than all the other States, but many more relatively to the other States than they now have. The people & strength of America are evidently bearing Southwardly & S. westwdly." Wilson had then added, "The majority of people wherever found ought in all questions to govern the minority. If the interior Country should acquire this majority, it will not only have the right, but will avail themselves of it whether we will or no."

Discussion of new states from the West resumed the next morning. Elbridge Gerry "wished . . . that the attention of the House might be turned to the dangers apprehended from Western States. He was for admitting them on liberal terms, but not for putting ourselves into their hands. They will if they acquire power like all men, abuse it. They will oppress commerce, and drain our wealth into the Western Country. To guard agst. these consequences, he

Elbridge Gerry

thought it necessary to limit the number of new States to be admitted into the Union, in such a manner, that they should never be able to outnumber the Atlantic States."[3] Rufus King seconded Gerry's motion.

Although they did not mention them specifically, Gerry and King, like Gouverneur Morris, seemed more focused on the Southwest territories below the Ohio, where accepted wisdom dictated that immigration would flow, than on those to the north. Still, why the two delegates from Massachusetts had suddenly become so reticent about expanding the Union was something of a mystery.

Objection to Gerry's motion to limit the number of new states came not from a southerner, but rather from Roger Sherman, who "thought there was no probability that the number of future States would exceed that of the Existing States." Sherman added, "We are providing for our posterity, for our children & our grand Children, who would be as likely to be citizens of new Western States, as of the old States. On this consideration alone, we ought to make no such discrimination as was proposed by the motion."

Gerry snapped back: "If some of our children should remove, others will stay behind, and he thought it incumbent on us to provide for their interests. There was a rage for emigration from the Eastern States to the Western Country, and he did not wish those remaining behind to be at the mercy of the Emigrants."

Despite his dire prediction, Gerry's motion failed 5-4, with Virginia, both Carolinas, and Georgia voting nay. The only northern state to vote no was obstructionist New Jersey. At least for the moment, any new states that might be admitted would enter the Union as equals.

The impact on the Senate of an equal admission of new states would depend on whether voting was by state or by population. If it turned out to be the former, the more states that were admitted, the more senators. From a sectional point of view, whether those senators aligned for or against slavery might determine the balance of power in the entire government. The North, already with the small states of Connecticut, New Hampshire, Delaware, and even absent Rhode Island, would enjoy a big initial advantage in such a configuration, while the slave states would have to find some way to ensure that more new states were admitted from the South than from the North.

All of which bore on the proceedings in Congress, ninety miles away in New York.

On July 13, the day after the three-fifths clause was approved in Philadelphia, Congress enacted "An Ordinance for the government of the Territory of the United States northwest of the River Ohio." The Northwest Ordinance, as it came to be known, was passed with only one congressman opposed, Abraham Yates Jr. of New York, the older brother of Robert Yates, who had tromped out of Philadelphia a week earlier.[4]

The Northwest Ordinance is a remarkable piece of legislation—all the more so for the near unanimity with which it was approved—and has often been called the single most noteworthy accomplishment of Congress before the adoption of the Constitution. Not only did the ordinance open up territory roughly equal to that of the thirteen original states, it was, until that time, perhaps the most progressive declaration ever issued by a governing body.

It included an article affirming freedom of religion, another guaranteeing habeas corpus and trial by jury, another that encouraged education, and still another that forbade the taking of Indian lands without their consent. The sanctity of contract was affirmed, as was the right of inheritance. But, most remarkable of all was Article VI, the final article, which explicitly stated, "There shall be neither slavery nor involuntary servitude in the said territory, otherwise than in the punishment of crimes whereof the party shall have been duly convicted."[5] At the time that the Northwest Ordinance was enacted, not one of these provisions was part of the legal code of the nation at large.

That an ordinance with a provision that banned slavery was passed by Congress on a day when nine of the eighteen members present were southerners,[6] over which a southerner was presiding, with every southerner voting aye, has puzzled not only historians, but even the Massachusetts congressman who inserted Article VI into the plan. Couple that with the pronouncements of the southern delegates about slavery at virtually the same moment down the road in Philadelphia, and not surprisingly some have seen the Northwest Ordinance as one prong of a compromise with the other being agreement by northern delegates to the three-fifths clause.[7]

Solid reasons exist to suspect that the timing was more than a coincidence. Several delegates to the convention were also members of Congress,[8] and they often shuttled back and forth between the two bodies. Travel between New York and Philadelphia was constant, and news was regularly relayed between the two most important cities in the United States. But most of all, suspicion that the three-fifths clause and the Northwest Ordinance were somehow related has revolved around the actions of one man, the Reverend Dr. Manasseh Cutler of Ipswich, Massachusetts, and the disposition of the rich and fertile country west of Pennsylvania and north of the Ohio River.

Cutler, part clergyman, part lawyer, part healer, part scientist, part social visionary, and part swindler, was another of those remarkable figures who seem to surface whenever a nation is in upheaval. He was born in Connecticut in 1742, the son and grandson of ministers. Instead of religion, which seemed too tame, he chose to attend Yale and study law. After graduation, he worked as a store clerk and schoolteacher in addition to trying his hand at legal work, but decided he didn't like any of those and returned to religion. He landed a position as minister in the Congregational Church in Ipswich in 1771, a post he held until his death fifty-two years later.

Cutler served as a chaplain in various units during the early years of the Revolution, but returned home in 1778 to oversee his parish. In August of that year, the severe depreciation in the buying power of paper money—it was by then worth only 10 percent of face value—induced Cutler to learn a new career to supplement his income as a minister. "I have spent considerable effort in pursuit of an estate in support of my family," he wrote, "and am now driven to the practice of physic."[9] While maintaining a full schedule in his parish, Cutler pored through the best medical books he could find and accompanied a doctor friend on visits to his patients. By the end of the year, he was sufficiently knowledgeable to see patients independently and soon afterward found himself pressed into service during a smallpox outbreak. At one point in early 1779, he had forty afflicted parishioners under his care.

Manasseh Cutler

As the war headed south toward the Carolinas, Cutler remained in Ip-swich and turned his ravenous curiosity to science. He experimented on an "electrical machine" (a contraption that produced a static charge, which, due to Benjamin Franklin's experiments, was all the rage at the time), became a proficient amateur astronomer, studied natural phenomena through a micro-scope, and, most of all, made himself into one of the most accomplished botanists in America. Cutler produced the first serious record of New England plant life, identifying and categorizing hundreds of different species. For his scientific work, Cutler was made a member of the newly formed American Academy of Arts and Sciences.

But Cutler's most important contribution emanated from progressive so-cial theories, not science, medicine, or religion. He had for a time turned his at-tention to education, founding a private boys' boarding school, when, in late 1785, he met up with Rufus Putnam and, together with some other New En-glanders, they developed a plan for the future of America.

Putnam, an engineer by trade, whose cousin Israel had become famous for his "Don't fire until you see the whites of their eyes" admonition at Bunker Hill, had risen from lieutenant colonel to general during the war. As the con-flict dragged on, he had dedicated himself to obtaining fair treatment for junior officers and enlisted men. Almost no one in either of these groups had been paid in anything but virtually worthless government paper, if they had been paid at all. Some officers had not received a cent in six years. In the early 1780s, Putnam seized on the idea of compensating these men by granting them title to acreage in the western territories. Congress had agreed with the notion in principle—it was better than paying out cash the government did not have— but Congress, as often happened in those days, dithered and failed to produce anything concrete.

In frustration, Putnam had helped draft in 1783 what became known as the Newburgh Petition, in which 288 officers at the Continental army head- quarters in Newburgh, New York, demanded that they be paid immediately in land grants. When once again Congress refused to act, the officers threatened to march south with the army and replace the government by force. Washington, who sympathized with the officers' plight and had even transmitted the peti- tion to Congress with his recommendation for approval, quelled the incipient rebellion by showing up unannounced at a meeting of the officers and persuad- ing them to abandon their plans.

The failure of the Newburgh petition did not deter Putnam, who contin- ued to work ceaselessly to settle the West with war veterans.[10] After the war, he got a job as a government surveyor and in that role personally visited the Ohio Territory, helping to plot future settlements. He also began to speculate in land. More convinced than ever of the potential for his idea, Putnam succeeded in interesting some like-minded New Englanders and, on March 1, 1786, at the Bunch of Grapes Tavern in Boston, with ten others including Cutler, most of them veterans, Putnam helped found the Ohio Company of Associates.*

Cutler's social vision soon melded with Putnam's knowledge of the area to produce a plan of far greater scope than Putnam had originally envisioned. The new Ohio settlement would not simply be a refuge and new beginning for war veterans who had been cast aside by the government they had served—this new settlement would be a model of progressive thought and enlightened vision. Cutler's plan was to capitalize on the recently completed surveys to create a settlement that would promote education, social betterment, religious obser- vance, and the New England virtues of simple values, frugality, and hard work. Unlike the idealistic Putnam, however, Cutler understood that visions could rarely be achieved without a healthy dose of pragmatism.

They were an odd pair in other ways as well. Putnam dressed simply, spoke slowly, and cut a generally unimpressive figure, while Cutler was a smooth- talking raconteur, partial to velvet suits and silver-buckled shoes. One thing they

---

*This Ohio Company was completely unrelated to George Mason's Ohio Company of Virginia.

did share, in addition to a desire to expand America, was an abhorrence of the institution of slavery.

Cutler, Putnam, and the fledging Ohio Company of Associates drafted Articles of Agreement that began, "The design of this association is to raise a fund in continental certificates for the sole purpose and to be appropriated to the entire use of purchasing lands in the western territory belonging to the United States, for the benefit of the company, and to promote a settlement in that country."[11]

As soon as the articles were finalized, Cutler began a lobbying effort by cultivating a member of the Massachusetts congressional delegation, Nathan Dane. Dane, a native of Ipswich and ten years Cutler's junior, shared Cutler's desire to populate the Ohio Territory with industrious New Englanders before slothful, slaveholding southerners moved in and took control.

The timing for such a scheme could not have been better. The nation was virtually bankrupt and Congress was pleased to listen to almost anyone who would promise to pump funds into the treasury. Moreover, the western lands were in no way proving to be the financial bonanza that had been expected. Land sales had been great disappointments, with few pioneers willing to pay for claims in the West. Settlers could be given no guarantee of protection from the tribes, or even the British, who continually made noises about reclaiming lost territory. In addition, few wanted to pay for something that could be had for free. Squatters had been pouring across the frontier and grabbing up the best land, undermining the entire western movement.[12]

On March 16, 1786, Cutler wrote to Dane. "There [are] a large number of persons who intend to be adventurers in the new company, in this part of Massachusetts and New Hampshire, provided a purchase of lands can be made that will be agreeable to them," the letter began. Cutler then said that the company's agent, Samuel Parsons, a seasoned Ohio explorer, would be making an application on the company's behalf. "The directors," Cutler went on, "entertain hopes that Congress, notwithstanding their land ordinance, will not refuse to make a private sale to this company, as it will greatly accelerate the settlement, save the company a large expense, and enable them to purchase the whole in one body."

But Cutler and his associates were not simply going to throw money at Congress for the privilege of owning land in Ohio. He cautioned Dane that "the high price at which Congress have set the federal lands has operated much against the company ... if the lands could be immediately purchased on the terms the Company propose, we have the fullest assurance that the subscription for one million dollars will be complete in a short time ... The spirit of emigration never ran higher with us than at this time [but] if they are disappointed in their expectations westward, they will turn their attention to some other quarter."

Cutler concluded, "We should be happy in obtaining your influence in favor of the Company, and have the fullest confidence of your readiness to second the wishes of so large a number of the inhabitants of the New England States."[13]

Although Dane dutifully became an eager advocate for the Ohio Company in Congress, Parsons, the company's agent, failed to impress Dane's fellow legislators or make any headway in securing the 1.5 million acres that the company sought. (That in itself was down from the 5 million acres that the Associates had originally wanted.) "Our principal fears of a disappointment are that Congress may dispose of these lands before it may be in our power to apply for them," Cutler wrote on May 30. Suspicions arose that Parsons had "views separate from the interest of this Company."[14]

Three weeks later, the company's fortunes had not improved, and all agreed that the gruff, plainspoken Parsons would not do. So, to take his place, the Ohio Company appointed an agent who had been described as "easy, affable, and communicative . . . given to relating anecdotes and making himself agreeable."[15] On Friday, July 6, 1787, while the Philadelphia convention was tied in knots trying to devise a formula for representation in the lower house of the legislature, the affable and agreeable Manasseh Cutler rode into New York City.

Cutler spent his first weekend there delivering letters of introduction and dining with the likes of Arthur Lee and Henry Knox. On Monday morning, he met with Thomas Hutchins, the lead surveyor on the parties in which Rufus Putnam had participated, who told him the land where the Muskingum River forked off the Ohio "was decidedly, in his opinion, the best part of the whole of the western country."[16]

Later in the morning, when Congress convened in its meeting chamber, "an apartment in the second story of the City Hall," to debate the terms of the ordinance for the Northwest (the day before the census would be introduced into the debates in Philadelphia), Cutler was in attendance. The members, he observed, "were so wide apart that there seems to be little prospect of closing a contract."[17]

After adjournment and into the evening, Cutler made himself affable and agreeable to the legislators. By the following day, he had persuaded them to give him a copy of the proposed ordinance "with leave to make remarks and propose amendments." The draft Cutler received said nothing about slavery.

Cutler submitted his amendments that same day—he never specified precisely what they were—and first thing the next morning, July 11, left New York for Philadelphia and the Constitutional Convention because, as he put it, "I thought this the most favorable opportunity." Those amendments and that journey have been the source of the greatest mysteries surrounding the coincidental passage of the three-fifths compromise and the Northwest Ordinance on successive days.

Cutler arrived late on July 12, just after the three-fifths rule had been adopted, and took a room at the Indian Queen. He met until midnight with a number of delegates, including Madison, Mason, Rutledge, and Charles Pinckney, sharing his vision for the western territories. After most had retired, Cutler then huddled privately with some Massachusetts delegates—Gerry, King, and Gorham—until 1:30 in the morning.[18] A day later, Gerry and King opened the July 14 session of the debates by moving to limit the number of new states admitted from the western territories.

On July 13, while Cutler continued to chat up delegates in Philadelphia, Congress in New York passed the Northwest Ordinance. Inserted at the last minute, almost certainly by Nathan Dane, was Article VI, banning slavery which, much to Dane's surprise, was approved.[19] Soon afterward, Cutler settled his account at the Indian Queen and, on the morning of July 16, embarked on the return trip to New York.

Cutler arrived on July 19 to find that "the amendments I proposed have all been made except one," the exception being an even more favorable method of taxation.[20] The wording to his liking, he set to work obtaining a contract from Congress for the purchase of the prime land the company sought, where the Muskingum River flowed into the Ohio.

Congress, Cutler soon discovered, was not so liberal-minded on location and payment as it had been on terms of the ordinance.[21] The agreed-upon price was $1 per acre, which many congressmen demanded in hard currency. In addition, a number of the legislators didn't want to give up perhaps the best land in the entire territory and suggested other, less favorable locations for the company's settlements.

Cutler was livid. He thought it understood that payment for the grant would be in military warrants, paper then worth about the same 10 percent of face value that had forced him to supplement his ministerial salary with medical fees. He consulted with Hutchins, who urged him to settle for nothing less than the Muskingum land.

Cutler had solid allies in Congress, some of them southerners like Richard Henry Lee.[22] Treasury Secretary William Duer and the president of the Congress, Arthur St. Clair, were also supporters, but many others had begun to see Cutler as nothing more than a fast-talking hustler. Even the loyal Dane was proving to be not so malleable. After listing the members of Congress he could trust, Cutler wrote in his diary, "Dane must be carefully watched, notwith-standing his professions." He added, "Clarke, Bingham, Yates, Kearney, and Few are troublesome fellows. They must be attacked by my friends at their lodgings. If they can be brought over, I shall succeed; if not, my business is at an end."[23]

For the next week, Cutler lobbied furiously, alternating threat and charm, but not moving the Ohio Company investors any closer to the sweetheart deal they expected. On July 27, a disgusted Cutler visited Congress one last time "and informed them of my intention to leave the city that day. My expecta-tions of obtaining a contract, I told them, were nearly at an end." Richard Henry Lee urged Cutler to wait while he called one final meeting on the com-pany's offer.

Congress caved in. "At half-past three," Cutler reported, "I was informed that an Ordinance had passed Congress on the terms stated in our letter, with-out the least variation, and that the Board of Treasury was directed to take Or-der and close the contract."[24]

The agreement between Congress and the Ohio Company was one of the great giveaways in American history. The investors received a grant of 5 million acres, 1.5 million for the Ohio Company and the remainder for private specula-tion. The purchase price was officially $3.5 million, $1 per acre minus one-third allowance for bad land and to defray expenses. But Congress had agreed to ac-cept payment almost entirely in military warrants, making the actual price about eight cents per acre. For the company's 1.5 million acres, only $500,000 (once again in warrants) was payable up front so, in return for the most valu-able open land in the United States, an almost-bankrupt government received only about $42,500 in real money.

As an additional inducement, in order to create a kind of demilitarized zone between the coming white settlers and the tribes, Congress threw in an addi-tional 100,000 acres within which any adult white male could obtain 100 acres of free land. This came to be known, fittingly, as the "Donation Tract."

Most important to Cutler, the settlements were indeed going to be social experiments. According to the charter, company investors were required to re-serve "one lot of six hundred forty acres per township, for the purposes of reli-gion; an equal quantity for the support of schools; and two townships of twenty-three thousand and forty acres each, for a university."

In December 1787, Rufus Putnam led the first group of settlers to Ohio and in April of the following year established Marietta, named, in the spirit of freedom, for Marie Antoinette.[25] Cutler visited the settlement later that year and studied the natural history of the area. He then returned to Massachusetts and never visited Ohio again.

The combination of Cutler's shuttle diplomacy, a South-dominated Congress agreeing at the last minute to open the Northwest territories to antislavery New Englanders, and the northern delegates in Philadelphia agreeing to the apportionment of three-fifths of the South's slaves, certainly has the appearance of a deal. The timing of events, however, makes such an explanation unlikely.[26]

Although certain select delegates in Philadelphia might have been aware of Cutler's proposed "amendments" to the ordinance—and Gerry and King almost certainly were—they could not have known for certain that an antislavery provision, not even officially proposed until Cutler had left New York, would be included in the final product. Congress, although aware that a three-fifths provision was under active consideration, would not have known of its approval only one day after it was passed—ninety miles was a long way in 1787. Nonetheless, despite the absence of an arranged compromise, a relationship likely existed between the two events, the nature of which may be found in Article V of the ordinance, "There shall be formed in the said territory, not less than three nor more than five States," and in Article VI itself.

In 1784, Thomas Jefferson, then a member of Congress, submitted a plan that would place all the western territories from the Canadian border to Florida on a grid divided into sixteen regions. Two would go to extending South Carolina and Georgia westward and the other fourteen would be set aside for new states, at least eight of which would lie north of the Ohio. He suggested names for ten of these, two of which, Michigania and Illinoia, more or less survived, while the others, including such baroque offerings as Pelisipia, Assensipia, and Cherronesus, were mercifully consigned to history's dustbin. Among the provisions that would apply to all these new states was one that stated, "after the year 1800 of the Christian era there shall be neither slavery nor involuntary servitude . . . otherwise than in punishment of crimes, whereof the party shall have been duly convicted to have been personally guilty."[27] Another provision allowed the admission of any new states on an equal footing with the old.

Since voting was by state under the Articles, if Jefferson's plan had been accepted as written, free states could ultimately have outnumbered slave states by a total of twenty-two to five. In addition, since slavery was already in place in much of the western territories—"The Western people are already calling out for slaves for their new lands," George Mason was to say at the convention—an approval of the plan would have meant eliminating slavery where it already existed.

Not surprisingly, Congress found Jefferson's plan unacceptable. The following month, the plan was altered to eliminate at least one of the states above the Ohio and to drop the slavery prohibition altogether. Some of the same men who were to approve Article VI of the Northwest Ordinance were instrumental in removing any mention of slavery from the 1784 plan.

The next year, another land ordinance was passed, this one laying the groundwork for settlement. Surveys would be conducted of any potential settlement area and the land would be divided into townships, six miles square, with a grid laid out at one-mile intervals on each side. Of the thirty-six resulting subsections, two were to be reserved "for the maintenance of public schools." Prices were set at $1 per acre.[28]

Northerners, led by Rufus King, tried to reinstate the slavery provision, making the date of prohibition immediate instead of waiting until 1800. As a sop to the slaveholders, he also inserted a clause requiring the authorities in any free state to return any escaped slave upon petition of the authorities, an extension of a similar clause in the Articles of Confederation.

That year, a young Virginia congressman named James Monroe decided to travel to the Ohio Territory to see the region for himself. He returned to Congress in December 1785, convinced that the plan of division in the Ordinance of 1784 was flawed. The territory north of the Ohio, vast as it was, should, he thought, yield no more than a maximum of five states. His call was soon echoed by another Virginian, William Grayson, who drew up a plan for those five states—now Ohio, Indiana, Illinois, Michigan, and Wisconsin—that is almost identical to the eventual boundaries. By early 1786, when Grayson submitted his plan, many believed that the territories south of the Ohio would yield as many as ten states. Under the Articles of Confederation, within a couple of decades the South could thus have dominated the one-state-one-vote Congress.

But Grayson's plan was unacceptable to congressmen from the North, who could count as well as anyone. They would not approve a plan that would add two slave states for every free state in a legislature where every state had an equal vote.

The situation in Philadelphia was different, however. Only proportional representation had been agreed to. Under such a system, the number of states admitted did not matter; the only thing that counted was population. Of the northern delegates, only Gouverneur Morris, who had been warning of a flood of admissions of new states for weeks, seemed to understand that some by-state formula would have to be incorporated into any acceptable document. He regularly cautioned his northern brethren not to allow an unlimited number of new states to enter the union as equals with the current thirteen.

This became another slave-state/free-state issue as southern delegates were equally insistent that new states enter without restriction. Mason, for example, at the height of the debate on apportionment, stated, "Strong objections had been drawn from the danger to the Atlantic interests from new Western States . . . If the Western States are to be admitted into the Union, as they arise, they must, he wd. repeat, be treated as equals, and subjected to no degrading discriminations." Randolph added, "If a fair representation of the people be not secured, the injustice of the Govt. will shake it to its foundations . . . Congs. have pledged the public faith to New States, that they shall be admitted on equal terms."[29]

"Equal terms," to the Virginians, obviously meant as slave states, an objective that Article VI unintentionally advanced. By enacting a prohibition of slavery north of the Ohio, the ordinance created a tacit acceptance of the institution south of the Ohio. "The South seemed reconciled to the Northwest Ordinance since it implied an open door to slavery in its own adjacent territories, where the institution had already taken root."[30]

Manasseh Cutler became the wild card in these maneuverings. Just what he told to whom in his intrigues to obtain a favorable deal for the Ohio Company of Associates remains a mystery. But that he engaged in intrigues there can be no doubt. In those early morning hours of July 13, he certainly tipped Gerry and King that the Northwest territories would be restricted to five states, and probably that an antislavery provision might be inserted as well.

As Cutler returned to New York on the morning of Monday, July 16, the convention, to open the session, approved an equality of votes in the second house by a 5-4 vote, with Massachusetts divided. Delaware, New Jersey, Maryland, and Connecticut voted in favor. Virginia, South Carolina, and Georgia, each of which would have benefited if both houses were apportioned by population, voted against, as did Pennsylvania, but North Carolina unaccountably voted in favor. Gerry and King, privy to Cutler's plan, voted on different sides of the issue, Gerry in favor and King, long opposed to equal representation, against.

After the acrimony of Saturday's debates, that this vote was taken on the opening of the session is surprising. Madison did not even indicate in his notes that anyone specifically called for a vote. In all likelihood, groups of delegates met extensively on Saturday evening and during the day on Sunday to hammer out a deal. What part, if any, Cutler's visit and the information that he imparted played in that deal will never be known.

And the after-hours wrangling was not done. After his notes for the July 16 session, during which a number of delegates, including Randolph, expressed outrage at the vote on the Great Compromise, Madison later inserted an extended footnote, the only such entry in his journal.[31] In it, he revealed that the next morning, Tuesday, July 17, before the day's session was to convene, "a number of the members from the larger States" met "by common agreement" to discuss what steps could be taken "in consequence of the vote in favor of an equal Representation in the 2d. branch." Of particular concern was "the apparent inflexibility of the smaller States on that point." Madison then noted that a number of delegates from small states attended as well, although he never indicated which states were represented or who specifically was present.

"The time was wasted in vague conversation on the subject, without any specific proposition or agreement," Madison went on, because "the opinions of the members who disliked the equality of votes differed so much as to the importance of that point." Some of the large-state delegates at the meeting seemed to prefer dissolving the convention to acceding to equal representation in the second house, while "others seemed inclined to yield to the smaller States, and to concur in such an act however imperfect & exceptionable." The former group believed that as "no good government could be built" from a legislature in which one house voted by state and as "a division of the Convention into two opinions was unavoidable," that "the side comprising the principal States, and a majority of the people of America, should propose a scheme of Govt. to the States," and another plan should be proposed by those who wish compromise with the small states.

Madison then concluded cryptically, "It is probable that the result of this consultation satisfied the smaller States that they had nothing to apprehend from a union of the larger, in any plan whatever agst. the equality of votes in the 2d. branch."

Madison seems to have suggested that the small-state delegates were mollified only because some of the large-state delegates preferred to split into two countries, which is odd, as it is unclear why the small states needed to be mollified at all. They were the ones who had just triumphed. The delegates from the large states who preferred to split the nation than accede to the compromise were the ones in need of persuasion. Madison never expanded on the details of this meeting, nor ever explained precisely what he meant.[32]

Whatever the explanation, an hour or so later when the delegates took their seats for the opening of the July 17 session, Gouverneur Morris made a motion to reconsider the entire issue and it was not seconded. Both the three-fifths clause and the Great Compromise had become part of the formula for the legislative branch of the United States.

13. Not a King, but What?

With the composition of Congress at least tentatively settled, the delegates moved on to the executive. How to make the transition from a king to a different sort of leader had been discussed since the opening sessions with even less agreement than on the legislature. Another committee of eleven had been appointed to consider the issue, and when its report was considered on the morning of July 17, nothing had been settled. Length of term, pay, powers, how the executive was to be chosen, whether the executive could be re-elected, even whether or not it would be a single person—all remained open questions.

The last issue was settled first, when the convention agreed without dissent that the executive would be a single person. This was a mild defeat for George Mason, who had floated the idea of a triumvirate, with one member each from the North, Upper South, and Lower South, although Mason had been less than forceful in suggesting it and did not seem to really believe it would be adopted. From there the delegates moved on to how the executive would be chosen, the key issue since the method of election would determine whose interests the executive would represent. There were three basic alternatives—election directly by the people, by the state legislatures, or by Congress.

Direct election would obviously mean that whatever states or sections of the nation held the greatest number of qualified citizens, rich or poor, would control the office.[1] There was little sentiment for popular election—for all the talk of democracy, this was not a group that had a good deal of trust in the common man. The committee of eleven had specifically rejected popular election. No one, however, opposed popular election more vehemently than the southerners. Although the southern states had obtained legislative apportionment for three-fifths of its slaves, that formula would not be applied in a popular vote for the executive. A man who owned a slave would not get 1.6 votes, nor would 60 percent of the slaves be allowed to line up at the ballot box. If election were by popular vote, presidents (except perhaps Washington, whom just about everyone assumed would hold the office initially) would most certainly come from the North until such time as the South could secure a majority of the white population.

Despite the lack of sentiment for direct election, Gouverneur Morris, always happy to thrust a thumb in the eye of slaveowners, asserted that the executive "ought to be elected by the people at large, by the freeholders of the Country . . . If the people should elect, they will never fail to prefer some man of distinguished character, or services; some man, if he might so speak, of continental reputation. If the Legislature elect, it will be the work of intrigue, of cabal, and of faction; it will be like the election of a pope by a conclave of cardinals; real merit will rarely be the title to the appointment."[2]

Sherman demurred, using the small-state argument. Freeholders, he insisted, "will generally vote for some man in their own State, and the largest State will have the best chance for the appointment." When Wilson supported Morris, Charles Pinckney said that he "did not expect this question would again have been brought forward; An Election by the people being liable to the most obvious & striking objections. They will be led by a few active & designing men. The most populous States by combining in favor of the same individual will be able to carry their points." Pinckney favored election by Congress. "The Natl. Legislature being most immediately interested in the laws made by themselves, will be most attentive to the choice of a fit man to carry them properly into execution."

Morris once again spoke in favor of popular election, then Mason, who just weeks earlier had issued a passionate plea for direct election for the legislature, retorted that "It would be as unnatural to refer the choice of a proper character for chief Magistrate to the people, as it would to refer a trial of colours to a blind man."[3]

After Wilson supported Morris once more, Williamson repeated Sherman's objection, but noted, "The people will be sure to vote for some man in their own State, and the largest State will be sure to succeed. This will not be Virga. however. Her slaves will have no suffrage."

Morris's motion failed. Only Pennsylvania, coincidentally the state with the largest free white population, voted aye. Luther Martin then moved that the executive be chosen by electors appointed by the various state legislators. Martin clearly intended that each state would be allowed to appoint the same number of electors but his motion failed, with only Maryland and Delaware voting in favor. At this point, the convention unanimously agreed that the executive would be chosen by the national legislature.*

After that, the delegates tried to come to some consensus as to the term of the executive and whether he was eligible for reelection. A motion was made to have an executive serve "during good behavior,"[4] but eventually a seven-year term was agreed to and consideration of reelection was put off for an unspecified period.

The essential problem with delineating a description of the executive was that there was so little agreement on anything specific, no base from which to proceed. Those who thought that a seven-year term was too long insisted on eliminating a right of reelection. Others thought that the possibility of reelection was vital to ensuring good behavior, but were split on how long the first term should be. Still others believed that a president should serve indefinitely unless he was found to have misused the office. A similar range of opinion was voiced over whether the executive could veto acts of the legislature and what the limits on veto power could be.[5]

Two days after consensus had been attained on a single executive with a seven-year term and no eligibility for reelection, the convention decided to re-examine the entire issue. Once again, after much bickering, other than agreeing that the executive should be one person and settling on seven years as a term, the delegates could agree on nothing.

At one point, Ellsworth reintroduced Luther Martin's notion of electors, this time apportioning electors by population, between one and three per state.[6] Conspicuously absent was whether or not slaves would be counted in this formula and Rutledge, taking no chances, immediately objected and insisted that only the "national legislature," where slave apportionment was assured, could choose the executive. Gerry picked up the notion of electors, proposing twenty-five in total, again between one and three per state, and that they be appointed by state legislatures.[7]

The motion on appointment by electors passed, with only the three southernmost states voting nay. A motion that the electors be appointed by state legislatures also passed by an impressive margin, but when they came to decide how many electors should come from each individual state, and how that ratio should be chosen, the delegates unanimously voted to put the question off.

---

*Election by Congress rather than by state legislatures had great significance in a federal system. Under the former, the executive would be equivalent to a prime minister, dependent on the legislative branch for his office, while under the latter, the executive would gain the office independent of the legislative branch, thus creating separation of powers.

With one issue partially settled, they went right back to length of term, shortening seven years to six.

Bickering about the executive continued for another week, the delegates achieving little more than placeholder compromises. Still, compared with the mire of early July, this was definite progress.[8]

Interspersed with deliberations on the executive were debates on the nature of the judicial branch and a sprinkling of other issues, one of which revealed how the delegates often camouflaged questions of slavery in seemingly general terms. On July 18, the convention took up the resolution, "That a Republican Constitution & its. Existing laws ought to be guarantied to each State by the U. States." After Gouverneur Morris voiced an objection to guaranteeing the constitution of Rhode Island, James Wilson assured him that "the object is merely to secure the States agst. Dangerous commotions, insurrections and rebellions."[9]

This was one provision that slaveholders did not have to persuade northerners to adopt. Although the North had seen a number of incipient insurgencies before 1786, southerners were most fearful of insurrection by slaves. Northerners had been unanimous in their refusal to send troops or militia to aid in putting down a slave uprising. But suddenly, eight months before, northerners realized that they too might be in need of support to put down a rebellion and a bond of understanding developed between northern capitalists and southern planters.

Not surprisingly, a Massachusetts delegate pushed hardest for this. Without mentioning the name "Shays," Nathaniel Gorham "thought it strange that a Rebellion should be known to exist in the Empire, and the Genl. Govt. shd. Be restrained from interposing to subdue it. At this rate an enterprising Citizen might erect the standard of Monarchy in a particular State, might gather together partisans from all quarters, might extend his views from State to State, and threaten to establish a tyranny over the whole & the Genl. Govt. be compelled to remain an inactive witness of its own destruction." Tobacco farmers Daniel Carroll and George Mason also weighed in, Carroll observing, "Some such provision is essential. Every State ought to wish for it," and Mason adding, "If the Genl. Govt. should have no right to suppress rebellions agst. Particular States, it will be in a bad situation indeed."

Even Luther Martin, who generally balked at every clause favorable to slaveholders, had no problem here. Although he was "for leaving the States to suppress Rebellions themselves," he later wrote in *Genuine Information* that his objection was based not on a hesitance to employ the central government in quelling insurrections, but rather on an unwillingness to place a state's entire militia under national control.

14. DETAILS

*A*lthough the delegates had reached tentative settlement of some major issues, as July drew to a close, the debates were spinning in ever-decreasing orbits.[1] In an attempt to move the discussions forward, on July 26, the delegates decided to appoint a five-member committee to both revise and amend the agreed-upon resolutions and to flesh out specifics—in other words, to produce a full working draft of a new constitution. The Committee of Detail, as it was called, was instructed not only to use the convention's product to date, but also to draw on Paterson's New Jersey Plan and Charles Pinckney's plan, extracting or adapting whatever it felt was appropriate to the new government. The convention specified no other restrictions, effectively allowing these five men to set the guidelines for any further debate, including or omitting whatever specific powers or prohibitions that they wished.

The willingness of the convention delegates to entrust the production of a prototype to this committee was the most important single act of the entire four months. It would not only create practical boundaries for the resolution of all the contentious specifics with which the delegates had yet to deal, but it would also remove any remaining vestiges of the philosophical symposium that Madison and his allies preferred. That the delegates understood precisely the task at hand and the type of product they expected can be discerned from the men they chose for the assignment.

The five were elected by secret ballot. Rutledge was chosen to chair, with Ellsworth, Gorham, Wilson, and Randolph the remaining members. A strong nationalist bent was unmistakable and, except for Randolph, all were also powerful negotiators and pragmatic deal makers.[2] The Committee of Detail was equally notable for who was not selected. Anyone who might descend into theory or stall the committee's progress was left off. Madison was not chosen, nor were Gouverneur Morris, Gerry, or Mason.

From these choices and nonchoices, the delegates made it clear that they

Nathaniel Gorham

were, from this point on, interested only in results. This was not so much colloquium as cabal. For weeks, Ellsworth and Rutledge had been supporting each other in the debates and it was no secret that, along with Sherman, they had been meeting on the sidelines. Rutledge and Wilson, living under the same roof, spoke every evening. Gorham and Wilson came down on the same side of almost every issue. As for Randolph, any important committee had to have a representative from the largest state in the Union (three-fifths of the slaves included). By selecting Randolph over Mason or Madison, the delegates gave Rutledge and the rest an eager and malleable nationalist who lacked the intellect or temperament to successfully outflank the other four.

There is also no mistaking the significance of Rutledge as chair. His fellow delegates could not have had a scintilla of doubt that when they elected Dictator John, they were guaranteeing that the document that emerged from the committee would be strongly proslavery. The convention contained no more unabashed a defender of slavery, nor anyone better equipped to wield power. By appointing a weak member for Virginia and none at all from either Maryland or North Carolina, any compromises that were forthcoming would most certainly favor Lower South planters and northern capitalists.

To allow the committee members even more latitude, they were given a charter that was left intentionally broad. Before it began its work, the committee was provided with an outline titled "Proceedings of the Convention, June 19-July 23,"[3] in which many of the key compromises that had been hammered out over

Edmund Randolph

the previous weeks were not even included. For example, in its resolution on representation in the lower house, the three-fifths clause was omitted. Instead it read, "That the Right of Suffrage in the first Branch of the Legislature of the United States ought not to be according to the Rules established in the Articles of Confederation but according to some equitable Ratio of Representation." Rutledge was therefore free once again to try to include a full counting of slaves, or at least use it as a bargaining chip with the northerners. The convention then called an eleven-day recess to allow the committee to complete its task.[4]

There are no notes or minutes from the meetings of the Committee of Detail. True to the spirit of the endeavor, many of the "meetings" were informal sessions in the evening at the Indian Queen or at Wilson's home. A number of surviving work papers, however, provide substantial insight into the committee's progress and the evolution of the product the members were to distribute to the convention on August 6.

Rutledge appears to have asked Randolph to play the same role for him as Randolph had earlier played for Madison, to produce an outline from which the committee might work."[5] At the very start, Randolph included a "how-to" on the writing of the draft Constitution. "Two things deserve attention," he wrote.

"1. To insert essential principles only, lest the operations of government should be clogged by rendering those provisions permanent and unalterable . . . 2. To use simple and precise language, and general propositions, according to the example of the several constitutions of the several states."[6]

Even as he assigned this task to the young Virginian, Rutledge was aware that Wilson was working on a plan of his own, this one not an outline, but a fully fleshed-out series of proposals for government.[7] Wilson's draft survives as well and also contains corrections and additions in Rutledge's hand. There is substantial overlap between Randolph's outline and Wilson's draft, so much so that Rutledge likely shuttled back and forth between the two, drawing on the ideas of one to make suggestions to the other. By the time the two versions reached the full committee, most of the provisions were therefore pretty well agreed upon.

How much Gorham and Ellsworth actually contributed is unknown, but the draft that emerged contained at least one key provision threatening northern profits that each of them found sufficiently unacceptable to have compelled them to reject the plan unless it was changed. Neither of these two men was known for reticence or political naïveté, so possibly they allowed the provision to emerge from the committee knowing that it would be rejected in the debates.

Whether or not Rutledge discussed the committee's progress with any delegates not on the committee is also unclear. General Pinckney had gone into the countryside during the recess and Butler had left town, but Charles Pinckney remained in Philadelphia. There were reports that other delegates who were still in Philadelphia wandered in and out of the committee's official sessions at the State House, although specific evidence for this is scant.

By August 4, the committee had completed its work. The final product, a corrected draft by Wilson, was taken to John Dunlap, a Market Street printer who also published the *Pennsylvania Packet* and would later be engaged to print the completed Constitution. Dunlap produced a proof that the committee further corrected (the corrections are in Randolph's handwriting) from which a final draft was printed. Dunlap produced about sixty copies of the report. On Monday, August 6, the convention reconvened and Rutledge handed each of the delegates a printed copy. The delegates immediately adjourned for the day to read the report.

The document they received was a detailed formulation, in "simple and precise language" of the powers, limitations, and makeup of the three branches of the new government. The executive, called the "President of the United States," was to be elected for a seven-year term by the national legislature (thus allowing

W E the People of the States of New-Hampſhire, Maſſachuſetts, Rhode-Iſland and Providence Plantations, Connecticut, New-York, New-Jerſey, Pennſylvania, Delaware, Maryland, Virginia, North-Carolina, South-Carolina, and Georgia, do ordain, declare and eſtabliſh the following Conſtitution for the Government of Ourſelves and our Poſterity.

ARTICLE I.

The ſtile of this Government ſhall be, " The United States of America."

II.

The Government ſhall conſiſt of ſupreme legiſlative, executive and judicial powers.

III.

The legiſlative power ſhall be veſted in a Congreſs, to conſiſt of two ſeparate and diſtinct bodies of men, a House of Repreſentatives, and a Senate; ~~each of which ſhall, in all caſes, have a negative on the other. The legiſlature ſhall meet on the firſt Monday in December in every year.~~

IV.

Sect. 1. The Members of the House of Repreſentatives ſhall be choſen every ſecond year, by the people of the ſeveral States comprehended within this Union. The qualifications of the electors ſhall be the ſame, from time to time, as thoſe of the electors in the ſeveral States, of the moſt numerous branch of their own legiſlatures.

Sect. 2. Every Member of the House of Repreſentatives ſhall be of the age of twenty-five years at leaſt; ſhall have been a citizen in the United States for at leaſt ~~three~~ years before his election; and ſhall be, at the time of his election, ~~a reſident~~ of the State in which he ſhall be choſen.

Sect. 3. The House of Repreſentatives ſhall, at its firſt formation, and until the number of citizens and inhabitants ſhall be taken in the manner herein after deſcribed, conſiſt of ſixty-five Members, of whom three ſhall be choſen in New-Hampſhire, eight in Maſſachuſetts, one in Rhode-Iſland and Providence Plantations, five in Connecticut, ſix in New-York, four in New-Jerſey, eight in Pennſylvania, one in Delaware, ſix in Maryland, ten in Virginia, five in North-Carolina, five in South-Carolina, and three in Georgia.

Sect. 4. As the proportions of numbers in the different States will alter from time to time; as ſome of the States may hereafter be divided; as others may be enlarged by addition of territory; as two or more States may be united; as new States will be erected within the limits of the United States, the Legiſlature ſhall, in each of theſe caſes, regulate the number of repreſentatives by the number of inhabitants, according to the proviſions herein after made, at the rate of one for every forty thouſand.

Sect. 5. All bills for raiſing or appropriating money, and for fixing the ſalaries of the officers of government, ſhall originate in the House of Repreſentatives, and ſhall not be altered or amended by the Senate. No money ſhall be drawn from the public Treaſury, but in purſuance of appropriations that ſhall originate in the House of Repreſentatives.

Sect. 6. The House of Repreſentatives ſhall have the ſole power of impeachment. It ſhall chooſe its Speaker and other officers.

Sect. 7. Vacancies in the House of Repreſentatives ſhall be ſupplied by writs of election from the executive authority of the State, in the repreſentation from which they ſhall happen.

V.

Report of the Committee of Detail

the slave states maximum influence) with no eligibility for reelection. He was to be called "Your Excellency."* The legislature was assigned a list of eighteen distinct powers, most of which had been either specifically discussed or alluded to in the debates. Some, however, were new. The last of the eighteen stated, "And to make all laws that shall be necessary and proper for carrying into execution the foregoing powers, and all other powers vested, by this Constitution, in the government of the United States, or in any department or officer thereof."[8] Called the "elastic clause" or the "necessary and proper clause," it seemed innocuous at the time, but was to cause no shortage of mischief in the coming years since it effectively gave the central government almost unlimited lawmaking powers. That Rutledge would allow the inclusion of an enabling clause that granted the central government sweeping, unspecified powers indicates that he was, by this time, fully in the nationalist camp and saw the government as a benefit to slaveholders rather than a threat.

After the enumeration of powers, prohibitions were listed, some of which were also new. Section 4 stated, "No tax or duty shall be laid by the Legislature on articles exported from any State; nor on the migration or importation of such persons as the several States shall think proper to admit; nor shall such migration or importation be prohibited." Export taxes had come up, but no one had agreed to guarantee continuation of the slave trade. That section promised to be unpopular with northerners (except shippers) and even more unpopular in Virginia.[9] Section 6 then stated, "No navigation act shall be passed without the assent of two thirds of the members present in each House." This provision promised to be particularly disagreeable to northerners (particularly shippers).

Section 2 was also original. It began, "Treason against the United States shall consist only in levying war against the United States, or any of them; and in adhering to the enemies of the United States, or any of them."

Treason had not been discussed in the convention before the Committee of Detail's report—neither the New Jersey nor the Virginia plans had addressed it—but the subject had certainly crossed everyone's mind. By including the phrase "or any of them," Rutledge and the committee were proposing that each state be left free to define treason and that each definition had to then be accepted by the other states. Rutledge doubtless had in mind another provision of the committee's report, Article XV, adapted from the fugitive slave provision in the Articles of Confederation. It read, "Any person charged with treason, felony or high misdemeanor in any State, who shall flee from justice, and shall be found in any other State, shall, on demand of the Executive power of the State from

---

*One can only wonder how much Rutledge saw himself in the role.

which he fled, be delivered up and removed to the State having jurisdiction of the offence."

Treason as thus defined would not be confined to runaway slaves but could be applied equally to whites who were seen to incite slaves, or who allowed them privileges contrary to the Negro Act of 1740. There were no restrictions on state definitions of treason. As a result, according to this statute, the national government would be forced to respect an indictment for treason in, say, South Carolina, which might consist of nothing more than opposing slavery. By incorporating a state definition of treason into the Constitution, Rutledge was seeking a guarantee that the central government would become party to maintaining order within the slave states.

When the delegates returned on August 7, no one expected the committee's plan to simply be rubber-stamped, and there was certain to be debate on specifics, but neither did any of the delegates expect this report to be scrapped and the convention to return to square one. Whatever they decided in the coming weeks, whichever provisions of this report were accepted, rejected, or altered, would form the plan for a new government of the United States. With the sense of urgency inside the chamber apparent, the rhetoric quickly became even more contentious. The delegates began with the most fundamental and controversial issue of all, suffrage, and spent two acrid days hammering it out.

In the committee's report, individual states would decide who could vote for members of the lower house as long as qualifications for voting for congressmen were the same as those for voting for state legislators. Gouverneur Morris moved that voting be restricted to freeholders, those who owned land or other property.

Morris had proposed the same standard in voting for the executive. If the motion had been adopted, a large number of tenant farmers in slave states—and a lesser number in free states—who could vote in state elections would have been ineligible to vote nationally, unless they owned some land or buildings on the side.* But the rule would also have disenfranchised commercially powerful merchants and artisans, in this case overwhelmingly northerners. "Give the votes to people who have no property," Morris said, "and they will sell them to the rich who will be able to buy them. We should not confine our attention to the present moment. The time is not distant when this Country will abound

---

*Although initially suffrage throughout the nation had been limited to freeholders, by the time of the convention, nine of the states had broadened their criteria to extend beyond real property and the remaining four were on their way to doing so.

with mechanics & manufacturers who will receive their bread from their employers. Will such men be the secure & faithful Guardians of liberty? Will they be the impregnable barrier agst. aristocracy?"[10]

Delegates as diverse as Sherman, Mason, Franklin, Gorham, and Pierce Butler lined up against Morris, but Madison, whose democratic bent was often difficult to quantify, supported Morris's view. The motion to enfranchise freeholders only was defeated, with Delaware alone voting in favor.

The following day, the delegates stayed on the issue of who could vote and who could run for office. They debated residency of potential representatives and how long a person needed to have resided in a state to be eligible for office. Then they got to apportionment.

What followed was a short exchange, crucial and intense, characterized by two denunciations and one vote that brought the convention's attitude toward slavery into sharp focus. Rufus King began.[11]*

The admission of slaves was a most grating circumstance to his mind, & he believed would be so to a great part of the people of America. He had not made a strenuous opposition to it heretofore because he had hoped that this concession would have produced a readiness which had not been manifested, to strengthen the Genl. Govt. and to mark a full confidence in it. The Report under consideration had by the tenor of it, put an end to all those hopes. In two great points the hands of the Legislature were absolutely tied. The importation of slaves could not be prohibited—exports could not be taxed. Is this reasonable? What are the great objects of the Genl. System? 1. defence agst. foreign invasion. 2. agst. internal sedition. Shall all the States then be bound to defend each; & shall each be at liberty to introduce a weakness which will render defence more difficult? Shall one part of the U. S. be bound to defend another part, and that other part be at liberty not only to increase its own danger, but to withhold the compensation for the burden? If slaves are to be imported shall not the exports produced by their labor, supply a revenue the better to enable the Genl. Govt. to defend their masters? There was so much inequality & unreasonableness in all this, that the people of the Northern States could never be reconciled to it. No candid man could undertake to justify it to them. He had hoped that some accommodation wd. have taken place on this subject; that at least a time wd. have been limited for the importation of slaves. He never could agree to let them be

---

*Both speeches are included in their entirety. They are crucial to an overall understanding of the dynamic of the convention.

imported without limitation & then be represented in the Natl. Legislature. Indeed he could so little persuade himself of the rectitude of such a practice, that he was not sure he could assent to it under any circumstances. At all events, either slaves should not be represented, or exports should be taxable.

This was the most unmitigated indictment of slavery to date and a call to both undo the three-fifths clause and outlaw the slave trade. King had even threatened to withhold approval unless slavery ceased to enjoy a favored position in bargaining. If other northerners had supported King, the convention could have cleaved in two.

Instead, Sherman quickly tried to mediate. He "regarded the slave trade as iniquitous; but the point of representation having been settled after much difficulty & deliberation, he did not think himself bound to make opposition." Slavery and the slave trade, then, were a price that Sherman was willing to pay to gain union.

Madison tried to change the subject, returning to the formula of one representative for every forty thousand inhabitants, advising that "the future increase of population if the Union shd. be permanent, will render the number of Representatives excessive." Gorham followed Madison's lead, and Ellsworth jumped in. Madison and Sherman then "moved to insert the words 'not exceeding' before the words '1 for every 40,000 [inhabitants],'" which was unanimously agreed to.

But Gouverneur Morris could not let slavery pass that easily. He moved to insert "free" before the word *inhabitants*. He then proceeded to launch into a diatribe that made King's pale and still stands as perhaps the most ferocious condemnation of slavery in the nation's history.

> He never would concur in upholding domestic slavery. It was a nefarious institution. It was the curse of heaven on the States where it prevailed. Compare the free regions of the Middle States, where a rich & noble cultivation marks the prosperity & happiness of the people, with the misery & poverty which overspread the barren wastes of Va. Maryd. & the other States having slaves. Travel thro' ye. whole Continent & you behold the prospect continually varying with the appearance & disappearance of slavery. The moment you leave the East. Sts. & enter N. York, the effects of the institution become visible, passing thro' the Jerseys & entering Pa. every criterion of superior improvement witnesses the change. Proceed south wdly & every step you take thro' ye. great region of slaves presents a desert increasing, with ye. increasing proportion of these wretched beings.

Upon what principle is it that the slaves shall be computed in the representation? Are they men? Then make them Citizens and let them vote. Are they property? Why then is no other property included? The Houses in this city [Philada.] are worth more than all the wretched slaves which cover the rice swamps of South Carolina. The admission of slaves into the Representation when fairly explained comes to this: that the inhabitant of Georgia and S. C. who goes to the Coast of Africa, and in defiance of the most sacred laws of humanity tears away his fellow creatures from their dearest connections & damns them to the most cruel bondages, shall have more votes in a Govt. instituted for protection of the rights of mankind, than the Citizen of Pa. or N. Jersey who views with a laudable horror, so nefarious a practice.

He would add that Domestic slavery is the most prominent feature in the aristocratic countenance of the proposed Constitution. The vassalage of the poor has ever been the favorite offspring of Aristocracy. And What is the proposed compensation to the Northern States for a sacrifice of every principle of right, of every impulse of humanity. They are to bind themselves to march their militia for the defence of the S. States; for their defence agst. those very slaves of whom they complain. They must supply vessels & seamen in case of foreign Attack. The Legislature will have indefinite power to tax them by excises, and duties on imports: both of which will fall heavier on them than on the Southern inhabitants; for the bohea tea used by a Northern freeman, will pay more tax than the whole consumption of the miserable slave, which consists of nothing more than his physical subsistence and the rag that covers his nakedness. On the other side the Southern States are not to be restrained from importing fresh supplies of wretched Africans, at once to increase the danger of attack, and the difficulty of defence; nay they are to be encouraged to it by an assurance of having their votes in the Natl. Govt. increased in proportion, and are at the same time to have their exports & their slaves exempt from all contributions for the public service. Let it not be said that direct taxation is to be proportioned to representation. It is idle to suppose that the Genl. Govt. can stretch its hand directly into the pockets of the people scattered over so vast a Country. They can only do it through the medium of exports imports & excises. For what then are all these sacrifices to be made? He would sooner submit himself to a tax for paying for all the negroes in the U. States, than saddle posterity with such a Constitution.

The delegates must have been stunned. Although both Morris and King had also enumerated practical reasons for rejecting slavery, here, for the first time, two members of the convention had plainly challenged the convention to place morality over pragmatism.

Sherman once again tried to soften the rhetoric and Charles Pinckney attempted to enumerate northern parochial interests that also placed a drain on the nation's resources, but no one else dared speak, not Mason, not Madison, not Dickinson, who had written of conscience on July 9. Even Rutledge sat in silence.

Morris's motion came to a vote. How would the delegates handle this call to principle, this test of their integrity as champions of democracy and the rights of man?

They voted Morris down. Ten states, including Massachusetts, Connecticut, Pennsylvania, and New Hampshire, refused to insert "free" before inhabitants. Only New Jersey voted "aye." After that vote, any pretense of an appeal to higher morality was done.

August 1787 has been labeled "special interests month," but it was also "unlikely brotherhoods month."[12] Even during the recess, groups of delegates had stepped up their intrigues, although alliances were difficult to conclude since the particulars of the plan were not yet clear. With the distribution of the Committee of Details' draft, groups could easily form around specific issues.

One of the most significant—and strangest—of these groups was headed by Luther Martin. A few days after the report was distributed, Martin began convening a nightly conclave in his rooms. The participants varied. A number of delegates from the republican states of New Jersey, Delaware, and Martin's Maryland drifted in and out, but the core group was not republican at all, consisting of Charles Pinckney, Edmund Randolph, Elbridge Gerry, and George Mason.

A more unlikely crew could not be imagined. Mason, Randolph, and Pinckney were slaveholders, while Martin and Gerry tenaciously opposed slavery.[13] Mason, Randolph, and Gerry were later to become the three most prominent nonsigners of the Constitution (Martin went home at the end of August), while Pinckney would be one of its most vocal proponents.

The only thing these men had in common was dissatisfaction at the turn of the proceedings, although the reasons for their unhappiness differed greatly. Luther Martin had a genuine dread of centralized authority. He found anathema the entire notion of abandoning a by-state system of representation for one in which the more populous states could, in his view, wield almost unlimited power. Gerry, who many had thought of as a nationalist going in, disliked enough specifics of the new plan that he had come to oppose it altogether. Both he and Mason announced that their opposition was in large part a response to the lack of a Bill of Rights, but in each case that was at best a half-truth.[14] Pinckney had no problem with the system of government—he was upset because he had not been either granted a more significant role or given sufficient credit in designing it. Mason and Randolph, both strongly in favor of redesigning the government when they had arrived in May, saw from the Committee of Detail report that Virginia was going to be squeezed between the North and the Lower South.[15]

Where Luther Martin went, so went alcohol, and there was no one, perhaps in the whole of American history, who could drink with Luther Martin.* Each night, the spirits flowed, and Martin, who was desperate to defeat the plan on philosophical grounds, had no trouble inciting the assembled malcontents. As the evenings wore on, inhibitions disappeared and tongues loosened. Every tongue, that is, except the host's. Martin's notion was to so divide the convention that it would break apart. He almost succeeded.[16] That he did not was the doing of an equally clever adversary, one whose powers of persuasion and negotiation were reliant on guile, not alcohol.

That adversary was John Rutledge, who was busy in another part of town cementing the unlikely bond between the Yankees and the rice planters. Roger Sherman had gone home during the recess, but as soon as he returned, he resumed his meetings with the South Carolinian. Ellsworth doubtless joined them on many occasions. Whether or not the three came to a tacit understanding or cut an actual deal, by the second week in August, Rutledge (and by association Butler and General Pinckney) and the two delegates from Connecticut had come to an agreement that would not only blunt Martin's attack, but also save the Constitution. The price would not be cheap, however, and to achieve success they would split the South apart and push the entire convention to the verge of collapse.

---

*Much later in his career, Martin was representing a Quaker in a property action. At the Quaker's insistence, Martin promised "not to drink a drop" for the duration of the trial. Martin discovered that he couldn't stand the strain, and sober he was sure to lose the case. And so the dilemma—to keep his word and lose for his client, or to break it and win. At the lunch break, Martin purchased a bottle of brandy and a loaf of bread. He poured the brandy over the bread and ate the 90 proof delicacy with a knife and fork. Having kept his word, he then walked back into court and won the case (Clarkson and Jett, *Luther Martin*, 280).

15. Dark Bargain: The Slave Trade and Other Commerce

*T*he episode began innocuously enough on August 16, with a debate over the power to tax exports. While no one disputed the need to raise revenue with a tax on imports, exports were a different matter. The southern states were opposed to such a provision, because their prosperity flowed directly from agricultural products that were exported to Europe. Not only would a tax on exports raise prices without raising profits, but it would also serve to subsidize the northern shippers who carried those goods across the Atlantic. As a result, Rutledge had specifically excluded taxes on exports in the Committee of Detail's draft.

Few northern delegates actually expected taxes on exports to pass—there was more than a little dissent about this question even within their own ranks—but the symbolic importance of the issue was unmistakable. The provision on export taxes was the first specific measure to come to the floor relating to the power of the new national government to regulate commerce and shipping, the first skirmish of what promised to be an intense battle over the vital and combustible issue of navigation acts.

If the new plan was adopted, the South, in a minority, would lack the votes to prevent the North from authorizing exorbitant rates or onerous restrictions on shipping. Richard Henry Lee had written to James Madison, "It seems clear to me that giving the congress the power to legislate over the trade of the union would be dangerous in the extreme to the five Southern or staple States whose want of ships and seamen would expose their freightage and their produce to a most pernicious and destructive monopoly."[1] The South's only recourse was to require an excessive majority to enact navigation or commercial legislation. Most southerners backed a two-thirds majority, although some suggested three-quarters.

But the Yankees hadn't spent three months mollifying the planters only to lose their ability to generate profits. As Gorham would note later, "The eastern states had no motive to union but a commercial one."

For the northern merchants, then, it was vital that navigation acts require only a simple majority in order to prevent the southern veto that the five slave states could easily muster. As Alexander Hamilton later observed in the New York ratifying convention, "The Southern [states] appear to possess neither the means nor the spirit of navigation. [They] wish to impose a restraint on the North, by requiring that two-thirds in Congress should be requisite to pass an act in regulation of commerce. They were apprehensive that the restraints of a navigation law would discourage foreigners, and, by obliging them to employ the shipping of the Northern States, would enhance their freight. This being the case, they insisted strenuously on having this provision ingrafted in the Constitution, and the Northern States were anxious in opposing it."[2]

While the draft plan called for the national government to have sole power over foreign and interstate commerce—inevitable, since commercial chaos was one of the key issues that had brought everyone to Philadelphia in the first place—it had also recommended the two-thirds majority in both houses to pass navigation acts.

Nonetheless, instead of the fiery rhetoric that many had expected when the trial balloon of export taxes came up, the August 16 discussion was brief, calm, and understated. Two asides, however, hinted that more rancorous debate was to come. The first was by George Mason. Fresh from Luther Martin's nightly get-togethers and imbued with a heightened fear of central authority, Mason thought the Committee of Detail's draft, which merely stated that "no tax or duty shall be laid by the Legislature on articles exported from any State," was not sufficiently specific to prevent the national legislature from finding a loophole and imposing such a tax. He moved to have the language strengthened by adding, "provided that no tax duty or imposition shall be laid by the Legislature of the U. States on articles exported from any State." Mason said that he "hoped the Northn. States did not mean to deny the Southern this security [to not tax exports]. It would hereafter be as desirable to the former when the latter should become the most populous."[3]

But the North needed no reminder. How to deal with the effects of a population shift had been the great conundrum for the New England merchants. Soon after Mason's pronouncement, Rutledge played his opening card and gave the Yankees—excepting Ellsworth and Sherman who doubtless already knew—a hint as to how it might be done.

The committee's draft had conveniently linked exports with slavery by adding after "No tax or duty shall be laid by the Legislature on articles exported from any State," the further stipulation, "nor on the migration or importation of such persons as the several States shall think it proper to admit; nor shall such migration or importation be prohibited."

"He should vote for the clause as it stood," Rutledge said, meaning without Mason's changes, "but on condition that the subsequent part relating to negroes should also be agreed to."

The slave trade, as the northern delegates already knew, was the one great issue where the South could not speak with one voice. Rutledge's comment, linking a rejection of Mason's restrictive language with the continuation of the slave trade, was the first public indication that the South Carolina planters would consider a quid pro quo with the northern merchants.[4]

Ellsworth and Sherman might have agreed in private, but would the other northerners go along? The inhumanity of slaving had become an open sore on the conscience of much of the nation. Rufus King and Gouverneur Morris knew that they were reflecting public sentiment in their harangues of August 8. Madison later wrote, "The African trade in slaves had long been odious to most of the states."[5] Most of the civilized world condemned the practice as well (although not so acutely that European shippers eschewed the profits).

There were practical considerations that had emerged as well. With the passage of the three-fifths clause, the slave trade had become a means by which Southern states could supplement their population and thus increase their power in the first house of the legislature. Then there was the issue of public safety. King and Morris had tried to exploit the very real fear of many northerners that continued imports of slaves would render the entire nation weaker, thereby increasing the danger of insurrection from within and invasion from without.

Nothing more was done that day. Rutledge's proposal engendered no additional comment and, after some minor squabbling with Gouverneur Morris, the question of taxes on exports was sent back to a committee of eleven for further consideration.

For the next four sessions, the delegates discussed a national treasurer, piracy on the high seas, counterfeiting, public debt, the makeup of the militia, and minor courts, but stayed away from both slavery and commerce. They also passed some interesting procedural motions. Apparently the citizens of Philadelphia were becoming impatient with the abbreviated length of the daily sessions—particularly since they were not allowed to know what was going on—and had expressed frustration at the sight of delegates sauntering in shortly before noon, only to leave in the early afternoon. Rutledge moved "that the Convention meet henceforward, precisely at 10 oC A. M. and that precisely at 4 oC P. M., the President adjourn the House without motion for the purpose, and that no motion to adjourn sooner be allowed."[6] Only two states voted nay, one of them, curiously, Pennsylvania.[7]

On the afternoon of August 20, the convention debated the treason provision. Gouverneur Morris, who had become a prominent presence as Madison had receded, "was for giving to the Union an exclusive right to declare what shd. be treason. In case of a contest between the U. S. and a particular State, the people of the latter must, under the disjunctive terms of the clause, be traitors to one or other authority."[8] All three delegates from Connecticut, as well as Wilson and Rufus King, supported this view. Mason was quick to disagree. "The United States will have a qualified sovereignty only," he noted. "The individual States will retain a part of the Sovereignty. An Act may be treason agst. a particular State which is not so agst. the U. States."

Morris continued to protest but, in the post-Shays environment, there was not much sentiment for weakening any clause pertaining to domestic security. The issue seemed to be breaking once again along sectional lines when Madison raised the specter of double jeopardy. "As Treason agst. the U. States involves treason agst. particular States, and vice versa," he observed, "the same act may be twice tried & punished by the different authorities."[9] Gouverneur Morris went along and the article was amended to read simply, "Treason agst. the U. S. shall consist only in levying war against them, or in adhering to their enemies." When the new wording was approved, the southern states lost the ability to individually define treason, and as a result Rutledge was for once turned back.[10]

The next day, August 21, the question of taxing exports was taken up once more. This time the debate was neither brief nor calm. John Langdon, the shipper from New Hampshire, possibly not yet fully acclimated after only four weeks in Philadelphia, two of them during adjournment, opened the discussion with a curious reading. He contended that "by this section the States are at liberty to tax exports," and he did not want New Hampshire, with only a tiny stretch of coastline, to be at the mercy of its neighbors to the south and east. He proposed a two-thirds or three-quarters majority to tax exports, which he also generously noted would prevent the northern states from "[oppressing] the trade of the Southn."[11]

Ellsworth agreed and in the process demonstrated how sympathetic he had become to the slaveowners' cause. "There are solid reasons agst. Congs. taxing exports. 1. it will discourage industry, as taxes on imports discourage luxury. 2. The produce of different States is such as to prevent uniformity in such taxes. There are indeed but a few articles that could be taxed at all; as Tobo. rice &

indigo, and a tax on these alone would be partial & unjust. 3. The taxing of exports would engender incurable jealousies."

Williamson added that the power to tax exports "would destroy the last hope of adoption of the plan." Gouverneur Morris tried to couch export taxes in the name of national government, stating that "local considerations ought not to impede the general interest," and Pierce Butler just as quickly shot it down, being "strenuously opposed to a power over exports; as unjust and alarming to the Staple-States." Sherman supported his new allies from South Carolina, agreeing that the legislature should be restrained in this area.

Madison, as always, tried to frame the discussion in philosophical terms of union. He noted, "As we ought to be governed by national and permanent views, it is a sufficient argument for giving the power over exports." Mason countered a bit later, "If we compare the States in this point of view the 8 Northern States have an interest different from the five Southn. States,—and have in one branch of the legislature 36 votes agst. 29 and in the other, in the proportion of 8 agst. 5. The Southern States had therefore good ground for their suspicions."

Immediately after the prohibition of taxes on exports passed by a vote of seven to four, with the five southern states united in the affirmative, Luther Martin rose to speak. Whether or not he knew that Connecticut and South Carolina were in cahoots or merely suspected it, Martin was never one to allow his fellow delegates to hide behind artifice. Anticipating the compromise to come, he tossed a bombshell into the mix.

He proposed "to vary the sect . . . so as to allow a prohibition or tax on the importation of slaves. 1. As five slaves are to be counted as 3 free men in the apportionment of Representatives; such a clause wd. Leave an encouragement to this traffic. 2. slaves weakened one part of the Union which the other parts were bound to protect; the privilege of importing them was thus unreasonable—3. it was inconsistent with the principles of the Revolution and dishonorable to the American character to have such a feature in the Constitution."[12]

One can almost see the Old Dictator leap to his feet. "Religion & humanity had nothing to do with this question," Rutledge thundered. "Interest alone is the governing principle with Nations—The true question at present is whether the Southn. States shall or shall not be parties to the Union. If the Northern States consult their interest, they will not oppose the increase of Slaves which will increase the commodities of which they will become the carriers." But could not tax, he might have added.

For more than three months, the convention had more or less succeeded in avoiding the slave trade. Like a dead mouse in the walls, the delegates had usually pretended the subject did not exist, despite the overpowering stink. Even Rutledge's rider to the export tax clause had engendered no comment other than his own. With one short statement, Luther Martin had ended all that.

With the issue finally on the floor, Ellsworth supported Rutledge. "Let every State import what it pleases," he insisted. "The morality or wisdom of slavery are considerations belonging to the States themselves."

Concluding debate for the day, Charles Pinckney asserted with typical subtlety that "South Carolina can never receive the plan if it prohibits the slave trade. In every proposed extension of the powers of Congress, that State has expressly & watchfully excepted that of meddling with the importation of negroes." Pinckney closed by offering an inducement. "If the states be all left at liberty on this subject, South Carolina may perhaps by degrees do of herself what is wished, as Virginia & Maryland have already done."[13]

When Pinckney had completed his remarks, the session was adjourned without a vote on Luther Martin's motion. As they left for their lodgings, George Mason and other planters of the Upper South must have been livid and more than a little nervous. Rutledge and Pinckney had been expected to insist on continuing the slave trade of course, but Ellsworth? If the African trade continued, the domestic slave trade, on which Virginia was banking so heavily, was doomed. Whether Mason visited Luther Martin's rooms or passed the time alone is unknown, but he must have spent the night stewing, because when he arrived at Convention Hall on August 22, he was in an obvious fury.

Roger Sherman opened the session. Speaking in his "strange New England cant," he asserted that he "disapproved of the slave trade; yet as the states were now possessed of the right to import slaves, as the public good did not require it to be taken from them, & as it was expedient to have as few objections as possible to the proposed scheme of Government, he thought it best to leave the matter as we find it."[14]

Mason spoke next. Jefferson, describing Mason's skills as an orator, had said, "His elocution was neither flowing nor smooth, but his language was strong, his manner most impressive, and strengthened by a dash of biting cynicism when provocation made it seasonable."[15] Never was provocation more seasonable, so, in his strongest, most impressive, and biting manner, George Mason delivered perhaps the best known, most impassioned, and most misunderstood address of the entire convention.

"This infernal traffic originated in the avarice of British Merchants," began the owner of more than three hundred human beings. "The British Govt. constantly checked the attempts of Virginia to put a stop to it. The present question concerns not the importing of slaves alone but the whole Union. The evil

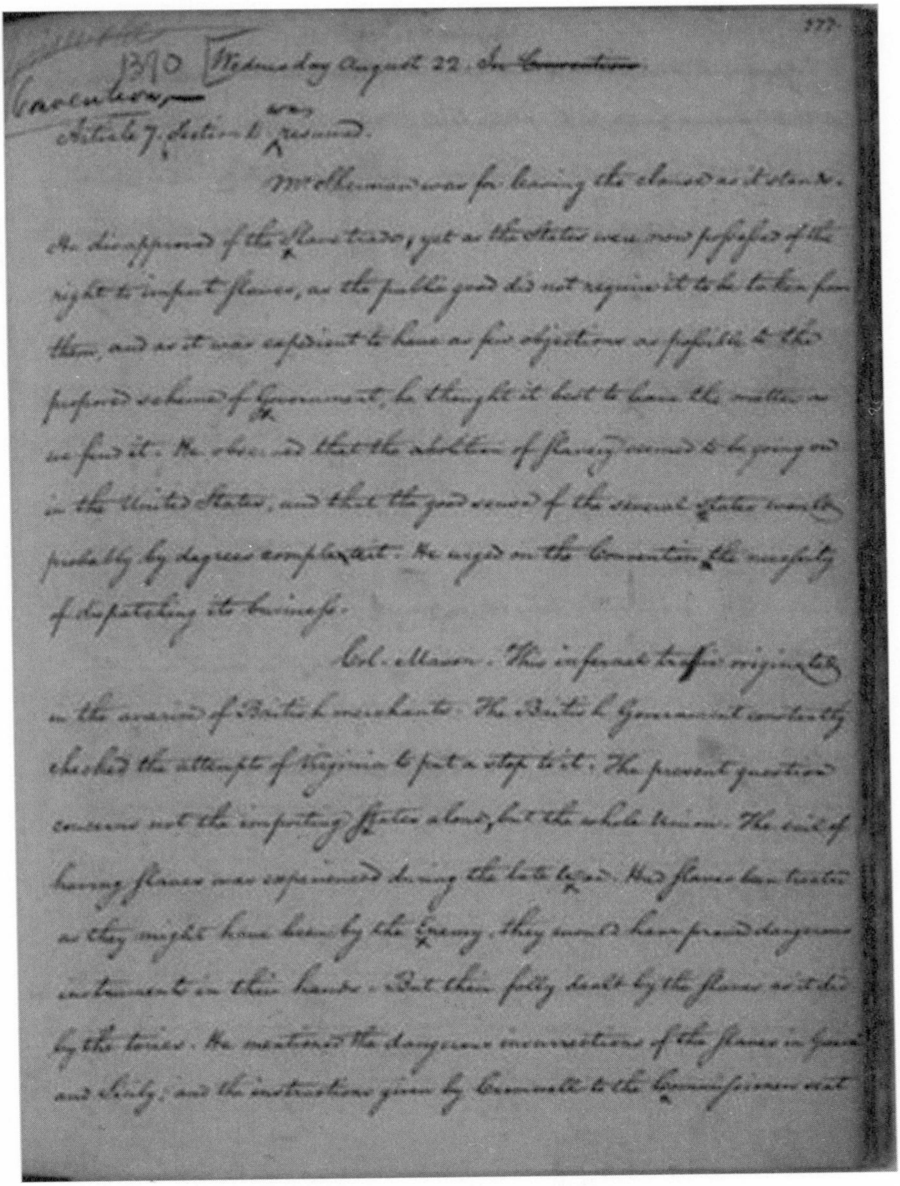

James Madison's notes on George Mason's speech on slavery

of having slaves was experienced during the late war. Had slaves been treated as they might have by the Enemy, they would have proved dangerous instruments in their hands . . . he mentioned dangerous insurrections of the slaves in Greece and Italy . . . Maryland & Virginia he said had already prohibited the importation of slaves expressly. N. Carolina had done the same in substance. All this would be in vain if S. Carolina & Georgia be at liberty to import. The Western people are already calling out for slaves for their new lands: and will fill that country with slaves if they can be got through S. Carolina and Georgia. Slavery discourages arts & manufactures. The poor despise labor when performed by slaves. They prevent the immigration of Whites, who really enrich and strengthen a Country. They produce the most pernicious effect on manners.

"Every master of slaves is born a petty tyrant," Mason bellowed. "They bring the judgment of heaven on a Country . . . He lamented that some of our eastern brethren had, with a lust of gain, embarked in this nefarious traffic . . . He held it essential in every point of view, that the Genl. Govt. should have the power to prevent the increase of slavery."[16]

These were essentially the same sentiments that Mason had voiced in Virginia, where he had received an excellent reception from his fellow planters. But this was not the Virginia legislature. Immediately after Mason had taken his seat, Oliver Ellsworth rose. Ellsworth, who seemed more attuned to other delegates' hypocrisies than his own, noted, "As he had never owned a slave, he could not judge the effects of slavery on character." He continued, "As slaves multiply so fast in Virginia and Maryland that it is cheaper to raise than import them whilst in the sickly rice swamps foreign supplies are necessary, if we go no further than is urged [restricting imports only] we shall be unjust towards South Carolina and Georgia. Let us not intermeddle." Ellsworth added, "If it was to be considered in a moral light, we ought to go further and free those already in the country."[17]

Mason was unused to such treatment and since freeing slaves was, needless to say, not at all what he had in mind, he did not respond. More than that, he did not open his mouth for the rest of the day, as unusual an occurrence in Philadelphia that summer as snow. Mason's pique did not end the debate. After Ellsworth, the Pinckneys weighed in. Charles noted all the advanced civilizations of antiquity in which slavery was common, and then repeated his offer to end the slave trade in South Carolina, even promising to vote for it. His cousin, however, was more to the point. "South Carolina and Georgia can not do without slaves," asserted the general. "As to Virginia, she will gain by stopping importations. Her slaves will rise in value and she has more than she wants . . . the importation of slaves," he went on, "would be for the interest of the whole union. The more slaves, the more produce to the carrying trade; the more consumption also and the more of this the more revenue for the common treasury."

Pinckney added that a prohibition of the slave trade would be tantamount to excluding South Carolina from the Union. Williamson of North Carolina and Abraham Baldwin of Georgia both agreed that their states could not agree to union if the extension of the slave trade were rejected.

Pennsylvania's Wilson could not resist pointing out that "if S. C. & Georgia were themselves disposed to get rid of the importation of slaves in a short time as had been suggested, they would never refuse to Unite because the importation might be prohibited." But Wilson was not so much asking for the slave trade to end as he was trying to raise revenue through it. "As the section now stands," he added, "all articles imported are to be taxed. Slaves alone are exempt. This is in fact a bounty on that article." Rufus King, modifying his stance from moral outrage to fiscal propriety, seconded Wilson's objection, noting, "the exemption of slaves from duty whilst every other import was subjected to it, was an inequality that could not fail to strike the commercial sagacity of the Northn. & middle States."

Then Delaware's John Dickinson rose. The man who had lamented how slavery branded America in the eyes of the world said that he "considered it as inadmissible on every principle of honor and safety that the importation of slaves should be authorized to the states by the Constitution." He hastened to add, however, that "the true question was whether the national happiness would be promoted or impeded by the importation."

After Langdon also expressed doubts about the Lower South ever terminating the slave trade on its own, General Pinckney felt the need to repudiate his young cousin. The general "thought himself bound to declare candidly that he did not think S. Carolina would stop importations of slaves in any short time." Then he made his offer to the New Englanders by moving "to commit the clause that slaves might be liable to an equal tax with other imports which he thought right & wch. wd. Remove one difficulty that had been started."

Rutledge added, by way of closing argument, "If the Convention thinks that N. C.; S. C. & Georgia will ever agree to the plan, unless their right to import slaves be untouched, the expectation is in vain. The people of those States will never be such fools as to give up so important an interest." He agreed that the matter should be committed.

The choice was clear. Northerners could choose to align themselves with the moral arguments of Virginia (hollow as they may have been) or the economic inducements of South Carolina. Gouverneur Morris, the man who had spoken with such vitriol less than two weeks earlier, let Virginia know what that choice was likely to be. He "wished the whole subject to be committed including the clauses relating to taxes on exports & to a navigation act. These things may form a bargain among the Northern & Southern States." Morris, like King and Dickinson, seemed willing to pay almost any price for union.

After Mason's jeremiad, the entire discussion had been conducted between northerners and delegates from the Lower South, as if they were hammering out their deal on the floor of the convention. Not only was Mason silent—no member of the Virginia delegation said anything at all until just before the vote to commit, when Edmund Randolph addressed the convention, his desperation obvious.

Randolph said he "was for committing in order that some middle ground might, if possible, be found. He could never agree to the clause as it stands. He wd. sooner risk the constitution. He dwelt on the dilemma to which the Convention was exposed. By agreeing to the clause, it would revolt the Quakers, the Methodists, and many others in the States having no slaves. On the other hand, two States might be lost to the Union. Let us then, he said, try chance of a commitment."

The motion to commit passed 7-3. Immediately thereafter, Pinckney and Langdon moved to also commit the section requiring two-thirds of each house to accede to any navigation act. Gorham protested. "Is it meant to require a greater proportion of votes?" he asked, fearing a three-fourths majority. He reminded the southerners of their end of the deal. "He desired it to be remembered that the eastern states had no motive to union but a commercial one. They were able to protect themselves. They were not afraid of external danger, and did not need the aid of southern states." To clarify, Wilson proposed commitment "in order to reduce the proportion of votes required."

Ellsworth did not want to take any chances on another committee wrecking the deal. He "was for taking the plan as it is. This widening of opinions has a threatening aspect. If we do not agree on this middle & moderate ground he was afraid we should lose two States, with such others as may be disposed to stand aloof, should fly into a variety of shapes & directions, and most probably into several confederations and not without bloodshed." Nevertheless, the motion to commit the rule on navigation acts passed 9-2.

Another committee of eleven was appointed to work out a compromise on navigation acts and the slave trade. Madison was chosen to represent Virginia and Luther Martin represented Maryland. This is how Martin later described the proceedings:

"I found the Eastern States notwithstanding their aversion to slavery, were very willing to indulge the Southern States, at least with a temporary liberty to prosecute the slave trade, provided the Southern States would, in their turn, gratify them by laying no restriction on navigation acts; and after a very little time the committee, by a very great majority, agreed on a report by which the general government was to be prohibited from preventing the importation of slaves for a limited time, and the restrictive clause relative to navigation acts was to be omitted."[18]

On August 24, the committee of eleven presented its report, although there was to be no discussion until the next day. The reworked clause read, "The migration or importation of such persons as the several states now existing shall think it proper to admit, shall not be prohibited prior to the year 1800 but a tax or duty may be imposed on such migration or importation at a rate not exceeding the average of duties laid on imports."[19] The section requiring a two-thirds majority to pass navigation acts was stricken.

The following morning, the elder Pinckney moved to extend the window on slave trading until 1808, a motion seconded by Gorham. To this point, Madison had stayed out of the debate. Nor did he seem to have participated much in the committee of eleven. Now, however, watching his beautiful edifice reduced to compromises over a repugnant practice and petty profiteering, he could sit by no longer. "Twenty years will produce all the mischief that be can apprehended from the liberty to import slaves," he observed tartly. "So long a term will be more dishonorable to the national character than to say nothing about it in the Constitution."[20]

The vote for the extension until 1808 passed easily, New England and the Lower South between them constituting a majority of the eleven states present. After the vote, Gouverneur Morris, whose wit could be lacerating, moved that the clause should read, "importation of slaves into N. Carolina, S—Carolina & Georgia." He said this "would be most fair and . . . he wished it be known also that this part of the Constitution was a compliance with these States."

Mason, thinking Morris serious, replied that while he was not against using the word "slave," he thought it would offend his good friends to the South to have their states named. Sherman also thought naming the states a bad idea. George Clymer, a Pennsylvania shipper, agreed, and North Carolina's Williamson, while assuring the delegates that "both in opinion and practice he was against slavery," thought it "more in favor of humanity" not to exclude South Carolina and Georgia from the Union.

Morris withdrew his motion.

As to the question of taxing the imported slaves, Mason quickly asserted, "Not to tax will be equivalent to a bounty on the importation of slaves." Were a sufficiently high tax imposed on African slaves, he hoped, Virginia slaves might begin to be more appealing.

Even the South Carolina delegates could not object, and a tax was approved. What was most interesting in this exchange, however, was a throwaway by Madison, who "thought it wrong to admit in the Constitution the idea that there could be property in men." Apparently it was not equally wrong that there indeed *was* property in men.[21]

Not until the following Wednesday, August 29, did the recommendation by the committee of eleven to strike the section requiring a two-thirds majority on navigation acts come up for discussion. As soon as the question was introduced, Charles Pinckney, always drawn to the outrageous, tried to renege on South Carolina's quid pro quo. "The power of regulating commerce was a pure concession on the part of S. States. They did not need the protection of the N. States at present."[22] He moved that the section read, "No act of the Legislature for the purpose of regulating the commerce of the U. S. with foreign powers, or among the several States, shall be passed without the assent of two thirds of the members of each House." Luther Martin seconded.

Charles Pinckney

Passage of Pinckney's motion might have saved Virginia. Like the slave system, navigation acts would have a vast economic impact on the South, and, perhaps to avoid their impact, South Carolina might have seen that realigning itself with its slaveholding brethren was preferable to doing business with the New Englanders.

But any such hope was soon dashed. Once again, the elder Pinckney was quick to rein in his cousin. "Considering the loss brought on the commerce of the Eastern States by the revolution, their liberal conduct towards the views of South Carolina, and the interest the weak Southn. States had in being united with the strong Eastern States, he thought it proper that no fetters should be imposed on the power of making commercial regulations." The general added that "he had himself . . . prejudices against the Eastern States before he came here but would acknowledge that he found them as liberal and candid as any man whatever."

Clymer and Sherman followed, both indicating that a two-thirds majority was a bad idea, neither mentioning the bargain that was by now enough of an open secret that Madison included it as a note in his records.[23] Richard Dobbs Spaight, a North Carolina planter, announced that he opposed Charles Pinckney's motion, as did Pinckney's fellow South Carolinian Pierce Butler.

George Mason tried again. "If the Govt. is to be lasting, it must be founded in the confidence & affections of the people . . . The Majority will be governed by their interests. The Southern States are the minority in both houses. Is it to be expected that they will deliver themselves bound hand & foot to the Eastern States and enable them to exclaim in the words of Cromwell on a certain occasion—'the Lord hath delivered them into our hands?' "

Wilson refuted Mason, noting that "the majority would be no more governed by interest than the minority." Madison delivered a long address, one of his few at this stage of the proceedings, noting both sides of the question but concluding that northern control over commerce would actually be a benefit to Virginia, as "the increase of the Coasting trade, and of seamen, would be favorable to the S. States by increasing the consumption of their produce."

After Rutledge also announced himself against Pinckney's motion, stating that "it did not follow from a grant of the power to regulate trade that it would be abused," and that navigation acts were necessary in "laying the foundation for a great empire," Edmund Randolph took the floor.

The putative author of the Virginia Plan spoke with despair. "There were features so odious in the Constitution as it now stands, that he doubted whether he should be able to agree to it. A rejection of the motion would complete the deformity of the system . . . He did not mean, however, to enter into the merits. What he had in view was merely to pave the way for a declaration which he might be hereafter obliged to make if an accumulation of the obnoxious ingredients should take place, that he could not give his assent to plan."

If the slave trade were continued and the North prevailed with a simple majority for navigation acts, Randolph and Mason were almost certain to refuse to endorse the plan. Patrick Henry was already on record as opposing the entire idea and the possibility began to loom that Virginia, one of the two most important states, might refuse to ratify the Constitution altogether. Still, northern shippers, having granted concessions on almost everything else, were not about to see their prosperity threatened. Gorham said, "If the government is to be so fettered as to be unable to relieve the eastern states what motive can they have to join in it, and thereby tie their own hands from measures which they could otherwise take for themselves."

If the convention fell apart, the New Englanders knew, the Lower South had the most to lose—it had been successful on virtually every point—but even Virginia, despite the loss on both ends of this latest deal, had made enormous gains in the ability to protect the plantation system. If the North walked out now, all those gains would be lost. Gorham's ultimatum was a risk worth taking for the shippers.

Pinckney's motion was defeated 7-4, South Carolina joining a solid North in voting nay. Thus the remaining three members of the South Carolina delegation must have joined in a rebuff of Charles Pinckney, sticking to the deal they had cut with the northern shippers. Immediately afterward, the motion to strike out entirely the section requiring a two-thirds majority to pass navigation acts was approved without dissent.

There was one more item on the slavery agenda. At the end of the previous session, "Mr. Butler and Mr. Pinckney moved 'to require fugitive slaves and servants to be delivered up like criminals.'" This was an important piece of the slaveholders' agenda. Although there was a fugitive slave provision in the Articles of Confederation, practically speaking, it was unenforceable. Congress had no real power to compel abolitionist Pennsylvania Quakers, for example, to return a fugitive slave, or even to prevent them from enticing slaves to flee to their protection. Under the new system, however, a fugitive slave provision would have teeth.

Wilson had protested against such a clause. "This would oblige the Executive of the State to do it at the public expence," he noted. Sherman added that he "saw no more propriety in the public seizing and surrendering a slave or servant, than a horse." Butler had then withdrawn his proposition "in order that some particular provision might be made apart from this article."

With the North comfortable with the navigation acts provision, Butler tried again. He "moved to insert . . . 'If any person bound to service or labor in any of the U__States shall escape into another State, he or she shall not be discharged from such service or labor, in consequence of any regulations subsisting in the State to which they escape, but shall be delivered up to the person justly claiming their service or labor.'"

Wilson, Sherman, and the other northerners quickly agreed to this wording without debate or dissent. With the compromise set and the fugitive slave clause in place, the business of slavery was complete. From that day forward, there was no more talk of slaves in Philadelphia.

16. Closing the Deal: September

$\mathcal{C}$ompromises are based on perception. When successful, both parties believe that what they have attained outstrips that which they have given up. They become very possessive of the deal and are willing, even eager, to resolve any remaining differences in order to avoid jeopardizing their gains. An unsuccessful compromise is just the opposite. Under what might be precisely the same terms, one or both parties believe that what they have given up is unacceptable compared to whatever minimal advantages may have been secured. Further conciliation becomes impossible. They tend to become stubborn and unreasonable, even about seemingly minor points, because they have decided that they have little or nothing to lose if the deal collapses, and are perhaps even looking for an excuse to make it collapse.

As the federal convention moved into September, many of the delegates had seen their views evolve from the latter to the former. Opponents who had been prepared to scotch the entire idea in May and June had come to see the new Constitution as a source of critical achievement. Small states had secured equal representation in the second house; large states had introduced the notion of proportional representation in the population-based first. Creditors saw the potential for a stable monetary system; debtors realized that the states would retain substantial power to enforce—or not enforce—contracts and financial obligations on an individual basis. Everyone saw a government pledged to put down insurrection, either black or white.

While northerners saw a new government that would encourage and protect commerce and shipping, slaveowners in particular had realized enormous benefits. Counting three-fifths of their slave population in the apportionment of seats in the first house was an incalculable victory, one that promised the southern states a huge disproportion of power in that chamber, not only for the present, but in perpetuity. With no plans in place to initiate a levy on the states, apportioning a similar percentage for taxation had no immediate impact and was therefore only a hypothetical.* The restrictions in the Northwest Ordinance on the number of new states north of the Ohio gave the South every reason to expect that it would also dominate in any chamber in which the states voted equally. These provisions, as well as those covering treason and fugitive slaves, benefited all the slave states equally. The extension of the slave trade was a victory for the rice planters of South Carolina over the tobacco growers of Virginia, but for most of the Upper South planters, the extension of the slave trade and the concessions to the North over commerce did not override the protections that the new government offered slaveowners in general.

Ellsworth, Sherman, and Rutledge, all reluctant nationalists in May, had become among the most ardent supporters of the new government.[1] The two delegates from Connecticut had been the authors of the two most significant compromises of the entire four months, and Rutledge had been able to secure almost every advantage that South Carolina had sought.[2]

Among the nationalists, the Annapolis triumvirate of Dickinson, Hamilton, and Madison, despite some setbacks, all viewed the new Constitution as a vast improvement over the Confederation. (Dickinson would leave early because of ill health but asked a fellow delegate, George Read, to sign the Constitution for him by proxy.) The Robert Morris surrogates, Gouverneur Morris and James Wilson, were enthusiastic supporters, as were the Massachusetts capitalists, King and Gorham. The quixotic Elbridge Gerry was a holdout, but since he was considered the convention's oddball (no mean feat with Luther Martin present), he was unlikely to influence anyone else.[3] Luther Martin, the new Constitution's most vocal and intractable opponent, had gone home in disgust.

Mason and Randolph, however, were different. Both had arrived in May with enormous personal prestige, especially Mason, and had been among the strongest supporters of a new government. Both found themselves inalterably opposed to the convention's product. In each case, despite some earlier misgivings, the August compromise ensured that opposition. Randolph's resistance would prove ephemeral—he supported the Constitution in the Virginia ratifying convention, doubtless having been persuaded to see the glass half-full by supporters of the plan like Madison.[4] Mason, however, remained obdurate. He had been looking into the future for years and seeing catastrophe, and he was certain that the commerce-importation compromise could well provide the tinder to destroy the Virginia he knew. Even worse, the three-fifths rule, seemingly

_____

*As it would remain.

slavery's biggest victory, in his view would accelerate Virginia's downfall since, while it provided a boon to southern legislative clout, it would also encourage the continued propagation of the slave population. On the final day of debate, Mason would make one final effort to restore a two-thirds majority for navigation acts, but was summarily voted down. He thereafter announced that he would not put his name to the document.

Mason's warnings were irrelevant to northerners and brushed off by his fellow southerners. So, with a new sense of purpose and cooperation, in that first week of September, the delegates tackled the last major unresolved issues— the powers and selection of a president, and how to admit new states.

As of August 24, the working definition of the executive had still been, "The executive power of the U. S. shall be vested in a single person. His stile shall be 'The President of the U. S. of America' and his title shall be 'His Excellency.' He shall be elected by ballot by the Legislature. He shall hold his office during the term of seven years; but shall not be elected a second time." Few actually favored this wording but the delegates still could not agree on how to improve upon it. A motion to change "legislature" to "the people" failed miserably. After some squabbling, the delegates agreed to insert "joint" before "ballot," thus involving both houses of Congress in the product.

No one was terribly enthusiastic about this plan and Gouverneur Morris then objected to the entire notion of allowing the national legislature to choose the executive. "If the Legislature have the Executive dependent on them, they can perpetuate & support their usurpations by the influence of tax-gatherers & other officers, by fleets armies &c. Cabal & corruption are attached to that mode of election," he observed. Morris instead proposed that "to guard against all these evils . . . the President 'shall be chosen by Electors to be chosen by the People of the several States.' "[5] The only aspect of the question enjoying even tentative acceptance was that the people should not choose the executive. Morris's motion failed 6-5, after which the provision was postponed again.

By August 28, nothing had changed. The only thing the delegates could agree on was that every proposed means of selecting a president was unacceptable. This time, popular vote did not even come up, and no one was really comfortable assigning the task to either state legislatures or the national legislature. Once again, election and powers of the president were assigned to a committee of eleven, but when the matter was reported out, the best the convention could do was, upon a motion by Sherman, assign a new committee of eleven to try to find a solution. Shortly before, Mason had declared "that he would sooner chop off his right hand than put it to the Constitution as it now stands."

On August 31, the committee presented its report, which did nothing to break the deadlock, so the delegates tried again, passing the question off to yet another committee of eleven.[6] By then, however, the importation-commerce compromise had been completed and there was an eagerness to solve the problem of the executive that had not been present previously. As a result, this new committee was stocked with delegates who had a better chance of arriving at a workable solution, or at least a solution that might be accepted as workable. The members included King, Sherman, Gouverneur Morris (instead of the ineffectual Thomas Fitzsimmons), Dickinson, Madison (instead of the combustible Mason), and Butler. The committee incorporated the notion of a joint legislative ballot, while returning control of electors to the individual states. The result was in many ways a mirror of the Connecticut Compromise for the legislative branch.

The executive, they proposed on September 4,

... shall hold his office during the term of four years, and together with the vice-President, chosen for the same term, be elected in the following manner, viz. Each State shall appoint in such manner as its Legislature may direct, a number of electors equal to the whole number of Senators and members of the House of Representatives to which the State may be entitled in the Legislature. The Electors shall meet in their respective States, and vote by ballot for two persons, of whom one at least shall not be an inhabitant of the same State with themselves; and they shall make a list of all the persons voted for, and of the number of votes for each, which list they shall sign and certify and transmit sealed to the Seat of the Genl. Government, directed to the President of the Senate—The President of the Senate shall in that House open all the certificates; and the votes shall be then & there counted. The Person having the greatest number of votes shall be the President, if such number be a majority of that of the electors; and if there be more than one who have such majority, and have an equal number of votes, then the Senate shall immediately choose by ballot one of them for President: but if no person have a majority, then from the five highest on the list, the Senate shall choose by ballot the President. And in every case after the choice of the President, the person having the greatest number of votes shall be vice-president: but if there should remain two or more who have equal votes, the Senate shall choose from them the vice-President. The Legislature may determine the time of choosing and assembling the Electors, and the manner of certifying and transmitting their votes.[7]

And so, the Electoral College was born.

Debate on specific items relating to the executive ensued for the next three days. The only notable change came at the suggestion of Roger Sherman, that the House of Representatives, voting by state, rather than the Senate, choose the president if either of two candidates with a majority were tied or if no candidate received a majority.

Of greater significance than the changes, was the atmosphere within which these debates were conducted. Where, in the past, one group of delegates or another had attacked every proposed change or alteration of the formula, delegates were now equally aggressive in rejecting changes. They refused to alter the manner of appointing electors, the number of electors, the percentage of the electors necessary to elect a president, and a number of other minor provisions—and this all in one day.

Provisions for the admission of new states had been agreed to with the same dispatch. At the end of the August 29 session, immediately after agreement on the fugitive slave clause, the delegates had taken up the question of the admission of new states, and by early morning of the next day had resolved it. Even Gouverneur Morris was conciliatory. New states were to be admitted on an equal footing with the original thirteen, with the proviso that no new state could be carved from within the boundaries of another without the consent of both the national legislature and the state's legislature, a measure necessary to maintain balance of power in the Senate.

All this newfound bonhomie did not mean that the delegates had ceased to pay attention. During discussion of one of the final issues, how to amend the Constitution, Madison proposed inserting the clause, "The Legislature of the U. S. whenever two thirds of both Houses shall deem necessary, or on the application of two thirds of the Legislatures of the several States, shall propose amendments to this Constitution, which shall be valid to all intents and purposes as part thereof, when the same shall have been ratified by three fourths at least of the Legislatures of the several States, or by Conventions in three fourths thereof, as one or the other mode of ratification may be proposed by the Legislature of the U.S." Hamilton seconded and it seemed that the motion would be quickly approved.[8]

Rutledge, however, quickly asserted that "he never could agree to give a power by which the articles relating to slaves might be altered by the States not interested in that property and prejudiced against it." So, he proposed adding the phrase "provided that no amendments which may be made prior to the year 1808, shall in any manner affect the 4 & 5 sections of the VII article," which the delegates inserted without debate.[9]

By the end of the day on September 8, the delegates had covered the entire plan. A Committee of Style was appointed to compile all of the draft provisions and create a finished document. The convention was taking no chances at this late date and appointed five nationalists—Johnson of Connecticut, King, Madison, Hamilton, and Gouverneur Morris. The task of actually turning the working notes into a flowing document was given to Morris, considered the most graceful writer of all the delegates.

He did not disappoint. On September 12, printed copies of the finished Constitution were distributed to the delegates. From the famous preamble, "We, the People of the United States, in order to form a more perfect union, to establish justice, insure domestic tranquility, provide for the common defence, promote the general welfare, and secure the blessings of liberty to ourselves and our posterity, do ordain and establish this Constitution for the United States of America," to the final Article VII, "The ratification of the conventions of nine States, shall be sufficient for the establishment of this constitution between the States so ratifying the same," the American Constitution is a stylistic masterpiece.

As to clarity, however, history has demonstrated that interpreting the intent of the convention from the finished document has not been as easy as marveling over the prose. In fact, Morris's version sometimes muddied the intent of the men who agreed to the plan, but by the time they received it, most were too worn out to debate semantics.

Morris also added a provision of his own. Perhaps as a favor to Robert Morris, in Article I, Section 10, which enumerates powers denied to the states, such as coining money, or entering into "any Treaty, Alliance, or Confederation," he inserted that no state shall pass laws "altering or impairing the Obligation of Contracts." It passed unnoticed (except by Gerry), or at least unchallenged, at the time, but the contract clause would spawn a body of law all its own over the years. And in the end it did not even help Robert Morris, whose paper empire imploded despite the sanctity of contract.

There were a number of minor changes to Morris's draft, most notably the reduction to two-thirds from three-fourths as the majority needed to override a presidential veto. The convention unanimously refused to authorize preparation of a Bill of Rights, deciding that the powers of the central government did not extend to questions like freedom of speech or the press—

those were reserved for the individual states—and a Bill of Rights was therefore unnecessary.*

For the next three days, the delegates, straining to finish, moved with amazing speed through the Committee of Style's report, refusing to make all but a few minor changes.[10] At the close of business on Saturday, September 15, the convention agreed to the product. It was returned on Monday, September 17, 1787, signed (except by Gerry, Mason, and Randolph) and sent on to Congress.[†]

After four months and three days, the Convention of 1787 was over. For Madison, Hamilton, and Dickinson, it was the culmination of more than two years of work that had begun in a poorly attended, largely overlooked meeting in Annapolis.

---

*Mason's refusal to sign the Constitution predated the convention's final rejection of a Bill of Rights, rendering his subsequent rationale hollow.

†After all the provisions had been agreed to, John Dunlap printed a proof copy of the new Constitution and gave it to Washington to check. Everything was in order, with one exception. In Article I, Section 9, instead of "1808" as the date until which the slave trade would be permitted, Dunlap had printed "1708." Whether this was a simple typographical error or an attempt by the antislavery Dunlap to register displeasure with the extension of the slave trade will never be known. In any event, Washington caught the mistake and a correction was made before Dunlap printed the finished copy (see opposite).

[4]

Sect. 3. He shall from time to time give to the Congress information of the state of the union, and recommend to their consideration such measures as he shall judge necessary and expedient ; he may, on extraordinary occasions, convene both houses, or either of them, and in case of disagreement between them, with respect to the time of adjournment, he may adjourn them to such time as he shall think proper ; he shall receive ambassadors and other public ministers; he shall take care that the laws be faithfully executed, and shall commission all the officers of the United States.

Sect. 4. The president, vice-president and all civil officers of the United States, shall be removed from office on impeachment for, and conviction of, treason, bribery, or other high crimes and misdemeanors.

III.

Sect. 1. The judicial power of the United States, shall be vested in one supreme court, and in such inferior courts as the Congress may from time to time ordain and establish. The judges, both of the supreme and inferior courts, shall hold their offices during good behaviour, and shall, at stated times, receive for their services, a compensation, which shall not be diminished during their continuance in office.

Sect. 2. The judicial power shall extend to all cases, in law and equity, arising under this constitution, the laws of the United States, and treaties made, or which shall be made, under their authority; to all cases affecting ambassadors, other public ministers and consuls; to all cases of admiralty and maritime jurisdiction; to controversies to which the United States shall be a party; to controversies between two or more States, between a state and citizens of another state, between citizens of different States, between citizens of the same state claiming lands under grants of different States, and between a state, or the citizens thereof, and foreign States, citizens or subjects.

In all cases affecting ambassadors, other public ministers and consuls, and those in which a state shall be party, the supreme court shall have original jurisdiction. In all the other cases before mentioned, the supreme court shall have appellate jurisdiction, both as to law and fact, with such exceptions, and under such regulations as the Congress shall make.

The trial of all crimes, except in cases of impeachment, shall be by jury; and such trial shall be held in the state where the said crimes shall have been committed; but when not committed within any state, the trial shall be at such place or places as the Congress may by law have directed.

Sect. 3. Treason against the United States, shall consist only in levying war against them, or in adhering to their enemies, giving them aid and comfort. No person shall be convicted of treason unless on the testimony of two witnesses to the same overt act, or on confession in open court.

The Congress shall have power to declare the punishment of treason, but no attainder of treason shall work corruption of blood, or forfeiture except during the life of the person attainted.

IV.

Sect. 1. Full faith and credit shall be given in each state to the public acts, records, and judicial proceedings of every other state. And the Congress may by general laws prescribe the manner in which such acts, records and proceedings shall be proved, and the effect thereof.

Sect. 2. The citizens of each state shall be entitled to all privileges and immunities of citizens in the several states.

A person charged in any state with treason, felony, or other crime, who shall flee from justice, and be found in another state, shall, on demand of the executive authority of the state from which he fled, be delivered up, to be removed to the state having jurisdiction of the crime.

No person held to service or labour in one state, under the laws thereof, escaping into another, shall, in consequence of any law or regulation therein, be discharged from such service or labour, but shall be delivered up on claim of the party to whom such service or labour may be due.

Sect. 3. New states may be admitted by the Congress into this union; but no new state shall be formed or erected within the jurisdiction of any other state; nor any state be formed by the junction of two or more states, or parts of states, without the consent of the legislatures of the states concerned as well as of the Congress.

The Congress shall have power to dispose of and make all needful rules and regulations respecting the territory or other property belonging to the United States; and nothing in this Constitution shall be so construed as to prejudice any claims of the United States, or of any particular state.

Sect. 4. The United States shall guarantee to every state in this union a Republican form of government, and shall protect each of them against invasion; and on application of the legislature, or of the executive (when the legislature cannot be convened) against domestic violence.

V.

The Congress, whenever two-thirds of both houses shall deem it necessary, shall propose amendments to this constitution, or, on the application of the legislatures of two-thirds of the several states, shall call a convention for proposing amendments, which, in either case, shall be valid to all intents and purposes, as part of this constitution, when ratified by the legislatures of three-fourths of the several states, or by conventions in three-fourths thereof, as the one or the other mode of ratification may be proposed by the Congress; Provided, that no amendment which may be made prior to the year one thousand ▪▪▪▪ hundred and eight shall in any manner affect the first and fourth clauses in the ninth section of the first article ; and that no state, without its consent, shall be deprived of its equal suffrage in the senate.

VI.

All debts contracted and engagements entered into, before the adoption of this Constitution, shall be as valid against the United States under this Constitution, as under the confederation.

This constitution, and the laws of the United States which shall be made in pursuance thereof; and all treaties made, or which shall be made, under the authority of the United States, shall be the supreme law of the land; and the judges in every state shall be bound thereby, any thing in the constitution or laws of any state to the contrary notwithstanding.

The misprint of the Constitution, noting 1708 as the date by which slavery would be abolished

17. SUPREME LAW OF THE LAND

*A*rticle VII of the Constitution was the shortest of all. It stated simply, "The Ratification of the Conventions of nine States, shall be sufficient for the Establishment of this Constitution between the States so ratifying the Same." It seemed straightforward enough. If conventions in nine states approved, the Constitution would take effect, only, of course, for those nine, while any of the four remaining states that ratified later would be admitted as equals. If one or more of them refused, they would no longer be considered part of the United States.

But brevity was deceptive.[1] Endorsement by Congress, where approval was by no means certain, was required before the document could even be introduced in state legislatures. If the Constitution survived the congressional test, a state's legislature might pack a ratifying convention with opponents of the plan or even refuse to authorize a ratifying convention at all.[2]

Even as the delegates held a celebratory dinner at the City Tavern on the evening of September 17, the battle for ratification began. John Dunlap had printed three thousand copies of the six-page Constitution, and these were soon officially on their way to Congress and unofficially to the legislatures and citizenry of each of the thirteen states. In Pennsylvania's case, the journey was short, since the state legislature was meeting on the second floor of the State House, just upstairs from the convention chamber, and received copies almost before the ink was dry.[3] It was a good thing too, since Pennsylvania's approval, crucial to the overall scheme, hinged on getting the process started quickly.

At that moment, the Pennsylvania legislature was dominated by federalists, as supporters of the new Constitution were called, but on September 29, less than two weeks later, the legislative session would end.[4] A new session with new members would begin in November and no one knew if that assemblage would be as amenable as the current group to abandoning the Articles of

The Pennsylvania Packet, *and Daily Advertiser.*

[Price Four-Pence.]   WEDNESDAY, September 19, 1787.   [No. 2690.]

WE, the People of the United States, in order to form a more perfect Union, establish Justice, insure domestic Tranquility, provide for the common Defence, promote the General Welfare, and secure the Blessings of Liberty to Ourselves and our Posterity, do ordain and establish this Constitution for the United States of America.

ARTICLE I.

Sect. 1. ALL legislative powers herein granted shall be vested in a Congress of the United States, which shall consist of a Senate and House of Representatives.

Sect. 2. The House of Representatives shall be composed of members chosen every second year by the people of the several states, and the electors in each state shall have the qualifications requisite for electors of the most numerous branch of the state legislature.

No person shall be a representative who shall not have attained to the age of twenty-five years, and been seven years a citizen of the United States, and who shall not, when elected, be an inhabitant of that state in which he shall be chosen.

Representatives and direct taxes shall be apportioned among the several states which may be included within this Union, according to their respective numbers, which shall be determined by adding to the whole number of free persons, including those bound to service for a term of years, and excluding Indians not taxed, three-fifths of all other persons. The actual enumeration shall be made within three years after the first meeting of the Congress of the United States, and within every subsequent term of ten years, in such manner as they shall by law direct. The number of representatives shall not exceed one for every thirty thousand, but each state shall have at least one representative; and until such enumeration shall be made, the state of New-Hampshire shall be entitled to chuse three, Massachusetts eight, Rhode-Island and Providence Plantations one, Connecticut five, New-York six, New-Jersey four, Pennsylvania eight, Delaware one, Maryland six, Virginia ten, North-Carolina five, South-Carolina five, and Georgia three.

When vacancies happen in the representation from any state, the Executive authority thereof shall issue writs of election to fill such vacancies.

The House of Representatives shall chuse their Speaker and other officers; and shall have the sole power of impeachment.

Sect. 3. The Senate of the United States shall be composed of two senators from each state, chosen by the legislature thereof, for six years; and each senator shall have one vote.

Immediately after they shall be assembled in consequence of the first election, they shall be divided as equally as may be into three classes. The seats of the senators of the first class shall be vacated at the expiration of the second year, of the second class at the expiration of the fourth year, and of the third class at the expiration of the sixth year, so that one-third may be chosen every second year; and if vacancies happen by resignation, or otherwise, during the recess of the Legislature of any state, the Executive thereof may make temporary appointments until the next meeting of the Legislature, which shall then fill such vacancies.

No person shall be a senator who shall not have attained to the age of thirty years, and been nine years a citizen of the United States, and who shall not, when elected, be an inhabitant of that state for which he shall be chosen.

The Vice-President of the United States shall be President of the senate, but shall have no vote, unless they be equally divided.

The Senate shall chuse their other officers, and also a President pro tempore, in the absence of the Vice-President, or when he shall exercise the office of President of the United States.

The Senate shall have the sole power to try all impeachments. When sitting for that purpose, they shall be on oath or affirmation. When the President of the United States is tried, the Chief Justice shall preside: And no person shall be convicted without the concurrence of two-thirds of the members present.

Judgment in cases of impeachment shall not extend further than to removal from office, and disqualification to hold and enjoy any office of honor, trust or profit under the United States; but the party convicted shall nevertheless be liable and subject to indictment, trial, judgment and punishment, according to law.

Sect. 4. The times, places and manner of holding elections for senators and representatives, shall be prescribed in each state by the legislature thereof; but the Congress may at any time by law make or alter such regulations, except as to the places of chusing Senators.

The Congress shall assemble at least once in every year, and such meeting shall be on the first Monday in December, unless they shall by law appoint a different day.

Sect. 5. Each house shall be the judge of the elections, returns and qualifications of its own members, and a majority of each shall constitute a quorum to do business; but a smaller number may adjourn from day to day, and may be authorised to compel the attendance of absent members, in such manner, and under such penalties as each house may provide.

Each house may determine the rules of its proceedings, punish its members for disorderly behaviour, and, with the concurrence of two-thirds, expel a member.

Each house shall keep a journal of its proceedings, and from time to time publish the same, excepting such parts as may in their judgment require secrecy; and the yeas and nays of the members of either house on any question shall, at the desire of one-fifth of those present, be entered on the journal.

Neither house, during the session of Congress, shall, without the consent of the other, adjourn for more than three days, nor to any other place than that in which the two houses shall be sitting.

Sect. 6. The senators and representatives shall receive a compensation for their services, to be ascertained by law, and paid out of the treasury of the United States. They shall in all cases, except treason, felony and breach of the peace, be privileged from arrest during their attendance at the session of their respective houses, and in going to and returning from the same; and for any speech or debate in either house, they shall not be questioned in any other place.

No senator or representative shall, during the time for which he was elected, be appointed to any civil office under the authority of the United States, which shall have been created, or the emoluments whereof shall have been encreased during such time; and no person holding any office under the United States, shall be a member of either house during his continuance in office.

Sect. 7. All bills for raising revenue shall originate in the house of representatives; but the senate may propose or concur with amendments as on other bills.

Every bill which shall have passed the house of representatives and the senate, shall, before it become a law, be presented to the president of the United States; if he approve he shall sign it, but if not he shall return it, with his objections to that house in which it shall have originated, who shall enter the objections at large on their journal, and proceed to reconsider it. If after such reconsideration two-thirds of that house shall agree to pass the bill, it shall be sent, together with the objections, to the other house, by which it shall likewise be reconsidered, and if approved by two-thirds of that house, it shall become a law. But in all such cases the votes of both houses shall

The Constitution, as presented in the Pennsylvania Packet, September 19, 1787

Confederation in favor of this new system. Obtaining a vote to authorize a rat-ifying convention before the 29th was thus of vital importance.

By the time the Constitution made it to Congress in New York on Sep-tember 20, eighteen members of the convention had arrived as well, most with congressional credentials. They resumed their seats, ready to ram an approval resolution through. It was the largest turnout in Congress of the entire year. But the antifederalists were not without clout of their own. Led by Virginians Richard Henry Lee and William Grayson, and Melancthon Smith of New York, opponents of the new plan were determined to scuttle it. Lee and his cohorts stalled, brought up irrelevant measures, tried a number of procedural con-trivances, and finally attempted to maneuver Congress into backing a call for a second convention.[5] They succeeded in delaying the vote until September 28, but ultimately could not prevent a resolution from coming to the floor. After the vote to approve, which was recorded as unanimous, federalist congressmen dispatched a messenger to Philadelphia with the news. Riding all night, the messenger arrived early the next day and delivered the news to George Clymer, who passed it on to the speaker of the Pennsylvania assembly in time for the morning session.[6]

Pennsylvania antifederalists got the news just after Clymer. They knew they would be outvoted, but tried to prevent the measure from even coming to the floor by not showing up and thus denying the assembly a quorum. The speaker dispatched the sergeant-at-arms to round up the "seceding members," only two of whom were needed to provide the assembly a critical mass. Taking those instructions one step further, a mob of Philadelphia federalists set out to effectively kidnap two antifederalist deputies. They found the unfortunate leg-islators, James McCalmont and Jacob Miley, hiding in their homes, then dragged them bodily to the State House and literally dumped them in the as-sembly chamber. The assembly minutes merely state that McCalmont and Mi-ley "entered the house."[7] A quorum was achieved and the assembly quickly voted to authorize a ratifying convention for November.

Pennsylvania's ratifying convention began on November 20 and by De-cember 12 it had become the second state to approve the Constitution, voting 46-23 in favor. The reason it wasn't first was that Delaware, which had origi-nally sent its delegates to Philadelphia expressly forbidden from endorsing anything but a modest reform of the Articles of Confederation, had voted to ratify five days earlier. Six days after Pennsylvania, another "small state," New Jersey, endorsed the plan, and Georgia followed two weeks later.[8] One week af-ter Georgia, in a ratifying convention dominated by "the thunders of Oliver

Ellsworth's eloquence," to paraphrase John Trumbull, Connecticut also voted to approve the plan.

Ratification got a bit trickier after that. Of the remaining eight states, three—New York, New Hampshire, and Rhode Island—seemed set against ratification; three more—North Carolina, South Carolina, and Maryland—were on the fence; and in the two most important states in the Union—Massachusetts and Virginia—opposition was fierce.

Massachusetts became the pivot. After the provisions of the new Constitution had been debated in town hall meetings across the Commonwealth, the federalists still faced an uphill climb. Finally, they convinced the haughty and self-important John Hancock that he was in line to be Washington's vice president in the new government, maybe even president if the general declined to serve. Hancock experienced a sudden conversion to federalism and, with him speaking in favor, Massachusetts ratified on February 6.[9]

Maryland was next, but that vote was still two months away. Luther Martin and his fellow antifederalists campaigned tirelessly but, in the end, the vote for ratification was a surprising 63-11 in favor. After South Carolina ratified in May,[10] New Hampshire, considered almost as antifederalist as Rhode Island (which had voted to reject the Constitution in a popular referendum in February), nonetheless voted to ratify.[11]

The new United States had been born—minus Virginia, New York, and North Carolina. (No one cared that much about Rhode Island.) With the Constitution a fait accompli, eventually all four of those states went along, none more reluctantly than Virginia.

The ratification process was an exercise in pure advocacy. Throughout the thirteen states, federalists and antifederalists alike gave speeches, wrote articles, and published pamphlets filled with distortions, half-truths, and outright lies. Those who had been among the fifty-five delegates present in Philadelphia were guiltiest of all. Ellsworth's fabrications in the *Landholder* essays, Gerry's equally slanted replies, Pinckney's overstatements in the South Carolina legislature, Luther Martin's screed in *Genuine Information*, all contributed to the propagandizing that characterized the ratification debate. In the *Federalist*, the best known of the postconvention essays, Hamilton, Jay, and especially Madison, parsed, quibbled, equivocated, and perverted the events in Philadelphia, all to convince New Yorkers of the virtues of strong government.[12] Of course,

"Brutus," to whom they were responding, if he was indeed Robert Yates, was no better.

The ratification process became so bitter that some of the men who had worked together in close quarters in more or less good faith for four months came to loathe each other afterwards. The most famous breakup was between Washington and Mason who, after almost four decades of friendship and mutual admiration, rarely spoke again, their contact reduced to short notes sent back and forth.* When Mason died in 1792, his estrangement from Washington was among his deepest regrets.

Mason had also alienated Madison, who had once been one of his most enthusiastic supporters. In a letter to Washington sent along with a printed copy of Mason's objections, Madison wrote, "As he persists in the temper which produced his dissent it is no small satisfaction to find him reduced to such distress for a proper gloss on it."[13]

There was such a disparity in the recollections of delegates who urged ratification and those who insisted upon rejection that it is hard to believe they had sat in the same meetings. As a result, any attempt to use postconvention rhetoric to work back to a meaningful analysis of any particular constitutional provision or the delegates' motives for including it is tenuous at best.

Clearly though, Pinckney, Ellsworth, Martin, Mason, and most of the rest of the delegates who were active in ratification were federalists or antifederalists only by coincidence. For them, the Constitution was a national document only secondarily. The forging of a nation was a far subordinate consideration to the welfare of their particular state, although they often equated the welfare of their state with that of the nation at large. In that regard, these men had advanced their thinking very little in four months in Philadelphia. They had arrived thinking of themselves as South Carolinians or Virginians or Connecticuters, and that is how they left.

This is not to say that there was no broader perspective, no idealism, no sense of higher purpose, in Philadelphia. Quite the contrary. Without the deep vision of some of the delegates, particularly Madison, Gouverneur Morris, Dickinson, and Hamilton—and even Mason, before events turned against him—the convention certainly would have failed to produce a result that enabled a nation. Madison especially saw the potential of a single, united republic. The prevailing

---

*Mason's notes were warm and friendly, while Washington's replies were chilly. Washington never forgave Mason for opposing the Constitution for self-serving reasons. He wrote to a mutual friend that Mason had been done in by pride and exhibited "a lack of manly candor" (Rutland, *Papers*, iii: 179).

sentiment in 1787 was that democracy could only succeed in a small, homogenous society, where no one faction could tyrannically impose its will on another. Madison believed just the opposite—that in a large, heterogeneous society with a powerful central government, shifting alliances could empower every point of view, and thereby exert the best control over the tyranny of a majority. With the passion of true belief, Madison and those who thought like him were willing to go to almost any lengths to see their vision achieved.

But that is precisely the point. Idealists like Madison, who see themselves as working for a higher good, are always at the mercy of pragmatists who care nothing for philosophy but simply want to win. At the convention, there was no more pragmatic a group of men than the slaveholders. They understood all too well how fervently those who favored union felt about a grand republic and, therefore, how much they could make them pay to get it. And make them pay they did. Planters like Rutledge, Butler, and the Pinckneys simply threatened to walk out if one demand or another was not acceded to. Gouverneur Morris, of course, tried the same tactic, but with less success. In response, northern entre-preneurs like Ellsworth, Sherman, and King—the very men who in public at-tacked slavery on moral and religious grounds—voted with slaveholders on the most fundamental elements of the new government, again not because of a higher vision, but only as a quid pro quo to the rice planters' willingness not to interfere with their ability to make money. Even Benjamin Franklin, presi-dent of the Pennsylvania Society for Promoting the Abolition of Slavery and the Relief of Free Negroes Unlawfully Held in Bondage, which had sent a bit-ter and scathing letter to the convention urging an end to the slave trade, en-dorsed a document that extended that trade for another two horrible decades.

Watching these compromises evolve, Madison, Gouverneur Morris, and the others who believed in the possibilities of America were left with a difficult choice. They could have either abandoned their dreams by opposing the crass self-interest before them, or grudgingly gone along, and then, after the conven-tion, defended the very compromises that they had found so repellent while in session.

When one compromises principles too much, however, the principles themselves cease to exist, and the idealists become indistinguishable from the pragmatists they scorn. This fate befell Madison. He took so many positions on the clause extending the slave trade, for example, that determining which, if any, he actually believed is impossible. In the convention, he opposed the slave trade bitterly, even allowing himself an uncharacteristic bit of sarcasm. "Twenty years will produce all the mischief that can be apprehended from the liberty to import slaves," he said famously on August 25. "So long a term will be more dishonorable to the National character than to say nothing about it in the Constitution."[14]

Once the convention ended and he was working for ratification, he made no further references to "dishonor on the national character" or the excessive "length of term" that the slave trade would remain permissible. In the *Federalist, 42,* Madison took up the same question, coming to a decidedly different conclusion:

> It were doubtless to be wished that the power of prohibiting the importation of slaves had not been postponed until the year 1808, or rather that it had been suffered to have immediate operation. But . . . it ought to be considered as a great point gained in favor of humanity, that a period of twenty years may terminate forever, within these States, a traffic which has so long and so loudly upbraided the barbarism of modern policy; that within that period, it will receive a considerable discouragement from the federal government . . . Happy would it be for the unfortunate Africans, if an equal prospect lay before them of being redeemed from the oppressions of their European brethren! Attempts have been made to pervert this clause into an objection against the Constitution, by representing it on one side as a criminal toleration of an illicit practice, and on another as calculated to prevent voluntary and beneficial emigrations from Europe to America. I mention these misconstructions, not with a view to give them an answer, for they deserve none, but as specimens of the manner and spirit in which some have thought fit to conduct their opposition to the proposed government.[15]

On Tuesday, June 17, 1788, in the Virginia ratifying convention, Madison took a different position still.

George Mason, the now-arch-antifederalist, opened the session with an assault on the slave trade clause in Article I, Section 9. "Mr. Chairman, this is a fatal section, which has created more dangers than any other," he began. "The first clause allows the importation of slaves for twenty years. Under the royal government, this evil was looked upon as a great oppression, and many attempts were made to prevent it; but the interest of the African merchants prevented its prohibition.

"As much as I value a union of all the states, I would not admit the Southern States into the Union unless they agree to the discontinuance of this disgraceful trade, because it would bring weakness, and not strength, to the Union." Mason then went on to repeat the same condemnations of slavery that had filled his convention speech and with which Virginians were well familiar. Then, however, in his desperation to defeat the plan, he presented an argument that he would never have made in Philadelphia, nor probably anywhere else.

And, though this infamous traffic be continued, we have no security for the property of that kind which we have already. There is no clause in this Constitution to secure it; for they may lay such a tax as will amount to manumission. And should the government be amended, still this detestable kind of commerce cannot be discontinued till after the expiration of twenty years; for the 5th article, which provides for amendments, expressly excepts this clause. I have ever looked upon this as a most disgraceful thing to America. I cannot express my detestation of it. Yet they have not secured us the property of the slaves we have already. So that "they have done what they ought not to have done, and have left undone what they ought to have done."[16]

Having spent two decades insisting that he was frantic to find a means of forcing his fellow Virginians to end their reliance on slavery, George Mason had here admitted that one of his reasons for refusing to endorse the Constitution was that it might well achieve that very aim. In doing so, he presented much the same arguments to Virginians that Rawlins Lowndes had in South Carolina—that the Constitution did not sufficiently protect the institution of slavery.

As General Pinckney had responded to Lowndes, it would now fall to a Virginia federalist to respond to Mason, to demonstrate that the Constitution was, in fact, a document that promoted and even encouraged slavery. Madison, the philosopher, the father of the Constitution, took on the task.

He dealt with the slave trade first. "We are not in a worse situation than before," he assured his fellows. "That traffic is prohibited by our laws, and we may continue the prohibition.... Under the Articles of Confederation, it might be continued forever; but, by this clause, an end may be put to it after twenty years. There is, therefore, an amelioration of our circumstances." As he soon made clear, the "circumstances" to which he referred was the need for Virginia to sell excess slaves to work the hellish rice plantations in South Carolina.

"The gentlemen from South Carolina and Georgia argued in this manner," he said. " 'We have now liberty to import this species of property, and much of the property now possessed had been purchased, or otherwise acquired, in contemplation of improving it by the assistance of imported slaves. What would be the consequence of hindering us from it? The slaves of Virginia would rise in value, and we should be obliged to go to your markets.' I need not expatiate on this subject."[17] Under the Constitution, Madison seemed to be assuring the planters, all Virginians needed to do was hang on for another twenty years, and those markets would spring open for them.

Madison also attacked Mason's contention that the Constitution did not protect the condition of slaves already in the country. "Another clause secures us that property which we now possess," he proclaimed. "At present, if any slave elopes to any of those states where slaves are free, he becomes emancipated by their laws; for the laws of the states are uncharitable to one another in this respect. But in this Constitution, 'no person held to service or labor in one state, under the laws thereof, escaping into another, shall, in consequence of any law or regulation therein, be discharged from such service or labor; but shall be delivered up on claim of the party to whom such service or labor shall be due.' This clause was expressly inserted, to enable owners of slaves to reclaim them."

To sum up, he observed, "From the mode of representation and taxation, Congress cannot lay such a tax on slaves as will amount to manumission . . . This is a better security than any that now exists. No power is given to the general government to interpose with respect to the property in slaves now held by the states. The taxation of this state being equal only to its representation, such a tax cannot be laid as [Mason] supposes."

Returning to the slave trade, Madison observed finally, "Great as the evil is, a dismemberment of the Union would be worse."[18] That he could appear as an enemy of slavery on practical grounds in Philadelphia, morally repulsed in the *Federalist*, and an ally of the planters in Virginia is testament to Madison's deftness and skill as a politician.

Madison has come to be known as the Father of the Constitution, because his vision and political philosophy are widely perceived to have set the mood for the convention and permeated the finished document. Certainly, no one was more involved with getting the convention called and setting its early tone. In the end, however, very few of Madison's major propositions were ultimately realized.

While a bicameral legislature was adopted, Madison was hardly the only delegate who favored two houses. On the other hand, he was unwavering that both houses of Congress be population-based, and spoke for hours on the subject, trying one formula after another (including the half-baked idea of an all-slaves/no-slaves division). Ultimately, however, he lost out to the Connecticut Compromise. He wanted the first branch to choose the second branch, but that idea failed as well. He wanted the executive chosen by the national legislature, but the convention opted to place the decision in the hands of electors from the individual states. He wanted a "council of revision" containing the executive and members of the judiciary to approve acts of the legislature, but the delegates

granted a veto to the executive alone. He certainly favored neither the continuation of the slave trade nor the ceding of navigation legislation to the North.*

As the convention wore on, Madison gave fewer and fewer speeches, and
when he did offer one of his philosophical discourses, it tended to be disre-
garded by his colleagues. And Madison was not alone. The convention paid little attention to Gouverneur Morris's denunciation of slavery and even less to
Mason's harangue against the slave trade. Hamilton, even after his return in
August, never gave a speech to match his daylong address of June 18. After the
Connecticut Compromise was adopted, Wilson read no more of Franklin's
musings into the record until the very last day, when Franklin urged unanimity
in accepting the convention's product, a wish that was ignored with regret by
Gerry and Randolph, and likely with secret relish by Mason.

If one man can truly be deemed Father of the Constitution, at least at the
convention, it is Rutledge. Of course, an unrepentant slaveowner as the Father
of the Constitution is far less appealing than a young and radiant philosopher
and future president, but Rutledge simply had far more influence on the final
product than did Madison. Moreover, Rutledge, by aligning with his fellow
slaveholders of the Upper South in the apportionment debate, and then with
the northerners in fashioning a compromise on the slave trade and navigation
acts, put South Carolina on the winning side in both contests. Madison got his
strong central government, it was true, but paid a significant price to do so.
Rutledge paid nothing.

If the Old Dictator is given patrimony, then Ellsworth and Sherman are
certainly uncles.† One or both of them either thought up or participated in
every important compromise, and thereby allowed the convention to avoid
collapse.

Rutledge's motivation in pursuing his agenda is apparent, as, for that matter, is Madison's and even Mason's. But what of Ellsworth and Sherman? Neither was a shipper or merchant, and Connecticut was not at the time a
commercial power.[19] What could have motivated two men of unquestioned integrity to put aside personal morality and forge bargains with slaveowners?

The answer once again is to found in Michelet, who, it will be remembered,
"always shows [remarkable men] in relation to the social group that has

---

*These defeats, among others, would cause Madison to famously break with the nationalists
only four years later and "repudiate the arguments of the *Federalist* for a strong national government" (Elkins and McKitrick, *The Age of Federalism*, 224).
†Charles Pinckney, if he indeed had as much to do with the end result as he later claimed, deserves similar mention.

molded them and whose feelings they are finding expression for, whose needs they are attempting to satisfy." Ellsworth and Sherman were creatures of their upbringing, their values, and the society in which they lived. They were in Philadelphia to protect and promote a way of life and this, not personal gain, or even a specific commercial advantage for Connecticut, prompted them to act as they did. Both men genuinely believed that their actions, even their compromises with slavery, were for the betterment of the society they represented and, as such, were also for the betterment of the United States.

The same is true of almost all the men who supported the Constitution. General Pinckney was not equivocating in his address to the South Carolina assembly. He urged his fellow slaveowners to support a system that ceded substantial powers to a central government over which they would have only one-thirteenth control because he saw that government as beneficial to South Carolina.

It was very much a case of the blind men and the elephant. Ellsworth, Sherman, and other northern merchants looked at the commerce provisions and saw a government that was pro-business, while Rutledge, General Pinckney, and the other rice planters looked at the present and future apportionment of power and saw a government that was proslavery. Not one of the delegates, even Madison, returned to his home state and urged his fellows to ratify the Constitution on the basis of higher principles, despite its being unfavorable to his state. Madison, as demonstrated by his variant defenses of the slave trade extension, was every bit the salesman, both in the *Federalist* and in the Virginia ratifying convention.

In one of the great ironies of American history, after all the intrigues, all the machinations, and all the compromises, so much worked out differently than was expected. Congress never did vote to impose a direct tax on the states, and so the North gave up three-fifths for nothing. If Mason and the other Upper South planters had known, they would surely have supported the South Carolinians and might have gained representation for all their slaves.

Population did not trend to the southwest, so the slaveholders never attained the majority in both houses that everyone expected. Only five new states from the Southwest entered the Union before the Missouri Compromise in 1820, against four from the North. Without a Southwestern majority to extend it, the slave trade was indeed outlawed in 1807, one year early. A government that was supposed to reside mostly in a southern-dominated legislature soon became executive driven, and the courts, thanks to John Marshall, assumed a much more active role in the government than anyone had foreseen. Slavery, of course, far from either withering away as the optimistic northerners expected, or attaining dominance as Rutledge intended, strangled and ulti-mately paralyzed the nation until a bloody war broke the deadlock.

Regardless of how events played out, sectionalism and slavery are key to un-derstanding the major debates and compromises in Philadelphia during the summer of 1787. Slavery, of course, did not precipitate every division at the con-vention, nor was every debate that did not include slavery trivial.

But in the central role it played, the weight of evidence leads inescapably to the conclusion that the Constitution was drafted by highly pragmatic men who were pursuing limited and self-interested goals. Philosophical concerns seemed to play only a minor role in the proceedings, and only then with but a few of the participants. Nonetheless, for all that, precisely because the dele-gates in Philadelphia were pragmatic, and were there to represent specific, parochial interests, they were able to draft a document that was workable, adaptable, and able to survive challenges that could never have been imagined in 1787. It is distinctly possible that had idealism dominated in Philadelphia, American democracy would have failed.

NOTES

Prologue: Fulcrum

1. Wright and MacGregor, *Soldier-Statesmen*, 119.
2. Farrand, *Records*, iii:96.
3. South Carolina was awash in Charles Pinckneys. The general's father was also named Charles, as was cousin Charles's father. Both earlier and later generations had their Charleses as well.
4. South Carolina, New Hampshire, Delaware, and Pennsylvania were states with presidents. South Carolina changed the title to *governor* in 1779 during Lowndes's term, New Hampshire in 1786, Pennsylvania in 1790, and Delaware not until 1792. Georgia, New York, and Maryland had no chief executive after independence until they elected their first governors in 1777, nor did Massachusetts until 1780.
5. The debate in the South Carolina legislature appears in Elliot, *Debates*, iv:271-86. Unless otherwise noted, all citations appear in those pages.
6. Lowndes's opinions did not moderate over time. He asked that his tombstone be inscribed, "Here lies the man that opposed the constitution, because it was ruinous to the liberty of America."
7. Unless Andrew Jackson, who claimed South Carolina as his native state, was actually born there. He may well have been born across the border in North Carolina. Georgia had to wait until 1976 for Jimmy Carter's election.
8. Southerners often argued that divine revelation showed inequality to the order of the universe. The Scriptures, they said, demonstrated that "an inferior race must live under the domination of the superior" (Elkins, *Slavery*, 36).

1. Devil in the Mist

1. Cutler and Cutler, *Life, Journals*, i:267.
2. Clarkson and Jett, *Luther Martin*, 193.
3. Delaware is sometimes listed as a slave state but, although slavery was not uncommon, according to the census of 1790, only 15 percent of the population was black, as compared to 40 percent in Virginia and 43 percent in South Carolina. Delaware also had a more thriving commercial economy than any of the five slave states to the south.
4. Madison was the first to use the word "miracle" to describe the process in a letter to Jefferson in October 1787 (Farrand, *Records*, iii: 131). The term has since been applied by any number of analysts and historians.
5. Abraham Lincoln was to say, "Slavery was hid away in the Constitution, just as an afflicted man hides away a wen or cancer, which he dares not cut out at once, lest he bleed to death" (quoted in Morris, *Witnesses*, 216).
6. Farrand, *Records*, ii:10.
7. Even those essays written by former delegates cannot be viewed as providing definitive evidence of the proceedings, since the authors were engaged in propagandizing and therefore took advantage of the secrecy of the convention to slant the facts in favor of their arguments. Of this, no one was more guilty than Madison.
8. Bancroft's remarkable output included poetry, philosophy, literary criticism, Greek and Latin grammars, and translations, particularly of German philosophers, in addition to American history. For seven years, he was the American ambassador to Prussia.
9. Bancroft, *History*, ii:75.
10. Wood, *Creation*, 131.
11. Farrand, *Framing of the Constitution*, 110.

12. *Dictionary of American Biography*, supplement II:262.

13. In 1987, an equally prodigious five-volume effort, *The Founders' Constitution*, was produced by Philip B. Kurland and Ralph Lerner, two University of Chicago professors. Drawing on the correspondence of delegates and nondelegates alike, pamphlets and other public documents of the period, and records of various debates and public statements, Kurland and Lerner divided their material by its pertinence to a particular clause or phrase in the Constitution and created what has been called the "*Oxford English Dictionary* of American constitutional history."

14. Farrand himself called it "my immortal work."

15. Beard was far from inactive, however, helping to found the New School for Social Research and serving terms as president of both the American Political Science Association and the American Historical Association.

16. While an improvement over Beard's, McDonald's focus on economics caused him to omit planters to whom slavery had become a burden but was nonetheless necessary to maintain a carefully constructed lifestyle. These men, centered in the tobacco-growing states of Virginia, Maryland, and North Carolina, would need to go against their own economic interests in order to maintain their way of life.

17. Slavery has not gone completely unnoticed. Jack Rakove in his Pulitzer Prize-winning *Original Meanings* seems so cognizant of the role of slavery that one wonders why he didn't make more of it. Only Paul Finkelman among modern historians has been unflagging in his insistence that slavery played more than a coincident role in the genesis of the Constitution.

18. Wilson, *To the Finland Station*, 5-6.

19. Ibid., 22.

2. Reluctant Nation: The Articles of Confederation

1. John Adams later said that the Connecticut proposal was written by Roger Sherman.

2. Dickinson was born in Delaware, but spent a good deal of his professional life in Pennsylvania. He would eventually serve as president of both states. He represented Pennsylvania in the Continental Congress and Delaware at the Constitutional Convention.

3. Slavery figured in no small part in the debates in Congress over the Articles, often in much the same way as it would in Philadelphia. See, for example, John Adams, *Papers*, ii:245-48.

4. Wood, *Creation*, 357.

5. Ibid.

6. Maryland would not have agreed that it was landless, asserting claims to a large block of territory that almost everyone else agreed belonged to Virginia, or perhaps Pennsylvania, or maybe even Connecticut.

7. See Clarkson and Jett, *Luther Martin*, 63.

8. Fiske, *Critical Period*. Fiske, who coined the phrase *Critical Period,* is of course referring to the American general Nathaneal Greene and Charles, Lord Cornwallis, of Britain.

9. Connecticut did not adopt a formal constitution until 1818 and Rhode Island until 1843, but each operated under extensions of colonial charters or laws unique to each state.

10. Boardman, *Roger Sherman*, 165.

11. Closing off the Southwest did not please land speculators either.

12. It had taken over two years to replace Livingston, an indication of just how ineffectual the government had become.

13. The Jay-Gardoqui affair is related in Jensen's *New Nation* and again, with typical sarcasm, in McDonald's *E Pluribus Unum.*

14. Jay's infatuation with Spain, ruled by "His Most Catholic majesty," was odd indeed. Jay's family were Huguenot émigrés who had fled Catholic persecution in France and Jay himself

had proposed denying Catholics equality in the new United States. He had been dissuaded from pressing the issue by Gouverneur Morris.

15. For the debate on the Jay-Garodqui treaty, see Ford, *Journals of the Continental Congress,* xxxi:574-613.

16. It would be reinstituted in 1795, eight years before Napoleon and the Louisiana Purchase rendered it moot.

17. Madison claimed not to hold out a great deal of hope that his fellow Americans would respond with enthusiasm but considered this "better than nothing."

18. Massachusetts did actually appoint delegates but, although the date of the meeting had been public knowledge for months, its delegation, after a leisurely trip south, did not arrive in time.

19. Hamilton wrote the first draft, which, not surprisingly, was considered too radical by his colleagues, so Madison and Randolph helped him tone it down.

20. Quoted in Boardman, *Sherman,* 223.

21. Rakove, *Original Meanings,* 33.

3. Rabble in Black and White: Insurrection

1. For a description of the tensions between eastern and western Massachusetts, Szatmary's *Shays' Rebellion* is by far most comprehensive source. More cursorily, see Fiske, *Critical Period;* McDonald, *E Pluribus Unum;* and Jensen, *New Nation.*

2. Szatmary, *Shays' Rebellion,* 86-87.

3. The spot is now marked by a tiny stone tablet on a road frequented by wealthy second-home owners from New York City.

4. Most of the leaders were pardoned almost immediately, and Shays was finally pardoned in June 1788.

5. Knox was married to his beloved and similarly rotund Lucy, and the Knoxes were perhaps the most corpulent couple in America. The general, who was not tall, weighed close to three hundred pounds, and Manassah Cutler described Knox's wife as "very gross" with a "military style, which to me is disgusting in a female."

6. Knox to Washington, December 1, 1786; quoted in Zinn, *History,* 95.

7. Herbert Aptheker wrote, "While there is a difference of opinion as to the prevalence of discontent among slaves, one finds nearly unanimous agreement concerning the widespread fear of servile rebellion" (*American Negro Slave Revolts,* 18).

8. Two whites known to be kind to their slaves were spared.

9. See Edgar, *South Carolina,* 75.

10. One incident of note occurred in Virginia in 1767, when some slaves poisoned their overseers, several of whom died. Four slaves were executed for the crime, "after which their heads were cut off, and fixed on chimnies of the court house; and it was expected that four more would soon meet the same fate." Some of the slaves likely belonged to George Mason. (See Aptheker, *American Negro Slave Revolts,* 199-200.)

11. The pervasive southern fear of slave uprisings is recounted, with some overstatement, in Aptheker, *American Negro Slave Revolts,* and also in Elkins, *Slavery.* Ulrich Phillips regularly provides a flavor for slaveowners' paranoia although, apologist that he can often be, he is less specific about labeling it as such.

12. Quoted in Aptheker, *American Negro Slave Revolts,* 20.

13. Madison, Hamilton, and Jay, *Federalist,* 293.

14. Haw, *John and Edward Rutledge,* 73.

15. Adams, *Papers,* ii:183.

16. Aptheker, *American Negro Slave Revolts,* 21.

17. Phillips, *Slave Economy*, 200.

18. Adams, *Papers*, ii:183.

4. Taming the West: The Ohio Company of Virginia

1. Farrand, *Records*, ii:3.

2. Ibid.

3. Miller, *George Mason*, 21.

4. "Slaves do not signify property. The young and the old cannot work," complained South Carolina's John Rutledge in 1776. South Carolina grew rice, not tobacco, but the principle was the same (Adams, *Papers*, ii:245).

5. Quoted in Phillips, *Slave Economy*, 137.

6. This contrasted with "Yankee skipper[s] . . . who made a genuine profit on every exchange and thriftily laid up his savings" (Phillips, *Economics of the Plantation*, 260). Phillips is almost totally ignored today. He was perhaps the most infamous perpetrator of the "sambo" image of enslaved Africans. Still, his studies of the slave economy and the sociopolitical effects of slavery on Southern life are unsurpassed.

7. McDonald, *E Pluribus Unum*, 118.

8. Freidenberg, *Life, Liberty*, 99.

9. In 1775, Michael would raise a company of volunteers whom he would lead on a forced march to Boston to support Washington, but die of exhaustion just before reaching Massachusetts. Michael also had an attractive daughter named Maria who would eventually marry a rising young Maryland lawyer named Luther Martin.

10. He also found a mammoth's tooth and ribs in his travels.

11. The French, who promised to limit settlement in the region, convinced the chiefs that an English victory would result in hordes of pioneers pouring over the mountains, which is precisely what happened.

12. Rowland, *George Mason*, i:78. Kate Mason Rowland was a great-great-great-grandniece of George Mason IV and created an excellent two-volume part biography and part collection of papers at the end of the nineteenth century. (She subsequently dropped the name Rowland and was known as Kate Mason until her death in 1916.) Robert Rutland's 1970 three-volume collection of papers is more extensive, but lacks some of Ms. Rowland's material, which had been lost in the interim. Still more of Mason's letters and other papers were lost in a fire in the mid-nineteenth century.

13. Mason's buying activities can be traced as far back as 1749, when, only twenty-four years old, he had bought up a large chunk of the newly laid-out city of Alexandria when lots were first put up for sale.

14. Mason and Franklin became "leading opponents in the ensuing rivalry between Pennsylvania and Virginia for the riches of the Ohio country" (Miller, *George Mason*, 181), and this competition between two of America's foremost citizens, the aristocratic southern slaveholder and the shrewd northern capitalist, personified the battle between slave states and free that would be waged in Philadelphia almost two decades later.

15. This made it far less painful for Virginia to give in to Maryland's demand and cede the land to the federal government. Virginians knew that their claims were moot anyway.

5. Sorcerer's Apprentice: Virginia and the Upper South

1. Morgan, *American Slavery*, 304.

2. Ibid., 304-5.

3. In the West Indies, slavery supplanted white labor when growers switched to sugar from tobacco and could not find enough whites willing to sign on for such grueling work.

4. Hawk, *Economic History*, 231.

5. Quoted in Miller, *George Mason*, 13.

6. Ibid., 6.

7. Rowland, *George Mason*, i:102.

8. Morgan, *American Slavery*, 307-8. Also see Elkins and McKitrick, *Age of Federalism*, 93.

9. Population figures before the census of 1790 vary widely and are notoriously unreliable. A widely circulated estimate put the white population at 252,000 while slaves numbered 280,000 and General Pinckney used this estimate in the South Carolina legislative debates. Other estimates have the slave population as a lower percentage as compared to whites, but not by very much.

10. Maryland, for example, in 1783, passed a law that made it "unlawful to import any slave for sale or to reside within this state: and any slave brought into this state contrary to this act shall thereupon immediately cease to be a slave and set free" (quoted in DuBois, *Suppression*, 226). In 1778, Virginia levied a £1000 fine for each newly imported slave (ibid., 226).

11. How George Mason I and Gerard Fowke advanced their positions in the colony, or whether they married wealthy widows or simply eligible daughters of successful planters, is not clear. By the time of George IV's birth, however, both the Masons and the Fowkes had prospered, the descendants of each well fixed in land and slaves. The Masons particularly had also become active in the political affairs of the colony.

12. Jefferson was another exception, beginning Monticello when he was twenty-six.

13. Rowland, *George Mason*, i:101.

14. Ibid., i:103.

15. Ibid., i:104.

16. Mason was beset with a lifelong case of gout. Flare-ups could be severe and debilitating and on many occasions he complained of ill health in his correspondence, especially to Washington during the war years. Whether or not this was prompted by guilt at not participating while his friend was enduring the hardship of war cannot be known. His illness was certainly the justification for declining military service.

17. Some biographers hypothesize that Mason was granted the title as recompense for his war work, but no documentary evidence backs that up.

18. Rutland, *Papers of George Mason*, i:61-62.

19. He would use the Roman example again in his famous August speech in Philadelphia.

20. Rutland, *Papers of George Mason*, i:173.

21. The *slave trade* was a different matter. That Mason wanted abolished immediately and forever. But the slave trade and slavery were two very different phenomena, as will be seen in chapter 15.

22. Rutland, *Papers of George Mason*, ii:448. Mason did not mean "all men" so much as "all men of property."

23. The second amendment provision about bearing arms originated at about this time—1774—with the resolutions to arm militias in the various states, steeped in what Rowland (*George Mason*, i:183) calls "abhorrence of standing armies, and their conviction that the militia is the true defence of the free country." Mason participated in the drafting of the Fairfax County resolution in January 1775, the first in Virginia, which said, "a well-regulated militia is the natural strength and stable security of a free government," language remarkably similar to the amendment to come.

24. Rutland, *Papers of George Mason*, ii:263.

25. Rowland, *George Mason*, i:188.

26. Rutland, *Papers of George Mason*, ii:498.

27. Ibid., ii:595.

28. That he did so until his death in 1792 is an indication that he never quite got over the sting.

6. Gold in the Swamps: South Carolina, Rice, and the Lower South

1. Barry, *Mr. Rutledge*, 103.

2. Butler was in fact the second son of an Irish baronet and had, in the fashion of those who would not inherit, pursued a career in the army. Butler had a notable military record, studied law, married well, and became one of the major slaveholding delegates in Philadelphia.

3. There is are only two serious modern works on John Rutledge, Richard Barry's *Mr. Rutledge of South Carolina* (1942), written as narrative with an extensive bibliography but no endnotes, and James Haw's 1997 *John and Edward Rutledge of South Carolina*, an overtly scholarly treatment. Although the plodding, sterile Haw dismisses Barry's more florid work as "unreliable," the two actually differ very little in substance. In addition, Barry's work was apparently reliable enough to be used as source material by Forrest McDonald and M. E. Bradford, among others. In any event, both Haw and Barry relied heavily on *History of South Carolina: from its first settlement in 1670 to the year 1808,* by planter, physician, and Rutledge's fellow legislator David Ramsay, but this treatment of Rutledge is so reverential that the Old Dictator's feet never seem to touch the ground. An example of Ramsay's prose: "When Rutledge spoke it was as if he transported us, by some magic, to an ancient place, far removed from all the feeling of the day. We were all like little boys listening to a revered headmaster, whose words were eagerly absorbed, so that they might be forever treasured."

4. Andrew Rutledge's exact lineage has never been established. He was possibly of humble beginnings from County Tyrone or descended from royalist aristocrats forced into hiding, or something different entirely.

5. Rutledge's exact birthdate is unknown.

6. Barry, *Mr. Rutledge*, 21.

7. Barry provides a florid and detailed description of the lives of the South Carolina elite. Even factoring in some overstatement, his account does not differ a great deal from that of Haw or Edgar.

8. Edgar, *South Carolina*, 162.

9. For an excellent overview of the rice economy, see Sirmans, *Colonial South Carolina.*

10. Quoted in Hawk, *An Economic History,* 94.

11. Hawk, *An Economic History,* 94.

12. With tobacco planters of the Upper South facing an increasing oversupply of slaves, and slaves to work rice plantations in constant demand, a natural market would have seemed to exist. But Upper South planters had accrued substantial costs in raising slaves to adulthood and the prices they asked of Lower South planters reflected the expense. Domestically raised slaves were more socialized to the culture, it was true, but with life expectancy so tenuous rice planters preferred the far lower-priced imports. Planters in the Upper South realized that they needed to find a way to eliminate competition from the African slave trade or the domestic market for their surplus would dry up.

13. It was in one of these cases that Rutledge lost in court for the only time in his career.

14. Barry, *Mr. Rutledge*, 58.

15. Adams, *Papers,* ii:119.

16. Ibid., ii:173.

17. Ibid., ii:151.

18. Barry, *Mr. Rutledge*, 211.

19. Ibid., 264.

20. Edgar, *South Carolina*, 244.

7. The Value of a Dollar: Connecticut

1. Rakove, *Original Meanings*, 86.

2. Collier, *Roger Sherman's Connecticut*, 197.

3. Ibid., 222.

4. Brown, *Life of Ellsworth*, 12. There is a remarkable paucity of biographical material on Ellsworth. Brown's study, now a century old, is still considered definitive. There is, unfortunately, no central collection of Ellsworth's papers.

5. One look at the portraits of the dour, glowering Ellsworth would be enough to convince any doubters that this was not a man given to pranks.

6. Brown, *Life of Ellsworth*, 26.

7. Ibid., 22-24.

8. He was well suited to the task, having grown to what was reported as a strapping six-foot-two, making him as tall as Washington and Gouverneur Morris.

9. Brown, *Life of Ellsworth*, 33.

10. Ibid., 35.

11. Ibid., 85.

12. Ibid.

13. In ruling for a married woman in a case in which she sought the right to dispose of her estate without it passing through to her husband, Ellsworth wrote, "Political considerations, therefore, so far as they can be of weight, serve to confirm the opinion" (Brown, *Life of Ellsworth*, 115).

14. Farrand, *Records*, iii:89.

15. Ibid., iii:88-89.

16. Adams, *Papers*, ii:173.

17. Contrary to popular belief, a man named Nathaniel Ames, not Benjamin Franklin, produced the most popular and humorous version.

18. Boardman, *Roger Sherman*, 117.

19. Adams, *Papers*, ii:247.

20. McDonald, *We the People*, 48.

21. Republicans wanted to maintain a loose confederation with a weaker central government. Nationalists, of course, favored a strong central government.

22. Farrand, *Records*, iii:33-34.

8. Philadelphia: The Convention Begins

1. For a description of Washington's arrival, see *Pennsylvania Packet*, May 14, 1787.

2. Postcolonial Philadelphia is excellently rendered in Weigley, *Philadelphia*, while a flavor for the city, including shipping news, real estate ads, lottery results, and criminal activity, can be acquired in just about any edition of the *Pennsylvania Packet*.

3. *Pennsylvania Packet*, May 23, 1787.

4. McDonald, *E Pluribus Unum*, 261.

5. If there was ever someone who did not know when to stop, it was Morris. His house of

speculative cards eventually collapsed and he ended up in debtors' prison. Morris died as he was born, destitute.

6. In the early days of the Supreme Court, justices "rode circuit," that is, visited assigned states twice yearly to hear cases in local jurisdictions.

7. According to the census of 1790, there were 2,648 slaves in Connecticut; 0 in Massachusetts; 157 in New Hampshire; 958 in Rhode Island; 21,193 in New York; 11,423 in New Jersey; 3,707 in Pennsylvania; 8,887 in Delaware; 103,036 in Maryland; 292,627 in Virginia; 100,783 in North Carolina; 107,094 in South Carolina; and 29,264 in Georgia. On a per-centage basis, slave population was no more than 6 percent of the total in the seven north-ernmost states, 15 percent in Delaware, and in excess of 30 percent in the five southernmost states. By 1790, slavery had either been abolished or was in the process of being phased out in all of the northern states, except Delaware.

8. Rutland, *Papers of Mason*, iii:881. Mason's enthusiasm cooled. Only ten days later, he wrote, "I begin to grow tired of the etiquette and nonsense so fashionable in this city."

9. In the absence of any convention sessions, Madison had convened the delegation at 3:00 p.m. each day to discuss, in Mason's words, "the great subject of our mission." In these meetings the Virginia Plan was put into the form that was later presented to the convention.

10. McDonald, *E Pluribus Unum*, 265-66.

11. Ann Gerry would live until 1842 and thus be the longest-surviving spouse of any delegate.

12. He moved there after the convention, set himself up as a minor potentate, then resorted to bribery, fraud, and chicanery to further improve his position. When Tennessee became a state, largely as a result of his efforts, Blount was elected to Congress and soon became the first man ever to be impeached by the House of Representatives and then expelled by the Senate.

13. He was to write on July 10, in a letter to Hamilton, "The Men who oppose a strong & ener-getic government are, in my opinion, narrow minded Politicians, or are under influence of lo-cal views" (Farrand, *Records*, iii:56). Despite his feelings, Washington was to play virtually no role in the debates, contenting himself with his duties as chair or, when the convention adopted a more informal structure "the Committee of the Whole," sitting without comment with his Virginia colleagues.

14. The distinction is figurative only. Paterson, generously listed at five-foot-two, was even tinier than Madison.

15. In all, fifty-five delegates from twelve states would participate in the debates. Of these, less than a third made substantive contributions, and they have been noted in the text. Few of the delegates attended all of the sessions and, even among those whose input was vital to the out-come—Hamilton and Ellsworth, for example—absenteeism was common.

9. June: The Colloquium

1. Text of the Virginia Plan is found in Farrand, *Records*, i:20-22.

2. The notion of wealth as a standard of both taxation and representation had been tossed about since debates on the Articles of Confederation in July 1776. Slaves were brought into the pic-ture when Samuel Chase asserted, "If Negroes are taken into the Computation of Numbers to ascertain Wealth, they ought to be in settling the Representation." It was here that Rut-ledge added, "I shall be happy to get rid of the idea of Slavery. The Slaves do not signify Prop-erty. The old and young cannot work. The Property of some Colonies are to be taxed, in others not. The Eastern Colonies will become carriers for the Southern. They will obtain Wealth for which they will not be taxed" (Adams, *Papers*, ii:245-46). Rutledge would take a different view of slaves as wealth in Philadelphia.

3. Madison never could figure out how to navigate between these two extremes. Eventually, he would simply try and include both in a bicameral legislature.

4. That was likely a bit too enfant terrible for a convention the average age of whose delegates was in the mid-forties. At his real age, thirty, Pinckney would have fit in well with Randolph, who was thirty-four, and the thirty-six-year-old Madison. Hamilton, the convention's other enfant terrible, was also thirty. Pinckney's plan was therefore lost to history until, thirty-two years later, in 1819, he re-created it for John Quincy Adams. In 1818, Adams was preparing the official record of the convention for publication (not including Madison's notes) and discovered that the Pinckney plan was missing. He asked Pinckney if he had a copy and some weeks later Pinckney sent him what he said was a copy of the original plan. This version of the "Pinckney Plan," however, was remarkably similar to the draft produced by the Committee of Detail, and other surviving members of the convention said it was bogus. Later historians, after carefully examining the debates, have concluded that Pinckney's ideas were, in fact, debated, with many finding their way into the Constitution.

5. McDonald, *E Pluribus Unum*, 166.

6. The June debates were the culmination of what Jack Rakove termed the "Madisonian Moment."

7. Bailyn, *To Begin the World Anew*, chapter 1.

8. On May 31, for example, George Mason rose to deliver a short lecture on democracy, arguing that one house of the legislature should be elected directly by the people. "[The legislature] ought to know & sympathise with every part of the community . . . we ought to attend to the rights of every class of the people. [I have] often wondered at the indifference of the superior classes of society to this dictate of humanity & policy . . . Every selfish motive, therefore every family attachment, ought to recommend such a system of policy as would provide no less carefully for the rights and happiness of the lowest than the highest orders of Citizens" (Farrand, *Records*, i:48-49). Mason took every opportunity to expound on the evils of tyranny, the meaning of liberty, and, ultimately, the horrors of the slave trade. But he was also well known as the convention's largest slaveholder, one of the most inveterate speculators, and a man who had bought up huge tracts of land and distributed not one square foot to those common people for whom he claimed to have such sympathy. But, since this was June and everyone was still being nice to one another, not one delegate commented on the inconsistencies between Mason's words and deeds. This would not be the case in August. Then, both the colonel's positions and his speeches received far less generous treatment, resulting in Mason radically changing his definition of the convention's mission.

9. Farrand, *Records*, i:35. Once again, Madison's notes—as well as those of Yates and the other delegates—sometimes refer to speakers in the first person, sometimes in the third person, and sometimes in both the first and third person within a single speech. Any speech in quotes has been rendered exactly as it appears in the record and represents, as precisely as we know, a delegate's actual words.

10. Ibid., i:36.

11. Unless otherwise noted, all citations from the June 11 debates appear in Farrand, *Records*, i:196-201.

12. This was made clear in Finkelman, *Slavery and the Founders*, 12.

13. In trying to count slaves for purpose of apportionment, a position to which he would doggedly adhere throughout the debates, Rutledge had changed his stance markedly since the Confederation debates of July 1776. Forgotten was his assertion that "slaves were not wealth" (Adams, *Papers*, ii:245).

14. The three-fifths clause had never been used for apportionment, only taxation.

15. Rutledge might then have passed on the formula to Charles Pinckney or perhaps Pinckney simply seized on it as a good idea.

16. According to Butler's notes, Gerry's comments were more provocative. "Are we to enter into a Compact with Slaves No!" (Hutson, *Supplement*, 70).

17. The New Jersey Plan is from Farrand, *Records*, i:242-45.

18. Madison's version of Hamilton's address is from Farrand, *Records*, i:283-92.

19. Yates's version of Hamilton's address is from Farrand, *Records*, i:294-301.

20. Rakove, *Original Meanings*, 64.

21. Debates of June 19 are from Farrand, *Records*, i:312-33.

22. The Great Compromise of July 16 eventually justified their decision to stick things out and was sufficient to persuade most of the states' rights delegates to support the new Constitution.

23. Some historians have contended that the first phase of the convention continued through the end of July, but June and July were two very different months in Philadelphia. With the apparent rejection of the New Jersey Plan—although different aspects of Paterson's proposals would continue to resurface—the delegates were ready to discuss a more nuts-and-bolts diagram of their proposed new government. When they did so, tempers in the chamber increased along with temperatures outside. As practical politics began to dominate the discussions, the artificial bonhomie of June gave way to partisanship, rigidity, and anger.

24. Madison's and Yates's versions are from Farrand, *Records*, i:337-41, but neither evidently gives anything but a cursory flavor of Martin's interminable and meandering rhetoric.

25. Ford, *Essays*, 183. Ellsworth (who was writing anonymously as a Landholder) took some serious liberties. First of all, Martin had actually arrived on June 9, three weeks before, and had spoken very little during that period. Second, not everyone had the same opinion of Martin's address.

26. Ibid., 130.

27. Farrand, *Records*, i:456. This statement appears in Yates's notes but not Madison's.

28. Ibid., i:452.

29. McDonald wrote, "The lineup was much more nearly sectional than large-versus-small: states south of the Potomac consistently voted with Madison's 'large states' bloc, 4 to 0; those north of it . . . voted as small states 6 to 2." (Massachusetts and Pennsylvania were the exceptions.) McDonald added that, when huge Virginia and tiny Delaware were factored out, the population of the "large" states was only 10 percent greater than that of the "small" (*E Pluribus Unum*, 274).

30. Farrand, *Records*, i:486-87.

31. Ibid., i:510-11.

32. Ibid., i:532-33.

10. Slavery by the Numbers: The Mathematics of Legislative Control

1. Debates of July 9 appear in Farrand, *Records*, i:557-62.

2. Twenty-six, if Delaware, which is sometimes considered a slave state, is included. Although slavery was, in fact widespread in Delaware, it had already begun to be more influenced by the industry to the north than by the plantations to the south.

3. Debates of July 10 appear in Farrand, *Records*, i:563-72.

4. New Hampshire was the easiest and most obvious target since its delegates had still not arrived, despite entreaties by a number of northern delegates that their presence was desperately needed.

5. Debates of July 11 appear in Farrand, *Records*, i:573-88.

6. Mason was to add later in the debate, "As soon as the Southern & Western population should predominate, which must happen in a few years, the power wd. be in the hands of the minority, and would never be yielded to the majority, unless provided for by the Constitution."

7. Mason prefaced his remarks by noting that he "could not agree to the motion, notwithstanding it was favorable to Virga. because he thought it unjust." Mason, as with almost all

his pronouncements about slavery, was a bit disingenuous here. Counting slaves as equal with freemen would in no way favor Virginia if slaves were also counted in full for purposes of taxation. Three-fifths would be all that most of the cash-strapped planters could bear. As for the injustice, Mason made it quite clear that he was referring to the black man's equality, not his enslavement.

8. Delaware's aye vote is bizarre unless one assumes that, doing everything it could to retain the Articles of Confederation, it voted for an obviously unacceptable proposal in the hopes that the entire plan might end up sufficiently odious as to be voted down by the states.

9. This was as blatant an attempt to appeal to Gouverneur Morris as Morris's hollow arguments against the census had been to appeal to Rutledge.

11. Sixty Percent of a Human Being

1. Hutson, *Supplement*, 158.

2. Debates of July 12 appear in Farrand, *Records*, i:589-97.

3. Davie overcame his objections and became instrumental in North Carolina's eventual (but belated) ratification in November 1789, the last of the original thirteen states to do so, except Rhode Island.

4. Debates of July 13 appear in Farrand, *Records*, i:598-606.

12. Balancing Act: Two Great Compromises

1. Delaware and New Jersey had consistently refused to have the second house apportioned by population. They had sometimes been joined by Maryland, sometimes by New York, sometimes by Massachusetts, and sometimes, when slavery was involved, by Southern states.

2. No similar sentiment existed among the smaller states in the South. Georgia, with its tiny population, usually voted as a large state and North Carolina, which shifted allegiances regularly, would provide the swing vote to enact the Great Compromise on July 16.

3. Debates of July 14 appear in Farrand, *Records*, ii:1-12.

4. Congress was as dysfunctional as ever. Although having more than fifty members whose credentials had been accepted, rarely were more than twenty in the chamber at any one time. Seven delegations were necessary to constitute a quorum and often as not Congress fell short and was forced to adjourn. To pass the Northwest Ordinance, eight states had delegations present, with three New England states—Connecticut, Rhode Island, and New Hampshire— not bothering to show up to vote on the most important piece of legislation in the preconstitutional period, which ironically was one of the few proposals that did not require either nine votes or unanimous approval to enact.

5. Article VI also said, "*Provided, always,* That any person escaping into the same, from whom labor or service is lawfully claimed in any one of the original States, such fugitive may be lawfully reclaimed and conveyed to the person claiming his or her labor or service as aforesaid," but even so, it was the first piece of national legislation to specifically outlaw slavery.

6. Eleven if Delaware's two delegates are included.

7. Staughton Lynd in *Class Conflict, Slavery, and the United States Constitution* attributes direct cause and effect to these two events, which he terms "the fundamental compromise of 1787."

8. Almost twenty delegates in Philadelphia also held credentials for the 1787 Congress. The list included Madison, Gorham, King, Charles Pinckney, Butler, Lansing of New York, and William Samuel Johnson of Connecticut, half the Georgia delegation and the entire delegation from New Hampshire. Most delegates spent more time in Philadelphia than New York, but almost all of them traveled north at some point in the summer.

9. Cutler and Cutler, *Life, Journals*, i:73.

10. His support of war veterans was not absolute. Later in 1786, he would head a regiment of the army Benjamin Lincoln led to suppress Shays' Rebellion (Szatmary, *Shays' Rebellion*, 86).

11. Cutler and Cutler, *Life, Journals*, i:181.

12. For an excellent dissertation of the western movement of the 1780s, see Onuf, *Statehood and Union*, especially chapter 2, "Squatters, Settlers and Speculators."

13. Cutler and Cutler, *Life, Journals*, i:195.

14. Ibid., i:196.

15. Linklater, *Measuring America*, 80.

16. Cutler and Cutler, *Life, Journals*, i:236.

17. Ibid., i:237.

18. Cutler was particularly impressed by Elbridge Gerry. "Few old bachelors, I believe, have been more fortunate in marriage . . . his lady is young, handsome . . . I should suppose her not more than 17, and believe he must be turned 55" (Cutler and Cutler, *Life, Journals*, i:255).

19. That Article VI was an amendment was indicated in the *Journals of the Continental Congress*, but these journals were only compiled between 1834 and 1856 from newspapers and other ancillary records. The Congressional Record was not begun until 1873. There were no official minutes kept of congressional sessions in 1787 and therefore just who proposed Article VI has been lost to history.

20. Cutler and Cutler, *Life, Journals*, i:293.

21. As it turned out, the slavery provision was widely ignored. There were slaves in Ohio until after the turn of the century and in Illinois until the 1820s.

22. Lee had given up on the claims of Virginia's Ohio Company and hoped that the treasury might make some money from this one.

23. Cutler and Cutler, *Life, Journals*, i:294.

24. Ibid., i:296.

25. This was Cutler's way of acknowledging French aid during the Revolution. Marietta was to remain as the touchstone of the American public land movement, while Marie Antoinette met quite a different fate in quite a different revolution.

26. Staughton Lynd, as noted, originated the "deal" theory, but Paul Finkelman persuasively laid out its flaws. Finkelman and Lynd do agree on two other possible reasons that southern congressmen supported the Northwest Ordinance. The first was that the South wanted to keep the northerners from competing in the tobacco and indigo markets—a sentiment also put forth by a Virginia congressman—although this seems climatically unlikely, especially as one moves farther north. The second was that the South expected the new states in the Northwest, once admitted, to vote with their agrarian cousins from the Atlantic South rather than the capitalists and small businessmen who dominated politics in the Atlantic North.

27. Barrett, Jay, *Evolution*, 22. This was the type of provision that Mason, had he been sincere in his desire to end slavery, might easily have proposed himself. He never did.

28. These were the sales that proved so disappointing two years later.

29. Farrand, *Records*, i:578-80.

30. Morris, *Witnesses*, 192. Staughton Lynd (in *Class Conflict*, 194) adds, "Thus while from the standpoint of the North the Ordinance appeared an antislavery triumph, to the South it may have seemed the end of the national government's attempt to prohibit slavery South of the Ohio."

31. Farrand, *Records*, ii:19-20.

32. Madison had made no secret of his distaste for the Connecticut Compromise. He likely had a greater role in assembling this group than he indicated here.

13. Not a King, But What?

1. "Qualified" because there was sharp disagreement on just who would be allowed to vote. Suffrage would be argued vociferously in the coming weeks.

2. Debates of July 17 appear in Farrand, *Records*, ii:21-36. This definition was not as broad as it seemed. By "freeholders," Morris meant only those men who owned property, and would exclude merchants and artisans, restrictions that would be hotly contested in early August.

3. This was in stark contrast to Mason's previously voiced sentiments on the nobility of lower classes.

4. The same term that was later applied to Supreme Court justices and other federal judges. There is no specific provision in the Constitution for a judge to serve for life, nor is there a definition of "good behavior."

5. Ultimately more than sixty votes were required to finalize what was to become Article II of the Constitution.

6. Farrand, *Records*, ii:58.

7. Ibid., ii:63.

8. The vow of secrecy that the delegates had taken was evidently being observed. During this period, when nothing could be agreed upon, and irritation was ubiquitous, the *Pennsylvania Packet* reported, "So great is the unanimity, we hear, that prevails in the Convention, upon all great federal subjects, that it has been proposed to call the room in which they assemble—UNANIMITY HALL." The *Packet* was not exactly impartial. The item also noted, "May the enemies of the new confederation, whether in Rhode Island or elsewhere, whether secret or open, meet with the same fate as the disaffected in the late war."

9. This debate is covered in Farrand, *Records*, ii:47-49.

14. Details

1. John Langdon and Nicholas Gilman of New Hamshire finally arrived during the last week of July, but the addition of another northern "small state" delegation did not infuse new energy into the proceedings.

2. Although Ellsworth and Rutledge were only lukewarm nationalists when they arrived, they were by then among the most robust supporters of a strong central government. Gorham and Wilson had been nationalists from the beginning, as had been Randolph, the ostensible author of the Virginia Plan. (Sherman had shifted his position as well. By this time, Ellsworth and Sherman were acting as one, and both had seen in Rutledge someone with whom they could do business.)

3. Farrand, *Records*, ii:129-33.

4. It was during this recess that Washington went fishing, not while the convention was in session, as is often said. Also, counter to conventional wisdom, although he originally fished for trout, he caught perch.

5. Randolph's completed outline, with corrections and additions by Rutledge, can by found in the George Mason papers.

6. Farrand, *Records*, iii:137.

7. Many of these documents were unearthed by Max Farrand, who then pieced together a speculative chronology of the committee's proceedings. Richard Barry in *Mr. Rutledge* provided a vivid account of the committee's affairs that, while glorious if true, unfortunately seems to be a complete flight of fancy.

8. Farrand, *Records*, ii:177-89.

9. Nothing bespeaks Randolph's lack of clout more than its inclusion.

10. Debates of August 7 appear in Farrand, *Records*, ii:193-212.

11. Debates of August 8 appear in Farrand, *Records*, ii:213-26.

12. "Special interests month" is from McDonald, *E Pluribus Unum* 174.

13. Martin, for all his faults, was one of the few delegates whose opposition to slavery was not for sale. According to McDonald, he "devoutly and genuinely opposed the institution" (*E Pluribus Unum, 180*).

14. Mason, as will be seen, had far greater problems with slavery and commerce issues, and Gerry, although more difficult to read, seems to have decided that the new government would turn despotic.

15. Randolph may well have passed this along during the recess, if not to Mason directly, then through Madison.

16. For a florid but splendidly Machiavellian rendition of Martin's soirées, see McDonald, *E Pluribus Unum*, 295-301.

15. Dark Bargain: The Slave Trade and Other Commerce

1. Burnett, *Letters of Members of the Continental Congress*, viii:181.

2. Elliot, *Debates*, ii:279-80.

3. Debates of August 16 appear in Farrand, *Records*, ii:303-311.

4. The degree to which the other delegates were surprised is unclear, but Rutledge had now brought the issue out of the backrooms and onto the floor.

5. Madison, Quoted in Farrand, *Records*, iii: 436.

6. Farrand, *Records*, ii:328.

7. On August 23, the *Pennsylvania Packet*, sensitive to the grumbling among the citizenry, wrote, "The punctuality with which the members of the Convention assemble every day at a certain hour, and the long time they spend the deliberations of each day (sometimes 7 hours) are proof, among other things, of how much they are entitled to the universal confidence of the people of America. Such a body of enlightened and honest men perhaps never before met for political purposes in any country upon the face of the earth." The next day, August 24, the delegates unanimously agreed to return the afternoon adjournment time to 3:00 p.m.

8. This debate of August 20 appears in Farrand, *Records*, ii:345-50.

9. Madison was the convention's chameleon. No one could ever be sure whether he would wear his nationalist philosopher's hat or his Virginia one, or attempt to wear both at once. Here he chose the first.

10. He did not give up entirely, however. The issue of fugitive slaves would be dealt with later.

11. Debates of August 21 appear in Farrand, *Records*, ii:352-65.

12. In a message to the Maryland legislature, Martin later noted, "It might be proper to take slaves into consideration when taxes were to be apportioned because it has a tendency to discourage slavery; but to take them into account in giving representation tended to encourage the slave trade and make it in the interest of the states to continue that infamous traffic."

13. The younger Pinckney and Butler suggested on several occasions that the Lower South might end the slave trade on its own, if only the rest of the nation would leave them alone. In fact, South Carolina had only done so for short periods through economic self-interest. General Pinckney, as noted, took a different view in the South Carolina ratifying convention.

14. Debates of August 22 appear in Farrand, *Records*, ii:366-95.

15. Rowland, *George Mason*, i:273.

16. Incredibly, this speech is regularly cited by historians to demonstrate that a man whose fortunes and prestige were completely based on the plantation system, a man who never freed a single slave, was actually against the practice. Mason's address to the Virginia ratifying convention nine months later is far more reflective of his real views on the subject.

17. Ellsworth was even more unsparing after the convention. Writing as "a Landholder," he observed, "Mr. Mason has himself about three hundred slaves, and lives in Virginia, where it is found by prudent management they can breed and raise slaves faster than they want them for their own use and could supply the deficiency in Georgia and South Carolina; and perhaps Mr. Mason may suppose it more humane to breed than import slaves . . . but his objections are not on the side of freedom, nor in compassion to the human race who are slaves" (Ford, *Essays*, 164).

18. Farrand, *Records*, iii:210-11. Most historians acknowledge the existence of a deal. McDonald, however, insists that the quid pro quo for the extension of the slave trade was South Carolina's recognition of northern land claims, but as Luther Martin was present at the committee meetings, it would seem more correct to take his word rather than someone writing two centuries after the fact. In any event, General Pinckney confirmed at least part of Martin's statement in a speech to the South Carolina ratifying convention. Referring to the meetings of the committee of eleven, he noted, " 'Show some period,' said the members from the Eastern States, 'when it may be in our power to put a stop, if we please, to the importation of this weakness, and we will endeavor, for your convenience, to restrain the religious and political prejudices of our people on this subject' " (Elliot, *Debates*, iv:285).

19. Ibid., ii:400.

20. Debates of August 25 appear in Farrand, *Records*, ii:408-21.

21. Luther Martin later wrote in *Genuine Information*, "The design of this clause is to prevent the general government from prohibiting the importation of slaves, but the same reasons which caused them to strike out the word *'national,'* and not admit the word *'stamps,'* influenced them here to guard against the word *'slaves.'* They anxiously sought to avoid the admission of expressions which might be odious in the ears of Americans, although they were willing to admit into their system those *things* which the *expressions* signified" (Farrand, *Records*, iii:210).

22. Debates of August 29 appear in Farrand, *Records*, ii:445-56.

23. Madison made a point to explain what General Pinckney had in mind when he referred to "liberal conduct." "He meant permission to import slaves. An understanding on the two subjects of *navigation* and *slavery* had taken place between those parts of the Union, which explains the vote on the motion depending, as well as the language of Genl. Pinckney & others."

16. Closing the Deal: September

1. Ellsworth left Philadelphia in late August, but was unstinting in his support for ratification. Not only did he write the *Landholder* essays, but the Constitution was approved in the Connecticut ratifying convention under his leadership.

2. He had not been able to persuade the convention to allow full counting of slaves, but savvy politician that he was, Rutledge had likely viewed that more as a bargaining position than a genuinely obtainable goal.

3. Ellsworth would devote a number of his *Landholder* essays to merciless—and unfair—attacks on Gerry and his opposition to the new plan. These would engender a counterattack by Luther Martin, which in turn caused Ellsworth to go after Martin. Many of Gerry's criticisms—like Martin's—were steeped in the fear that the new Constitution would lead to a far more pernicious concentration of power in the central government than the delegates had in mind, a point of view that history has shown to be all too accurate.

4. Even before he left Philadelphia, Randolph noted that he might support ratification of the plan. On the final day, he noted "that he did not mean by this refusal to [sign] that he should oppose the Constitution without doors."

5. Farrand, *Records*, ii:403-4.

6. Whenever the delegates could not move past an issue, they appointed a committee, and if that group could not produce a result, another committee was appointed, sometimes a third, and even a fourth. Sometimes the members of one committee were completely different from those of a previous committee; sometimes only one or two members changed. Sometimes, as in the committees of eleven, one delegate was appointed by each state; sometimes, as in committees of five, the members were elected by the convention. That there were three separate committees within days to deal with the presidency is an indication of how thorny the issue was for most of the delegates.

7. Farrand, *Records*, ii:497.

8. Ibid., ii:559.

9. Ibid.

10. At one point, Madison noted, "the members very impatient & calling for the question."

17. Supreme Law of the Land

1. Not only deceptive, but illegal. Unanimous consent, not just the approval of nine states, was required for a change to the Articles of Confederation, and a new Constitution certainly qualified.

2. It was in a debate in the South Carolina legislature to authorize a ratifying convention that General Pinckney triumphed in January 1788.

3. In any case, the *Pennsylvania Packet* included the entire text in its issue of September 19.

4. This is one of American history's great misnomers, since a "federalist" would normally be someone who supported a weak central government.

5. Richard Henry Lee wrote to George Mason, "I availed myself of the Right to amend, & . . . called the ayes & nays to fix them on the journal. This greatly alarmed the Majority & vexed them extremely—; for the plan is, to push the business on with great dispatch, & with as little opposition as possible: that it may be adopted before it has stood the test of Reflection & due examination" (Smith, *Letters of Delegates*, xxiv:459).

6. Clymer was more active in those twelve days than he had been during the entire four months in convention.

7. McMaster and Stone, *Pennsylvania*, 64.

8. The entire Delaware delegation and all but one of New Jersey's representatives, including Paterson, signed the Constitution. William Houston, the only nonsigner from New Jersey, had left the convention due to illness, but signed the report to the New Jersey legislature.

9. That Hancock would fall for such a trick is amazing. Twelve years earlier he had been equally convinced that he was to be named commander of the Continental armies and was flabbergasted when Washington was chosen instead.

10. South Carolina's ratifying convention, unlike the legislative session that authorized it, was an easy victory for the federalists. Lowndes stayed home and on May 23, 1788, the Constitution was approved by a vote of 149-73.

11. The vote was close and came only after ferocious campaigning by federalists both from New Hampshire itself and out of state. McDonald claims that a federalist victory was only assured after a lunch in which federalists got a number of their opponents so drunk that they missed the afternoon vote (*E Pluribus Unum*, 353-54).

12. John Roche noted, "The Federalist is probative evidence for only one proposition: that Hamilton and Madison were inspired propagandists with a genius for retrospective symmetry" (Levy, *American Constitutional Law*, 22).

13. Farrand, *Records*, iii:129.

14. Ibid.

15. Madison, Hamilton, and Jay, *The Federalist* 280-81.

16. Elliot, *Debates*, iii:452-53.

17. Ibid.

18. Ibid.

19. See McDonald, *E Pluribus Unum*, 185-91.

Selected Bibliography

Adams, John. *The Adams Papers,* L. H. Butterfield, ed. Cambridge, MA: The Belknap Press of Harvard University Press, 1962.

Adams, William Howard. *Gouverneur Morris: An Independent Life.* New Haven: Yale University Press, 2003.

Aptheker, Herbert. *American Negro Slave Revolts: On Nat Turner, Denmark Vesey, Gabriel, and Others.* New York: Columbia University Press, 1943.

Bailey, Kenneth P. *The Ohio Company of Virginia and the Westward Movement, 1748-1792: A Chapter in the History of the Colonial Frontier.* Glendale, CA: Arthur H. Clark Company, 1939.

———. *Thomas Cresap, Maryland Frontiersman.* Boston: Christopher House, 1944.

Bailyn, Bernard. *The Ideological Origins of the American Revolution.* Cambridge, MA: Harvard University Press, 1992.

———. *To Begin the World Anew: The Genius and Ambiguities of the American Founders.* New York: Alfred A. Knopf, 2003.

Bancroft, George. *History of the Formation of the Constitution of the United States of America.* New York: D. Appleton, 1882.

Barrett, Jay A. *Evolution of the Ordinance of 1787.* New York: G. P. Putnam's Sons, 1897.

Barry, Richard. *Mr. Rutledge of South Carolina.* New York: Duell, Sloan and Pearce, 1942.

Beard, Charles. *An Economic Interpretation of the Constitution of the United States.* New York: The Macmillan Company, 1913.

Beeman, Richard, Stephen Botein, and Edward C. Carter II. eds. *Beyond Confederation: Origins of the Constitution and American National Identity.* Chapel Hill: University of North Carolina Press, 1987.

Boardman, Roger Sherman. *Roger Sherman, Signer and Statesman.* Philadelphia: University of Pennsylvania Press, 1938.

Bradford, Melvin E. *Founding Fathers: Brief Lives of the Framers of the United States Constitution.* Lawrence: University of Kansas Press, 1994.

Brookhiser, Richard. *Gentleman Revolutionary: Gouverneur Morris, The Rake Who Wrote the Constitution.* New York: Free Press, 2003.

Brown, Robert E. *Charles Beard and the Constitution, A Critical Analysis of "An Economic Interpretation of the Constitution."* Princeton, NJ: Princeton University Press, 1956.

Brown, William Garrott. *The Life of Oliver Ellsworth.* New York: The Macmillan Company, 1905.

Burnett, Edmund C., ed. *Letters of Members of the Continental Congress,* 8 vols. Washington, DC: Carnegie Institution of Washington, 1921-36.

Clarkson, Paul S., and Jett, R. Samuel. *Luther Martin of Maryland.* Baltimore: The Johns Hopkins University Press, 1970.

Collier, Christopher. *Roger Sherman's Connecticut: Yankee Politics and the American Revolution.* Middletown, CT: Wesleyan University Press, 1971.

Cutler, William P., and Cutler, Julia P. *Life, Journals and Correspondence of Rev. Manasseh Cutler, LL.D.* Cincinnati: Robert Clarke & Company, 1888.

Dictionary of American Biography. New York: Charles Scribner's Sons, 1937-44.

DuBois, W. E. B. *The Supression of the African Slave Trade to the United States, 1683-1870.* New York: Russell and Russell, 1898.

Edgar, Walter. *South Carolina: A History.* Columbia: University of South Carolina Press, 1998.

Elkins, Stanley. *Slavery: A Problem in American Institutional and Intellectual Life.* Chicago: University of Chicago Press, 1959.

Elkins, Stanley, and McKitrick, Eric. *The Age of Federalism: The Early American Republic, 1788-1800.* New York: Oxford University Press, 1993.

Elliot, Jonathan. *The Debates in the Several State Conventions on the Adoption of the Federal Constitution as Recommended by the General Convention at Philadelphia in 1787.* Washington, DC: Constitution Society, 1836.

Farrand, Max. *The Framing of the Constitution.* New Haven: Yale University Press, 1913.

———. *Records of the Federal Convention.* New Haven: Yale University Press, 1911, 1937.

Finkelman, Paul. *Slavery and the Founders: Race and Liberty in the Age of Jefferson,* 2nd ed. Armonk, NY: M. E. Sharpe, 2001.

Fiske, John. *The Critical Period of American History 1783-1789.* Boston: Houghton Mifflin & Company, 1896.

Ford, Paul Leicester, ed. *Essays on the Constitution 1787-8.* Brooklyn, NY: Historical Printing Club, 1892.

Ford, Worthington C., ed., *Journals of the Continental Congress, 1774-1789,* 34 vols. Washington, DC: Government Printing Office, 1904-37.

Freidenberg, Daniel. *Life, Liberty, and the Pursuit of Land.* Buffalo, NY: Prometheus Books, 1992.

Genovese, Eugene. *The Political Economy of Slavery: Studies in the Economy and Society of the Slave South.* New York: Pantheon, 1965.

Haw, James. *John and Edward Rutledge of South Carolina.* Athens: University of Georgia Press, 1997.

Hawk, Emory. *An Economic History of the South.* New York: Prentice Hall, 1934.

Hunter, Lloyd A. *Pathways to the Old Northwest: An Observance of the Bicentennial of the Northwest Ordinance.* Indianapolis: Indiana Historical Society, 1988.

Hutson, James H., ed. *Supplement to Max Farrand's The Records of the Federal Convention of 1787.* New Haven: Yale University Press, 1987.

Jensen, Merrill. *The Articles of Confederation: An Interpretation of the Social-Conditional History of the American Revolution, 1774-1781.* 1940. Reprint, Madison: University of Wisconsin Press, 1970.

———. *The New Nation: A History of the United States During Confederation, 1781-1789.* New York: Alfred A. Knopf and Company, 1950.

Kurland, Philip B., and Lerner, Ralph, eds. *The Founders' Constitution.* Chicago: University of Chicago Press, 1987.

Levy, Leonard, ed. *American Constitutional Law: Historical Essays.* New York: Harper & Row, 1966.

Linklater, Andro. *Measuring America.* New York: Walker and Company, 2002.

Lynd, Staughton, *Class Conflict, Slavery, and the United States Constitution: Ten Essays.* New York: Bobbs Merrill, 1967.

McDonald, Forrest. *We the People: The Economic Origins of the Constitution.* Chicago: University of Chicago Press, 1958.

———. *E Pluribus Unum: The Formation of the American Republic 1776-1790.* Boston: Houghton Mifflin, 1965.

———. *Novum Ordo Seclorum: The Intellectual Origins of the Constitution.* Lawrence: University Press of Kansas, 1985.

McMaster, John Bach, and Stone, Frederick D. *Pennsylvania and the Federal Constitution, 1787-1788.* Philadelphia: Historical Society of Pennsylvania, 1788.

Madison, James; Hamilton, Alexander; and Jay, John. *The Federalist or The New Constitution.* New York: Heritage Press, 1945, originally published in 1788.

Miller, Helen Hill. *George Mason, Gentleman Revolutionary*. Chapel Hill: University of North Carolina Press, 1975.

Morgan, Edmund, *American Slavery, American Freedom: The Ordeal of Colonial Virginia*. New York: W. W. Norton & Company, 1975.

———. *Benjamin Franklin*. New Haven: Yale University Press, 2002.

Morris, Richard B. *Witnesses at the Creation: Hamilton, Madison, Jay and the Constitution*. New York: Holt, Rinehart and Winston, 1985.

Onuf, Peter S. *Statehood and Union: A History of the Northwest Ordinance*. Bloomington: Indiana University Press, 1987.

Pennsylvania Packet and General Advertiser, Early American Microfilm Collection, Ann Arbor, University of Michigan.

Phillips, Ulrich B. *American Negro Slavery: A Survey of the Supply, Employment, and Control of Negro Labor as Determined by the Plantation System*. 1918. Reprint, New Orleans: Louisiana State University Press, 1966.

———. *Life and Labor in the Old South*. Boston: Little, Brown and Company, 1929.

———. *The Slave Economy in the Old South: Selected Essays in Economic and Social History*. New Orleans: Louisiana State University Press, 1966.

Pinckney, Elise, ed. *The Letter Book of Eliza Lucas Pinckney*. Chapel Hill: University of North Carolina Press, 1972.

———. *Economics of the Plantation*. South Atlantic Quarterly, July, 1903.

Rakove, Jack. *Original Meanings: Politics and Ideas in the Making of the Constitution*. New York: Alfred A. Knopf, 1996.

Ramsay, David. *History of South Carolina: from its first settlement in 1670 to the year 1808*. Charleston: David Longworth, 1809.

Reardon, John, J. *Edmund Randolph: A Biography*. New York: MacMillan, 1975.

Rowland, Kate Mason. *George Mason: Life, Correspondence and Speeches*. New York: G. P. Putnam's Sons, 1892.

Rutland, Robert A. *The Papers of George Mason*. Chapel Hill: University of North Carolina Press, 1970.

Sirmans, M. Eugene. *Colonial South Carolina: A Political History, 1663-1763*. Chapel Hill: University of North Carolina Press, 1966.

Smith, Paul H., ed. *Letters of Delegates to Congress, 1774-1789*. Washington, DC: Library of Congress, 1976-93.

Szatmary, David P. *Shays' Rebellion: The Making of an Agrarian Insurrection*. Amherst: University of Massachusetts Press, 1980.

Van Doren, Carl. *Benjamin Franklin*. New York: Viking, 1938.

Weigley, Russell F., ed. *Philadelphia: A 300 Year History*. New York: W. W. Norton & Company, 1982.

Wiencek, Henry. *An Imperfect God: George Washington, His Slaves, and the Creation of America*. New York: Farrar, Straus and Giroux, 2003.

Williams, Francis Leigh. *A Founding Family: The Pinckneys of South Carolina*. New York: Harcourt, Brace and Jovanovich, 1978.

Williams, Frederick D. *The Northwest Ordinance: Essays on Its Formulation, Provisions and Legacy*. Lansing: Michigan State University Press, 1989.

Wilson, Edmund. *To the Finland Station: A Study in the Writing and Acting of History*. New York: Farrar, Straus and Giroux, 1972.

Wood, Gordon S. *The Creation of the American Republic 1776-1787*. Chapel Hill: University of North Carolina Press, 1969.

Wright, Robert K. Jr., and MacGregor, Morris J. Jr. *Soldier-Statesmen of the Constitution.* Washington, DC: Center of Military History, 1987.

Zahniser, Marvin R. *Charles Cotesworth Pinckney, Founding Father.* Chapel Hill: University of North Carolina Press, 1967.

Zinn, Howard. *A People's History of the United States: 1492-Present.* New York: HarperCollins, 2003.

ACKNOWLEDGMENTS

I cannot express enough my gratitude to everyone at Walker for making this not only the most rewarding publishing experience I have ever had, but also the most fun. They bring an enthusiasm and a professionalism to the process that are rare and irreplaceable. So thank you to Michele Amundsen, Peter Miller, Maya Baran, Krystyna Skalski, Marlene Tungseth, Diana Drew for crackerjack copyediting, and Jackie Meyer for a knockout cover design. But mostly, I owe this book to the indefatigable, obsessive, maddening, and utterly wonderful George Gibson, who, if I have my wish, I will be able to torment (and vice versa) for many books to come.

Henry Dunow also deserves a deep thank you for his willingness to champion a difficult book that needed just the right home. Judge John Kane and Emily Bazelon were kind enough to read the manuscript for me and ask the important questions.

Then, of course, there is my family, Nancy, Emily, and yes, even Darwin, without whom all this effort would not have much point.

INDEX

Page numbers in *italics* indicate illustrations.